| *Developmental* |
| MANAGEMENT |

BEYOND LEADERSHIP

REVISED EDITION

Developmental Management

General Editor: Ronnie Lessem

*For copyright reasons this edition is not available in the USA

Developmental
MANAGEMENT

Beyond Leadership

BALANCING ECONOMICS, ETHICS AND ECOLOGY

REVISED EDITION

WARREN BENNIS, JAGDISH PARIKH, AND
RONNIE LESSEM

BLACKWELL
Business

Copyright © Blackwell Publishers Ltd 1994

First published 1994
Reprinted 1995, 1996 (with corrections)

2 4 6 8 10 9 7 5 3 1

Blackwell Publishers Ltd
108 Cowley Road
Oxford OX4 1JF
UK

Blackwell Publishers Inc
238 Main Street
Cambridge, Massachusetts 02142 USA
USA

British Library Cataloguing in Publication Data

A CIP catalogue record for this book is available from the British Library.

Library of Congress Cataloging-in-Publication Data

Bennis, Warren G.
    Beyond leadership : balancing economics, ethics, and ecology /
Warren Bennis, Jagdish Parikh and Ronnie Lessem. – 2nd ed.
        p.   cm. – (Developmental management)
    Includes index.
    ISBN 1–55786–960–X (alk. paper)
    1. Industrial management.   I. Parikh, Jagdish.   II. Lessem,
Ronnie.   III. Title.   IV. Series
HD31.B394   1996
658 – dc20   96–5381
                                                                              CIP

Typeset in 11 on 13 pt Ehrhardt
by CentraCet Limited, Cambridge
Printed in Great Britain by TJ Press, Padstow, Cornwall

This book is printed on acid-free paper

Contents

To our respective heritages

Preface

Leadership at its best not only arises out of personal mastery but also results in group synergy. As such it fulfills two of the four purposes for which this book has been written. However, it does not necessarily lead to organizational learning and sustainable development. These are the other two purposes which we shall be addressing. In fact, such a combination of personal mastery, group synergy, organizational learning, and sustainable development needs to be maintained by an evolved sense of value. Such a sense and sensibility transcends mere business leadership, which is closely associated with economics and ethics, thereby balancing economics and ethics with ecology. In this context "ecology" serves as both an organizational metaphor for learning and a physical foundation for sustainability.

For a conventionally western, economically oriented manager, then, effective management is a matter of efficient resource allocation. Economic value is specifically added when a firm's financially accounted-for output proves to be worth more than the commercial value of its inputs in alternative uses. The "global" manager at whom this book is aimed, while taking due account of this economic reality, must go further. For a conventionally eastern, socially oriented manager – characteristically engaged in a large Asian (especially Japanese) manufacturing concern – wealth creation requires that an organization successfully develops, and brings to market, products and services which are not only a collection of physical and financial capital but also a distillation of the human values that go into their making. Such a process of value integration is essentially an ethical one, motivated by a search for purpose and meaning.

The global manager, however, while taking account of this act of morality, must go further. For he or she, in the final analysis, must achieve a balance between economic, ethical, and ecological value. Whereas what might be termed static patterns of value separate the economic, ethical, and ecological, dynamic patterns are integrative. Such an integration takes us beyond leadership toward a new form of business stewardship. "Eco-philosophy, perceived as global and comprehensive, is a process philosophy which is integrative, hierarchical and normative – self actualizing with regard to the individual and symbiotic with regard to the cosmos" (H. Skolimowski, *Living Philosophy*, London, Arkana, 1992, page 46).

Such a "global" manager then, to whom this book is dedicated, will aim for a balanced economic, ethical, and ecological approach. As a result he or she will not only transcend east and west, to realize a new globality, but will also go beyond leadership to bring about an integration of self-mastery, group synergy, organizational learning, and sustainable development.

The focus of this book, therefore, will be on the individual, group, organization, and society in the context of the new paradigm – beyond conventional leadership – which alone can ensure an ongoing balancing of economics, ethics, and ecology.

Warren Bennis, Jagdish Parikh, and Ronnie Lessem

Acknowledgments

We want to thank once again Richard Burton for his courage in championing the series, and Geoffrey Palmer and Janey Fisher for their endeavors during the copy-editing of the manuscript.

W.B., J.P., and R.L.

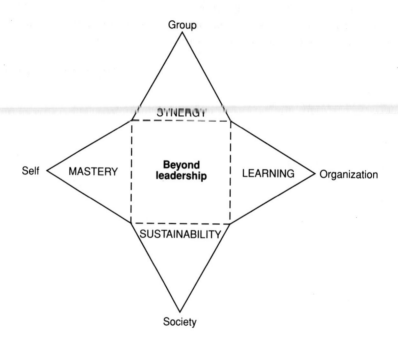

Frontispiece   Beyond leadership

PART I

Introducing the New Business Paradigm

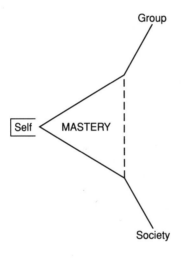

Introduction: From the Old Paradigm to the New

Ronnie Lessem

Change and Uncertainty, Conflict and Complexity

As the business world becomes more complex, more uncertain, more changeable and more conflict-ridden, so the requirements of managers proliferate. We are called upon, simultaneously, to manage complexity and uncertainty, change and conflict in ever larger doses. Our ability to cope with all of this should be enhanced by the multiplicity of concepts and techniques that have developed over the past 50 years. The trouble is that by now there are so many of them that it is difficult to know which way to turn. Moreover, for the discriminating manager it is not good enough merely to discard the old ideas in favor of the new. For much of the conventional wisdom still has value to this day.

What we shall be doing in this handbook for the "new paradigm" manager, therefore, is threefold. Firstly we shall be identifying, in this introductory chapter, the kinds of conventional management wisdom that we shall not be covering. Secondly, and at the same time, we shall identify those American (western) and Japanese (eastern) approaches to management which have already become part of the manager's stock in trade, and therefore do not warrant further consideration. Thirdly, and substantively within this book, we shall be focusing on those "global" concepts and methods that constitute the "new paradigm" in management.

- As far as the *individual manager* is concerned, what will distinguish extraordinary from ordinary management is the focus on self-mastery.
- As far as the *management team* is concerned, what distinguishes

old-paradigm teamwork from new-paradigm group interaction is the focus on social synergy.

- As far as the *managed organization* is concerned, what distinguishes old-paradigm structures and functions from new-paradigm structures and processes is the focus on organizational learning.
- Finally, what distinguishes old-paradigm social responsibility from new-paradigm environmental responsiveness is the focus on sustainable development.

What, though, is the conventional wisdom with which others, outside of this book, have been long concerned?

The conventional wisdom

We associate what we have termed the "northern" conventional management wisdom with prominent management thinkers of recent European heritage resident in America. The best known of these, in relation to the individual manager, is Peter Drucker, renowned for his work on the managerial skills of planning and organization, directing and control. With regard to management teams Rensis Likert at Michigan did pioneering work on effective teamwork, and participative management. With respect to formal organization, the doyen has been Harvard University's Alfred Chandler, with his revelations of the "visible hand" of hierarchical organization. Finally, when it comes to business and society, George Steiner in California has long championed the role of business's social responsibility, over and above the shareholder's financial responsibility.

Although many progressive managers might argue that the conventional wisdom has had its day, like Newtonian physics it still exercises a major influence on the middle-ground, stable-state approach to management and organization. Nevertheless, it is "old hat!"

The westerly way

In recent years, a westerly wind has been blowing over the conventional wisdom, overturning northern-style rationalism with a western style of entrepreneurism. The leader of this "people and enterprise" movement, related to the would-be "excellent" manager, has been the inimitable Tom Peters. Alongside him, and supplanting rationally based teamwork with emotively oriented shared values, have been the two Americans Deal and Kennedy, noted for their work on corporate cultures. At an organizational level, the shift in orientation from the vertical to lateral organization, and from hierarchy to network, is vividly depicted in Charles Handy's vision of the future of work, and the emerging aspirations of professionally based knowledge workers. Finally, from a societal perspective, George Gilder has established his reputation for reinventing the spirit of enterprise in a contemporary context.

It is important for us to emphasize, at this point, that this westerly movement away from an old paradigm, embodied in the conventional wisdom, does not actually take us to the new paradigm, as such. Rather it represents a transitional movement, as does the easterly one.

The easterly movement

While analytical management embodies the conventional wisdom, and entrepreneurial management the westerly way, total quality management is essentially a Japanese invention, most clearly exemplified by Toyota. The easterly movement, as we shall see, is more clearly represented by Japanese companies than by their individual management thinkers. Teamwork, in an easterly context, is best reflected in the "quality circles" beautifully illustrated by Shigeru Kobayashi, a one-time managing director at Sony. Similarly, and at an organizational level, the concept of "lean manufacturing" has been embodied by the Japanese in general, and by Honda most particularly. Finally, at a societal level, the Japanese American Robert Ozaki has recently emerged with his version of human capitalism, a third force in between conventionally based capitalism and socialism.

The global manager

While the westerly based management concepts remain too strongly vested with old-style capitalism, at least at a societal level, the easterly based approaches remain too Japanese in form and content to become much more widely spread. It is the globally based approaches, then, that transcend the limits posed by particular cultures. In other words, the new-paradigm manager is by definition transcultural in his or her approach to developing self-mastery within him or herself; in generating social synergy across a group; in engendering organizational learning within institutions, and in fostering sustainable development across the globe. Let us now review, more specifically, what this particular book will be about.

The New Paradigm Manager

Attributes of the new management paradigm

Don Beck (chapter 3), based at the Center for the Study of Values near Houston, Texas, is an American who has devoted much of the past 12 years of his working life to helping South Africa sort out its political and economic problems. Having become, therefore, a man of the west and the south, and a physical scientist with an interest in management, he has defined the new-paradigm thinker for us, in the following terms:

- you think in flow states and recognize that organizations and societies pass from one plateau to the next
- you have the scope, range, and power to manage the entire staircase of your own, of others', of your organization's and of society's history
- you recognize that everything connects to everything else
- your commitment is to the living planet: to traditions and collective memories, to people living today and as yet unborn, as well as to the environment
- you are a product of the information age, your sensory systems and those of your organization being constantly open to the flow of data from all possible sources
- you are skilled at recognizing, and dealing with, different levels of development, each in the process of change
- you respect competence, wherever it exists, and have a passion for doing things that are unique, by yourself and with others

Such a new-paradigm manager, as we have already said, possesses individual self-mastery (competence and uniqueness), fosters social synergy (flow and connectedness), engenders organizational learning (history and development), and engages in sustainable development (information age and living planet).

From uncertainty to self-mastery

Competence and uniqueness

Leadership and self-mastery, intuition and vision characterize the individual, new-paradigm manager. Our authority on visionary leadership, in this book, is Warren Bennis (chapter 4), who has gained a worldwide reputation in this field. The themes of developing vision, and of transforming vision into action, are dealt with by Jagdish Parikh and Fred Neubauer, in collaboration with Alden Lank (chapter 5) and by Ronnie Lessem (chapter 6). Parikh is an Indian businessman, educated in America and based in Asia, who has gained particular renown in Europe for his programmes on managing your self. Lessem is an African management thinker of central European heritage, also educated in America and resident in Britain, who has devoted himself to uncovering and releasing what he terms the global "business sphere". Parikh, moreover, with his eastern heritage, is well equipped to deal with the acquisition of self-mastery.

From conflict to social synergy

Flow and connectedness

The largely unsung exponent of conflict resolution in the west, Clare Graves in America, began working in the forties and fifties on ways of reconciling conflicting values. His work has in fact been taken on by Don Beck and Chris Cowan, Beck also being the author of our chapter on new paradigm thought. From Beck and Cowan in America we turn to Bernard Lievegoed (chapter 8) in the Netherlands, for further guidance on conflict resolution in the context of mergers and joint ventures. Lievegoed was probably Holland's most eminent management thinker, having created an internationally based consultancy, oriented toward his developmental ideas. Like Beck and Cowan, Lievegoed has focused on flow and integration. Finally in this section, we turn to Southern Africa's Albert Koopman (chapter 10), a business visionary in his own right, who has created the country's largest industrial democracy, Cashbuild, which to this day remains very profitable as well as socially synergetic.

From management complexity to organizational learning

History and development

The subject of organizational development (OD), the rightful domain of the new-paradigm thinker and strongly championed by Bernard Lievegoed, has been largely stillborn, because of its all too far-reaching implications for individual and institutional development. In recent years, in fact, it has been transcended by the concept of "the learning organization." Elliott Jaques (chapter 14), a Canadian psychotherapist and worldwide authority on bureaucracy, has emerged with his concept of "requisite organization."

In such an organization, hierarchy is geared toward mastering complexity rather than toward subordinating people. Ronnie Lessem's (1992a) approach to "developmental management" (chapter 12) and his concept of "total quality learning" (1992b; chapter 14) sets the scene here for Jaques' focus on a progressively layered approach to learning, both through the individual and in the organization. Charles Hampden-Turner (chapter 15) adopts a different approach to organizational learning, oriented toward the management of dilemmas. Hampden-Turner's recent focus has been upon the "seven cultures of capitalism."

From change to sustainability

The information age and the living planet

In the final section of this chapter we focus on society at large. The orientation toward "sustainable development" (chapter 16) is spearheaded by John Davis (1991), a senior manager from Shell who, in his latter years, has acted as a consultant around the globe with Britain's

Table 1.1 The evolution of management

	Old paradigm			New paradigm global
	Northern	Western	Eastern	
Individual manager	Effective management (Drucker)	Entrepreneurial management (Peters)	Total quality management (Toyota)	Self-mastery
Social group	Effective teamwork (Likert)	Shared values (Deal/Kennedy)	Quality circles (Sony)	Social synergy
Organization as a whole	Hierarchical organization (Chandler)	Networked organization (Handy)	Lean organization (Honda)	Organizational learning
Economy and society	Corporate responsibility (Chandler)	Free enterprise (Gilder)	Human capitalism (Ozaka)	Sustainable development

Intermediate Technology Development Group. Secondly, Yoneji Masuda (1990), probably the internationally best known Japanese futurologist, focuses on "managing in the information society" (chapter 17). Lastly Jagdish Parikh (1992) concludes by offering his own views on 'doing business in the new paradigm' (chapter 18).

Toward a New Paradigm of Management

In conclusion, we can identify a line of evolution, in management thought, from an old-paradigm (inclusive of "northern", "western" and "eastern" concepts and methods) toward a "global" new-paradigm orientation (see table 1.1).

In this book we shall be concerned with the what and the how of managing, while adopting a global perspective, in the new paradigm.

References

Beck, D. and Cowan, C. 1996: *Spiral Dynamics*. Oxford: Blackwell.
Bennis, W. 1985: *On Leadership*. New York: Harper and Row.
Davis, J. 1991: *Greening Business*. Oxford: Blackwell.
Jaques, E. 1992: *Executive Leadership*. Oxford: Blackwell.

Koopman, A. 1991: *Transcultural Management*. Oxford: Blackwell.

Lessem, R. 1989: *Global Management*. Englewood Cliffs, New Jersey: Prentice-Hall.

—— 1992a: *Developmental Management*. Oxford: Blackwell.

—— 1992b: *Total Quality Learning*. Oxford: Blackwell.

Lievegoed, B. 1991: *Managing the Developing Organization*. Oxford: Blackwell.

Masuda, Y. 1990: *Managing the Information Society*. Oxford: Blackwell.

Parikh, J. 1992: *Managing Your Self*. Oxford: Blackwell.

—— 1993: *Managing Intuition*. Oxford: Blackwell.

Hampden-Turner, C. 1990: *Charting the Corporate Mind*. Oxford: Blackwell.

2

New-paradigm Thinking
Don Beck and Chris Cowan

Crucible of Chaos

The world is a dynamic crucible the contents of which are – sometimes quite literally – exploding in the chaos of change. A crucible is a vessel in which elements are fused and transformed under intense heat, with high and focused energy. Millions of years ago this planet was itself a geothermal crucible, as volcanic activity created the physical characteristics we see today – mountain ranges, gold and ore-bearing reefs, diamond pipes, river valleys, agricultural lands. The man-made crucible so central to our global economic development is a reminder in miniature of those cataclysmic events so long ago: searing heat, the bubbling of minerals and molten metals, and the pungency of escaping gases. It is also an apt metaphor for today's human crucible, as the most disparate and often incompatible elements are forced by circumstance into fusion and transformation. A crucible melts down old systems, refines out impurities, forms new alloys, creates new entities, destroys old orders, contains and refocuses energy and sparks thresholds of change. This is a searingly hot and acrid process. One can almost smell burning as one reads of the assassinations in parts of Africa, Asia, or Europe and tries to absorb the virulent rhetoric and the torrents of accusation and counter-accusation. A crucible is not a comfortable place to be.

Into this human crucible are being poured some of the most explosive elements and forces to have plagued the planet itself through history – the legacies of colonial dispossession, bizarre racial theories, perceived historical slights and injustices, warped religious cults, zealotry, and ideologies with pretensions to transcendent truth. All the value systems which have developed over mankind's long psychological ascent are present in their pristine form across the globe, impinging on one another. Iron Age man mixes on a daily basis with the High Technology/Information Age person, along with others at the various stages and gradations in between. While certain minds are at home with space age technology, others are just joining the agricultural or industrial revolutions. Time and geography make conditions all the more volatile. The time frame is compressed. The world is being required to manage change, over years, which elsewhere has percolated over the centuries.

The global crucible boils and bubbles with several critical destabilizing forces and elements, any one of which is able to contribute to the unique turbulence and fluctuation. These destabilizers we call the "Seven Gs": gaps, gulfs, guilt, grudges, greed, glitches, and games.

- *Gaps* exist in the close proximity of grinding Third World poverty across the globe and the conspicuous consumption of the First World sector. In many cities ancient donkey carts and limousines travel the same roads, and affluent youths prowl modern shopping malls while impoverished children struggle in violent townships.
- *Gulfs* exist in the multiplicity of languages and cultures; in thought processes which are centuries apart. These create deep-seated differences in perception, understanding, and expectation. It will take generations to bridge these mental divides.
- *Guilt* lies in the remorse experienced by many privileged individuals who contemplate decades of deprivation, oppression, and mistreatment of others, based on culture or racial origin. It is both understandable and deadly. Decisions based on guilt are almost invariably bad, merely aggravating matters.
- *Grudges* have been bred by the bitterness, resentment, anger, and desire for revenge of those who have been deprived or mistreated. They are a breeding ground for demands for punishment, which solve nothing.
- *Greed* is present in the "sinking ship" syndrome. Businessmen squeeze what they can out of the public, by fair means or foul, because "everyone is doing it" and this might be the last chance. Correspondingly, people in government abandon the ethics and norms of the past, enriching themselves and entrenching their interests while they can.
- *Glitches* are the wild cards of social and political life, such as the Mafia funding politicians, other unpredictable exposés,

political violence, and assassinations. These always have the capacity to destabilize unexpectedly, and may emanate from the outside world as much as internally.

- *Games* are the activities of the players who use global issues to their own ends, which often do not have a great deal to do with our worldly interests. Players include politicians, men of the cloth, the media, and sports administrators all over the world. Americans off-load the guilt of their own racial feelings. The British condemn ethnic violence while failing to put their own house in order. African despots used to condemn apartheid as a distraction from their own shortcomings.

Has mankind in its long historical emergence ever had to deal with quite as much turbulence as today? The chaos is awesome, the complexity overwhelming.. Can there possibly be an order to bring sanity, stability, and progress?

Out of Chaos, Order

Douglas Hofstadler, the American physicist and pioneer in the theory of artificial intelligence, noted: "It turns out that an eerie type of chaos can lurk just behind a façade of order – and yet, deep inside the chaos lurks an even eerier type of order." Can one find that eerie order lurking within the global chaos? If so, where? Who will be its discoverers? One reads nothing of it in the press, academic journals, or books by the experts. Is the cause then hopeless? Is the world doomed to repeat the sins of its past (where there has been no lack of cataclysmic conflict) or experience the eruptions that have tarnished other civilizations? The analyses of political scientists, sociologists, and economists so far give few answers. There is a sterility, a sense of fatalism in the debate, little that is innovative. Politicians across the spectrum seem to be making yesterday's speeches, addressing yesterday's issues. One searches the sermons of the moralists and the commentaries of the pundits in vain for anything that is fresh and hopeful. The entire globe appears all too often to be in gridlock – witness Bosnia Herzegovina in the 1990s.

Or is there a key by which the people of the world can discover a common language for an escape from the confusion of this Tower of Babel? Perhaps Albert Einstein gives us a clue: "The world that we have made as a result of the level of thinking we have done thus far creates problems that we cannot solve at the same level as they were created." If that is so, we surely have to address the issues in the crucible from a different level, within a new perspective. The entire world seems to be searching for solutions from the same level of thinking as produced the problems they are attempting to solve. And in that case the entire world must be trapped in a cruel and destructive cul-de-sac. If we are to follow Einstein's advice and solve problems from a higher level than the one at which they were created, we need to operate within a new paradigm.

Emerging Paradigms

In *The Structure of Scientific Revolutions*, Thomas Kuhn has popularized the term "paradigm" as simply a model of society with which most people concur. He defines the expression as ". . . a constellation of concepts, values, perceptions and practices shared by a community which forms a particular vision of reality that is the basis of the way a community organises itself."

Individuals have "mindsets" or value systems while entire communities or cultures share a paradigm – the basic operating assumptions that hold the social system together. The assumptions are seldom, if ever, stated explicitly – yet they exist unquestioned and unchallenged. Once the paradigm emerges, we cling to it tenaciously since it impacts on virtually every area of our lives. But eventually new information enters our conceptual world, calling into question the older assumptions. At this point paradigm change becomes erratic, chaotic, and discontinuous. Paradigms emerge from crucibles of the mind.

Components of a paradigm

Much like the genetic code on the DNA of any living organism, a paradigm is designed, formed, and organized by a basic tool kit and a set of instructions. Each new paradigm is created and tailored to the conditions produced by unique crucibles, through these instructional prescriptions and variables. By organism we mean a single person, a group, a team or organization, or larger social systems such as cultures, communities, societies, and nations. By conditions we refer to the elements within the environment – all previous paradigms in their residual forms – and the potential for emerging paradigms. The key components of a paradigm for consideration are these.

World view

What is the world like? Is it a rainforest, an enchanted village, a dangerous jungle, a righteous cathedral, a market-place of opportunity, a caring commune, a natural habitat, a global village, or all and any of the above?

Command and control center

This is a critical mass, center of gravity, or bottom line that emits signals and commands to the rest of the organism to provide the correctly coded information at the right time. What is the proper motivational balance? What ratio of reward and punishment will be appropriate? How will the children be taught? What form will justice take? What will be the view and role of science? Who will rise into leadership positions?

Degree of complexity

How complex are the problems in the milieu? How can that level of complexity, or even greater, be created by the organism? The degree of complexity activated in the paradigm must not be too advanced or too primitive for the organism. First World systems and technology will fail within Third World environments.

Elaboration stream

How are those principles reflected "downstream" in religion, politics, economics, psychology, architecture, community development, athletics, philosophy, common-sense values, and many other areas?

Organizing principle

What kind of organizing system and model allows the paradigm to operate effectively? Should it be tribal order, an empire, a sacred hierarchy, a circle of equals, an integrated network, or the marketplace?

Potential

What are the available resources and competencies within the organism? Is the necessary thinking available, at least in its potential form? What happens if the demands in the conditions cannot be met by the resources in the organism?

Other paradigms

Which other paradigms are represented in their residual form? How strong are they? How do they color the dominant paradigm? How quickly can people downshift to the operating assumptions of the older paradigms?

Recognition patterns

What messages and information patterns can be detected by the paradigm? What communication codes and media are used in the sending and receiving of messages?

Healthy and unhealthy forms

Does the expression of the paradigm contribute to the overall health and well-being of the entire spiral of paradigms? Or are the expressive forms selfish and self-centered? Do they absorb energy from the total environment without replacing it with something better?

Time lines

Where is the time focus? Is it on the past, the present or the future? In what ratio? What determines how it measures time?

Flexibility factor

What will trigger change in each of the respective paradigms? What are the early signs of impending change? How can they be recognized and by whom? How can each paradigm be successfully moved on from or subsumed in the next? Is the paradigm rigid or flexible? Is it open or closed? What anchors hold it back? What antibodies does it possess? Where is it in its life cycle? Is it emerging, in its nodal stage or in decline?

Edward Harrison, a physicist at the University of Massachusetts, describes a paradigm (or "universe") as a view of the universe, a mask through which we perceive the world. "The universes," he wrote in *Masks of the Universe*, "are our models of the Universe. They are great schemes of intricate thought – grand cosmic pictures – that rationalise human experience. Each universe is a self-consistent system of ideas, marvelously organised, interlacing most of what is perceived and known."

When each universe or paradigm emerges, the believers are convinced it offers the ultimate view, the final word, the end of the quest, the last pinnacle. Everything now will become crystal clear. Pity the people of the future. They will have little to think about or do. But Harrison warns there is no end to the gallery of cosmic pictures. Each is simply the prelude to the next, then the next, then the next. He notes: "A universe rises, flourishes, then declines in the course of time and is superseded by another. Its decline and fall occur because the society is assaulted by an alien culture, or startling new facts and ideas emerge, or old problems erupt and refuse to stay suppressed."

To illustrate this, imagine if it were possible for your great-great-grandfather to join you at your breakfast table. He would look a little like you – rather different also. He would speak the same language as you – but not quite the same language. What would you find to talk about? Last night's television? If you attacked him for not solving the race problem in his time, he would probably reply: "What race problem?" And if it were possible for you to have your great-great-grandson at your breakfast table next day, he would look a little like you – rather different also. He would speak the same language as you – but not quite the same language. If he chided you for not solving the problem of pollution in outer space in your time, you would reply: "Pollution where?"

The assumptions within our paradigms are expressed in religion, education, the market-place, mores and traditions, sports, economic and political thought, virtually everywhere. Generational gaps may have little to do with time. They may have everything to do with contrasting paradigms.

Paradigm shifts, like major adjustments in the earth's tectonic plates, may be as turbulent and destructive as tremors and quakes. Everything is impacted on both immediately and in a series of delayed after-shocks. Many established structures and landmarks are demolished, the rubble is cleared and new ones are constructed. This could have much to do with what is happening in the world today.

The New Global Paradigm

A new and entirely different pattern of thought is beginning to emerge worldwide and in various fields of human activity, driven by a fresh set of conditions and challenges. The new paradigm is beginning to find expression in the natural and the social sciences, especially in education and philosophy and now in political thought as well. The end of the Cold War between east and west has unlocked forces which had been contained on both sides of the Iron Curtain. The Berlin Wall, focal point of more than 40 years of pressure and brinkmanship, almost overnight became the Berlin Mall. The Gulf area of the Middle East erupted in a war which nobody would have predicted only months earlier. Operations Desert Shield, then Desert Storm, were successfully prosecuted under the auspices of the United Nations Security Council and with the blessing of the former Soviet Union and China. Who could have predicted any such thing from within the recent paradigm of the Cold War? Who would have anticipated the rapid demise of the old Soviet Empire, or the peaceful emergence of a new non-racial South Africa?

The new paradigm is being shaped by contributions from a host of new and revitalized academic and scientific disciplines. Insights from quantum physics and chaos theory are being applied in understanding the functioning of the brain, social behavior, stock-market cycles and weather patterns. Traditionalists within the fields of economics, political science, psychology, sociology, and anthropology are being challenged by a new generation of integrative and open systems thinkers. New disciplines are emerging in political psychology, ecological evolution, general systems theories, and a host of others. Everything is being called into question once again. The sacred cows are no longer safe.

The imagery of a crucible suggests that something new is created within the fiery mixture of chemicals, gases, and base metals. Ilya Prigogine won the Nobel Prize in Chemistry for his concept of dissipative structures. A dissipative structure is an "open" thermodynamic (energy-processing) system that generates "order through fluctuations." When crucible-like conditions exist, torn by fluctuations or what are termed perturbations (things that literally "perturb" us), a threshold might be reached that will transform the system in the direction of more complex structural organizations and greater structural stability. In short, new forms of order emerge from the chaos, only to await the time when the process will repeat itself. When applied to large-scale social systems such as cultures, nations, or the entire human species, the "new forms of order" are actually new paradigms. New thinking arises, then, out of crucibles, chaos, dissipation, and fluctuation. The chaos of violence that has gripped parts of the globe over recent years is, we contend, one of the more tragically spectacular instances of misunderstood paradigm change.

The globe is full of perturbations and is experiencing dissonance and dissipation at a dangerous level. If diamonds are created by pressure, the social landscape should be littered with them. Evidence of major dissipation is to be seen in the violence in the former Yugoslavia, the turbulence within both white and black politics and the saintly, zealous discovery, in various quarters, of "the truth" (actually a new form of order) emerging out of doubt, turmoil, and conflict (discontinuous fluctuations within thermodynamic systems).

What we may be seeing, therefore, is our collective intelligence setting up the conditions for change as we seek to escape the fiery hell of the crucible to embrace a new order. But how does one deal with a planet the population of which is encountering different expressions of dissipative structures all along the continuum of psychological time? Different kinds of mini-crucibles are bubbling and boiling all over the world. Mini-crucibles are there waiting to form authoritarian empires, and to spew out the burning zeal of holy war. Others produce Dickensian squalor, still others are turbulent with conflicting ideologies, unscrupulous fortune-hunters, and exploitative foreign interests. As with the blazing oil wells of Kuwait in 1991, the fires will burn for some time while society searches for the models to deal with the entire spectrum of evolutionary change. But if all the fires could be put out at once, that would surely release the pent-up energy for constructive purposes instead of wasting it into the atmosphere or in fruitless clashes with authority.

The emerging paradigm must therefore have the capacity to deal with complexities of a magnitude greater than what has evolved so far in our planet's turbulent history. The new paradigm must indeed be equipped to cope with multiple and often conflicting levels of development in contemporary society on a simultaneous basis. It must have the power, resourcefulness, and range of operation to encounter each of the evolutionary crucibles while, at the same time, acting to preserve the integrity and the future of the entire organism.

Our world is in the throes of profound change as the older, parochial paradigm of separate development disintegrates. Politicians, academics, church leaders, businessmen, in fact all responsible citizens, search for a glimpse of the new order – the new paradigm. As the pillars of the old order crash down, what structures can be put in their place? What new wineskins can contain the new wine? How do new-paradigm people, whether as managers, economists, or politicians, think?

New-paradigm Thinkers: a Profile

The following are characteristics of new-paradigm thinkers.

Thinking in open systems in contrast with fixed, ideal states

Fixed-state thinkers believe there is an ideal condition that, once put into place, will solve problems now and in the future. Once the ideal condition is achieved, it must be defended at all costs. The fixed-state advocates carry the banners of fundamentalism, Marxist egalitarianism, free-market consumerism, western capitalism, and "New Age" communalism. Whenever fixed-state advocates become zealots for their particular cause, they lose perspective regarding the nature of change and become frozen and partisan in their view.

New-paradigm thinkers think in flow states and recognize that society passes from one plateau to the next. In doing so, they integrate what is appropriate from the past with what will be congruent in the future to move the organism and its respective subsystems along the human trajectory to greater complexity.

Integrating natural differences in an evolutionary flow

Millions of people are passing through different levels of development simultaneously. There are effectively different futures for different people. Across the globe, different segments of the population are looking into different "final states" at the same time. And for them, at that stage, the state is "ideal." It is not ideal for the entire organism, however, not for the total human parade.

New-paradigm thinkers therefore search for the integrated structures necessary to manage this long human march. Different population groups, with their differentiated needs and demands, are passing from pinnacle to pinnacle. Some are only now experiencing the trauma of detribalization. Others are passing through a minefield of anarchy and its savage consequences. Not a few are riding the yeasty crest of becoming true believers, with all the associated senses of conversion, commitment, and sainthood. Millions of others are leaving traditional orders in favor of pragmatic materialism, the quest for the best, and the competitiveness of "the game."

New-paradigm thinkers have the scope, range, power, and insight to manage the entire staircase of human history – a dynamic developmental spiral that characterizes the globe. They think and act for the entire population instead of for specific racial, ethnic, religious, or class-based groups or interests. They have the X-ray vision to see beneath the surface and detect the natural differences in people. As a result, they avoid being trapped in historic stereotypes and frozen categories regarding people and their values and priorities.

Connecting everything to everything else in quantum chunks

New-paradigm thinkers recognize that everything connects to everything else. One cannot deal with the street kids of the urban ghettos only through law enforcement. Everything has to be mobilized: the schools, the families, the churches, the business sector, and community organizations. Major problems cannot be handled in a fragmented, *ad hoc*, piecemeal fashion.

Organizations which isolate functions in compartments, divisions, levels, or territories are at serious risk. The new thinking in this decade points toward the need for common visions, integrated structures, and focused strategies and resources. Instead of becoming absorbed with small bits, the effective resolution of complex situations requires dealing with big chunks – therefore the use of insights from "quantum" thinking.

Acting for the entire organism in creating and distributing abundance

Practitioners of the new paradigm focus on the whole instead of the parts. They recognize that to deal with any one thing or small part one must be prepared to understand and influence virtually everything at the same time. They take the panoramic, wide-angled view. Their commitment is to the organism-call in the living planet: the people living today and those yet unborn; the history, traditions, and collective memories that provide safe and secure moorings and anchors; and the environment, natural resources, and living conditions. Likewise, they recognize the interdependence of the entire planet.

This positive thinking system is dedicated to the creation and distribution of abundance instead of the redistribution of scarcity. In this sense "abundance" refers to much more than material wealth or affluence. The standard of living and quality of life are impacted upon, as are the life of the mind, the health of the spirit, and the wealth of the visions and dreams.

Seeing everything by holographic scanning before acting

New-paradigm thinkers are products of the Information Age. Their sensory systems are constantly open to the flow of data from all possible sources. They disdain political games, territorial defensiveness, or other forms of information/distortion and blockage. They have the capacity to navigate on past, present, and future time lines – in all directions – to obtain a sense of perspective, continuity, and receptiveness to new ideas.

Employing a full range of tailored problem-resolution processes

Since new-paradigm thinkers are skilled at dealing with different levels of development, competing "final states," the process of change, and complex environments, they are adept at finding the right problem-resolution package for the right situation at the right time.

They draw from a rich background in decision-making techniques that can be tailored to resolve issues in diverse settings. In all cases they act on behalf of the entire organism for the greater good. They employ compromise or negotiated processes where relevant; authoritarian conduits where absolutely necessary; and complex problem-resolution formats where appropriate.

Having the attributes of resourcefulness, fearlessness, toughness, competence, and playfulness

A new kind of person is being forged in the crucible of the 1990s. These people, of all ages, from all races, ethnicities, sexes, and occupations, are experiencing quantum leaps in the quality of their thinking. The refining fire of the long global ordeal has charged the minds of an entire generation of global citizens with a creative power and range beyond that being produced in any other culture on the planet.

These 21st-century new-paradigm thinkers are easily recognized. Status, the revenge motive, feelings of guilt or shame, or the preoccupation with power are simply not valued. New-paradigm people rather display respect for competence wherever it exists, a preference for autonomy and personal freedom, an interest in what is personally challenging and engaging, and a passion and sense of joy in doing something which is unique. They do not have blind, unconditional loyalty to causes, or unthinking self-sacrifice. The new-paradigm thinker is his or her own man or woman. Just as little will they have self-serving motives or lack of ethics and responsibility. New-paradigm thinkers are by no means perfect, but they cannot be manipulated. They will take up a cause only if they decide it is of merit, and it is they who make that choice.

New-paradigm thinkers may not be visible in the usual corridors of influence and prestige. They may be found on the periphery of power, among normal people doing normal things, and they may be found in any occupation. They may or may not have academic backgrounds, professional qualifications, or certificates on their walls. One has to watch and listen carefully for them. They have no compelling urge to announce their presence until a problem draws them to respond. Having solved it, they tend to vanish from the scene.

In this chapter we have described the components of new-paradigm thought in general. In Parts II–V we turn to its business application in particular: an individual orientation toward visionary leadership; a group focus on social synergy; an institutional orientation toward the learning organization; and a societal focus upon sustainable development. The place to start, then, is with your Self.

PART II

As a Manager – From Uncertainty to Mastery

3

Toward Self-mastery
Jagdish Parikh

Overcoming Dissonance

In moving from an old-paradigm to a new-paradigm approach to life, and to work, you need to manage yourself differently.

Ask yourself, "What do I currently want from life, or from myself?" In other words, what is the objective of your self? The usual responses from managers to such questions are: wealth, health, power, success, happiness, family harmony, and satisfaction. The responses to the question "What is it that you usually get most of the time in your activity as a manager?" are usually: frustration, anger, problems, stress, satisfaction, and excitement.

While most managers maintain that they experience negative feelings for more than 50 percent of the time, some experience the opposite. Nevertheless, there seems to be a consensus that, irrespective of the actual ratio, they would like to reduce the negative experiences and enhance the positive ones. When we probed further with those managers who indicated that they wanted wealth, health, or power, we found that it was happiness or satisfaction that they were really seeking through these mediating factors. Moreover, ironically, as their responses indicated, their "satisfaction" had not increased despite their acquisition of more wealth or power. In other words, most managers, even the most successful ones, had less in the way of positive feelings of satisfaction than they wanted, despite their higher level of success.

Why should this be so? Why does "success" often not yield happiness, despite the fact that whatever we identify as success is ultimately sought to yield satisfaction? One of the reasons is that in the process of achieving success and pursuing it in the various roles

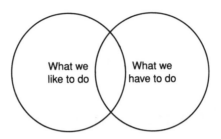

Figure 3.1   The dissonance factor

you play in your life, you have to undertake several things which are not to your taste. Unfortunately, in contemporary life this happens to a significant extent (see figure 3.1). This dissonance creates a lot of stress and frustration. To be able to reduce it, or increase the overlap between what you have to do and what you like to do, thereby maximizing satisfaction, is one of the aims of the "New-paradigm Manager," in *Managing Your Self*.

Beyond the Peter Principle

Another possible reason for poor self-management is the widely held belief that sooner or later we will reach our level of incompetence: this is also called "plateauing." There is a strong conviction, illustrated in figure 3.2, that everyone goes through a growth period (A) which is followed by a stable, or stagnant, period (B). This marks the "plateauing" phase which, in turn, is followed by a decline (C). It

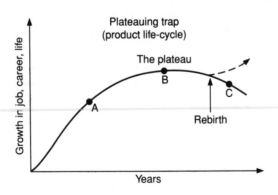

Figure 3.2   Beyond plateauing

appears that this endless cycle of birth, growth, stagnation, decay, and death is characteristic of all forms of individual and institutional life.

The prospect of plateauing, and then of decline, haunts career executives who have been in the same job for 10–15 years. Most of them see themselves as being between points B and C. Feelings of uncertainty and fear that they may have reached the plateau, or are on their way down, are not uncommon amongst managers in mid-career: the plateau is seen as inevitable. The growing complexity and demands on performance placed on them by the organization, in a contemporary environment of accelerating change, accumulates to such an extent that it makes them feel that in the not-too-distant future they will reach a stage at which they will no longer be able to respond to these demands effectively. This naturally results in frustration, fear, insecurity, and stress. Such feelings are by no means confined to people at points B and C – they occasionally assail people even at position A.

What we do not realize, or what a lot of us are not aware of, is that there is a way out of this apparently inevitable trap, by creating a perceptual change in our attitudes and belief systems. You can, at any stage in the cycle of your life, be "reborn" (psychologically). You can realize the possibility of perpetual renewal in virtually every aspect of your life through a perceptual process of rebirth. This requires a fresh look at the inner potential that each one of us possesses.

We narrow down the possibilities in our lives by having an extremely limited awareness of our true potential, which is, for the new-paradigm manager in all practical purposes, unlimited. On the basis of such ignorance, we limit our ambitions or aspirations, and because of our strong belief in our "inadequacies" or "limitations," almost as a self-fulfilling prophecy, we program ourselves into a very limited performance.

Our concept of "what we can do" is, to begin with, very limited. Within such a limited concept, we determine "what we want/should do"; and ultimately what we are "able" to do is only a fraction of this, as shown in figure 3.3.

It is convergence of what we "want" to do, together with what we feel in our hearts that we "should" do, with what we are actually "able" to do that yields the experience of "joy" or "satisfaction" (see figure 3.4).

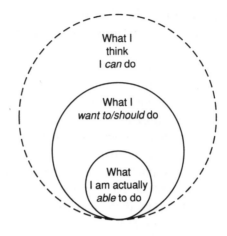

Figure 3.3   Self "imposed" limits

Tapping your Human Potential

The first step, therefore, is for you to become aware of your real potential, as a unique person in all aspects and dimensions of your self, and then to enhance the same. An outline of these parameters is given in table 3.1.

While, for instance, in your normal life you do not need to discriminate between eight million shades of colors or between 300,000 different tones, the information given in table 3.1 indicates the range of potential to which you have access. In other words, you

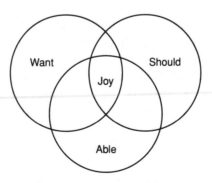

Figure 3.4   The realm of joy

Table 3.1 Human potential

Aspect	System	Capabilities
Physical	Senses	Eyes: can discriminate 8 million shades Ears: can discriminate 300,000 tones
	Muscles	When all 600 pinpointed, can pull 25 tons
	Bone	One cubic inch can stand 2 tons force
Mental	Brain	Super-computer with immense observing, recording, analyzing, recalling, and storing capacity equivalent to thousands of contemporary mainframes. Beyond computing, it has almost immeasurable learning, understanding-imaging, creative, and intuitive abilities
Emotional		Range of feelings
Neurosensory		Multisensory/intersensory capacity
Consciousness		Spectrum of fields and levels

need not continue to harbor the belief, and the consequent fear, of experiencing stagnation in your competencies or capacities.

Beyond categories: the "seed" principle

Several models of "human classifications" or "personality types" are prevalent today, a few of which are illustrated in table 3.2.

All of these, and other classifications or categories, can be very useful in making us aware of our predominant characteristics or orientations. Unfortunately, however, with such "typing" we are frequently left with a feeling that we are in one mold, or category, and have to live with it. In fact, in many organizations "teams" or "task forces" are formed on the basis of such classifications. This supposedly serves to ensure that all the qualities and competences that are required in the performance of any project or task are provided for by this grouping and balancing of different personality types in a team. This can be beneficial up to a point in that it may well lead to higher team performance. But, unless some conscious "balancing" training is given to each team member, to cultivate his or her less dominant characteristics or traits, that person is likely to

Table 3.2 Human classifications

Classification	Authors	Descriptors
Personality type	Friedman and Roseman	"A" or "B"
Personality type	Jungian/Myers-Brigg	Extrovert/introvert Sensing/intuitive Thinking/feeling Judging/perceiving
Orientation	Blake and Moulton	Task/people grid
Need hierarchy	Maslow	Physiological/sociological/ psychological/transpersonal
Life positions	Eric Berne	I'm OK/I'm not OK
Ego stages	Eric Berne	Parent/adult/child

be permanently blocked or locked in that limited "track," through such constant reinforcement at work.

It is therefore important to realize that, keeping in mind the almost unlimited human potential that you are gifted with in all your dimensions, you can change, evolve, blossom, and grow into a fuller, greater, richer human being (see figure 3.5). You *can* change – if you really want to.

The central point of this "new-paradigm" approach to managing

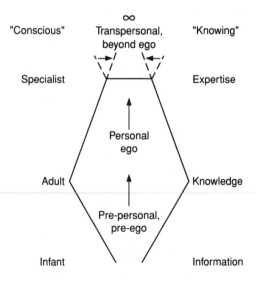

Figure 3.5 Model of personal growth

yourself is that you, as a human being, are like a "seed" with a tremendous amount of dormant potential. You have a choice: either feel the "comfort" or "security" of remaining a "seed" all your life or take a more dynamic and courageous attitude, and fertilize and nurture the seed. Then you will enable the "seed" to break through its "barriers," and blossom through various evolutionary stages into a fully grown plant or tree, with all the richness of its flowers or fruits.

From childhood you grow into adulthood and aspire to be a specialist, by converting information to knowledge and then to expertise, through primary, secondary, and advanced education. At this stage you have built up your "personal ego," based on several learnt beliefs and identities. You now have two choices. You can restrict your future growth by remaining like a seed that is trapped in the "box" of your restrictive beliefs or ego state. Alternatively, you may choose to "believe" in the possibilities of breaking through such psychological barriers into a different, higher, domain of existence, by cultivating a special expertise (knowledge plus skills plus attitudes), by converting work ethic into a growth ethic. This involves gaining access to and experiencing higher levels of consciousness and going beyond ego, thereby opening up alternative, but hitherto dormant, channels of knowing. This is what "managing your self" in the new paradigm is about.

The Master Manager: "Re-visioning"

Broadly speaking, managers can be classified into three categories: (a) the innocent manager, (b) the learned manager, and (c) the master manager (see figure 3.6).

1 Prior to the development of management as a profession and as a distinct educational discipline, most executives managed their business organizations through their common-sense and personal insights. If you operate at this level, you are an "innocent manager."

2 However, as the functions of business and the processes of management became more complex, it was found that intelligence alone was not enough: specialized expertise was now considered essential for effective management. With professional management training, in acquiring further knowledge and skills of business

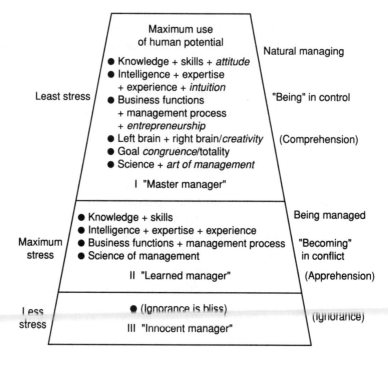

Figure 3.6 Levels of managing living

functions as well as management processes, you become a "learned" manager. However, as management becomes even more complex, and you become involved in multiple roles and responsibilities, there are concomitant conflicts. As you face up to these, a growing feeling of apprehension and stress often occurs. At this point the learned manager experiences, on the one hand, an escalating achievement orientation and, on the other, a growing dependence on external factors. At this stage, you experience maximum stress, in that while you are managing your organization you are also in a sense being "managed" by it.

3 Some managers do realize this, but their coping strategies are generally not appropriate, and therefore mostly ineffective. They usually deal with symptoms rather than causes, suppressing or transferring their stress. To break through and beyond this level of the "learned manager" before you break down and blow up, or burn out, you have to develop into a "master manager." What significantly differentiates the master manager from the learned manager are

certain attitudes, and the capacities of intuition, entrepreneurship, and creativity. An appropriate combination of these implies a comprehensive and integrated use of your full potential and the ability to understand and achieve a "goal" congruence amongst different and often conflicting roles. This implies an active synthesis of management as a science and an art. It can also be viewed as "natural managing," which causes the least amount of stress.

Level of living and managing

Such new-paradigm management fosters vision and commitment. With a deeper level of consciousness, your perceptions and attitudes generate a natural and spontaneous flow of behavior and performance, leading to an actualization of expertise. At the same time you are constantly in touch with your "being" level and experiences. The "master manager" experiences a joyous, self-dependent, and confident feeling of being in control, in stark contrast to the feelings of anxiety, uncertainty, and insecurity that the "learned manager," who generally operates from a "state of fear," normally experiences. Such a masterful performance can be compared with that of a maestro.

As a result, the new-paradigm manager experiences a minimum level of unhealthy stress. It is important to realize that the "quality" of management cannot be separated from the quality of life or the quality of the person who does the managing. The level of managing is, in fact, a consequence of the personal level-of-being of the manager. The competencies that are now being increasingly required, in order to cope with the changing demands of the environment, cannot be acquired by traditional training methods, but are largely a consequence of a different consciousness and vision of reality, of life, and of one's own self.

From this perspective, therefore, if you want to acquire managerial mastery, it is necessary for you to develop a conceptual understanding and insight into "reality," to understand the various dimensions and potential of a human being and the different levels of consciousness and identities of which you are capable. This will give you access to certain attitudes that result in behavioral qualities which are now being increasingly emphasized as essential, even by some "hard" management theorists. To a new-paradigm manager, such qualities "happen" to him. This master approach will not only enable you to

Table 3.3 The evolution of management thinking

Date	Concept of man	Management approach
1900–1925	Rational-economic man, social Darwinism	Carrot-and-stick approach, "scientific management"
1926–1950	Social man, "leaders are made, not born"	Human relations school, the Hawthorn experiment
1951–1975	Humanistic man, need hierarchy	Human resource management, Theories x and y, group dynamics, Maslow's need hierarchy
1976–1990	Holistic man, holarchy	Developmental management, Theory z, quality circles
1990–?	Integrated man, "being" and "becoming"	Transformative, synergistic approach, management

maximize the use of your potential but also to maximize the return on your life. There will be a natural synthesis in your multiple and often conflicting goals, roles, and responsibilities.

Levels of living and levels of managing are inseparable. You can only go beyond a certain level of managing if you are able to go beyond a certain level of living. This leads us on from the "what" of self-mastery to the "how" of managing by detached involvement, the route to becoming a new-paradigm manager.

Becoming a master manager

One of the most interesting features of emerging organizational cultures and managerial styles is the changing managerial role model. No longer is it enough for a manager to have only analytic or problem-solving skills. These are being increasingly met by computers, and by expert and knowledge-based systems. What is of growing significance, in the new managerial role, is self-mastery, particularly in these contemporary times of rapid and complex change.

In fact, if you reflect on the historical evolution of management, from the beginning of this century, you will find that managerial theory and roles, at any given time, have generally been based on the prevailing concepts of "man" (see table 3.3).

Management by Detached Involvement

From table 3.3 you can see that the new-paradigm concept of Man is "enlarging" beyond the "ego level" of a human being. Consequently, the emerging approach in management is one of integration and transformation. This involves a synthesis between your self-centered, ego-level needs and your self-less consciousness as a transcendent being. You then experience a kind of self-ness, operating from an integrated and "balanced" level of being. Such transformative and synergistic approaches alone can bring about the kind of goal congruence – at a micro- and macro-level – that is now being increasingly expected from organizations, and therefore from managers.

In fact, such "master managers" are expected to perform the multiple leadership roles of "focalizer," "facilitator", "synergizer," and "co-creator":

- *focalizer*, generating shared vision, mission, position, and attention
- *facilitator*, bringing about commitment, action, harmony, and growth
- *synergizer*, helping to achieve individual/organizational/societal role/goal congruence
- *co-creator*, positioning oneself as co-learner and co-shaper of success – the first among equals, not the "hero"

In that managerial capacity you need to balance, and integrate, the economic and technological goals of business with the ecological and psycho-social aspirations of society, through a shared vision and committed action. In order to understand the complexities involved, and be able to achieve such goal and role congruence, you need, as a manager, to develop a higher level of creativity, a deeper level of consciousness of detached involvement, and the associated knowledge, skills, and attitudes.

Knowledge

As such a new-paradigm manager, firstly you possess general insights into people, things, ideas, and events, as well as particular professional and managerial know-how. Secondly, you have greater insight into environmental forces and trends than is required for everyday business and management functions. Thirdly, you have in-depth insights into your own inner dynamics, covering the functioning of your body, mind, emotions, neurosensory system, and states of consciousness. In other words, you know enough about your own and your organization's internal dynamics to be able to effect harmony between the two.

Skills

The skills you have acquired, as a master manager, can be identified and exercised at three levels: personal, group or team, and cultural.

Personal

At the personal level, you possess skills that enable you to achieve inner balance and integration within the five dimensions of your self – body, mind, emotion, neurosensory system, and consciousness.

Team

At the team level you have three types of skills:

- The skill of motivating others in a group, by linking their interests and ideas to a common vision generated by the interaction of these very interests and ideas, which serve to galvanize the disparate group into a cohesive team.
- The skill of communicating: through a two-way process developed through listening. It is only through such two-way communication that you will enable every member of a team to learn where they fit into the general scheme of things. Similarly, through such mutual interaction, individual tasks and team objectives are aligned, toward the commonly perceived corporate goals and vision. This leads individuals to the kind of commitment required of them in order to function as a team.
- The skill of "facilitating": within the framework of the team,

developing a structure as well as processes which enable everyone to perform at their peak level, within the context of the common vision and mission.

Cultural

At the third, cultural level, you can develop alignment in the organization, and attunement within the individual. These two processes, when combined, serve to generate the necessary goal congruences and to develop and maintain the vision and the mission of both individual and organization.

Attitudes

Finally, as a master manager you have a particular set of attitudes. In fact, you shift from traditional, power- and problem-driven attitudes to vision-driven ones (see chapter 4). These attitudes arise from your commitment to certain purposes and values, which implies a shift from management style based on control and aggression to one centered upon caring and connection. Your thoughts, feelings, and actions are proactive and self-reliant, as opposed to the conventionally reactive postures of many "innocent" or even professional managers.

Creativity

The fourth dimension in the new-paradigm manager's mix is that of creativity, which comprises the following elements:

- the capacity for envisioning and an understanding of intuition
- the ability to have a much wider and deeper perception – the ability to see more than "what meets the eye"
- to see deeper significances and connections, which may not be obvious, and the ability to break old connections, and make new ones
- the skill to convert such connections into concrete applications relevant to the organization and its mission

In other words, creativity implies a capacity for vision, intuition, perception, connection, and application.

Consciousness

The fifth dimension is that of consciousness, the capacity to shift your "gear" into different levels of consciousness appropriate to the tasks and the situations in which you are involved. On the basis of your concept of reality and the self, you can develop an understanding as well as the capacity to access different states of consciousness, and lucidly tune into them whenever desired. This is possible when you are in touch with your deeper level of the self or consciousness, which is detached from your ego-self or from ego-related consciousness.

A master manager is usually neither "selfish" nor "selfless," remaining in touch with the deeper level of the self; that is, with his being-level. This could be described as "self-ness" – a kind of detached involvement. This removes the distraction of the ego-related "noise" and brings you in touch with your "inner music." Operating from such consciousness, you can access and achieve your deeper potential and perform with a "joy of doing" (not with a "fear of losing") so that you identify with current performance, in the context of the vision of the organization. This is the stuff of which sustainable peak performance is made. This is the most basic dimension of a leader, or "master manager," because it is this quality which inspires others. Finally, this is the level at which you experience alignment, attunement, and empowerment within the organization, and with its external environment. Such mastery is therefore more a mental state than a personality trait. It can be learnt or cultivated.

From this perspective, it is clear that the role of the new-paradigm manager has shifted and has been enlarged, significantly, from that of the traditional problem-solver to that of focalizer, facilitator, synthesizer, and synergizer. Such synergy, at both a micro- and macro-level, is an essential precondition for organizational effectiveness, over the long term. Such effectiveness incorporates high-level performance and satisfaction of the individual and, at the societal level, rising standards of living and higher standards of life.

The implication is that the master manager is one who is not only a good manager in a corporate context, but is also a good citizen in

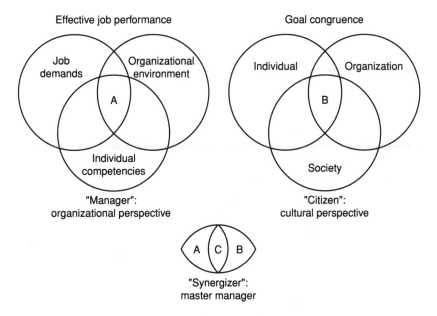

Figure 3.7   The master manager

the social context. As a manager, in the organizational perspective (shown in figure 3.7), for effective performance he needs those competencies "A" which synchronize his personal growth with his job demands and organizational enrichment. As a citizen, in the cultural perspective, to achieve goal congruence among the individual, the organization, and the society, he needs qualities "B." As a master manager or leader, therefore, he needs the core of both "A" and "B," namely "C." This is the mix of knowledge, skills, attitudes, creativity, and consciousness that we have just discussed. These are attainable and sustainable with detached involvement which implies a different level of living and managing. This means functioning from a larger, deeper, and richer vision.

On being vision driven

We have presented the entire concept of "managing your self" and becoming a master manager within the context of development at three levels: societal, organizational, and individual. At the societal

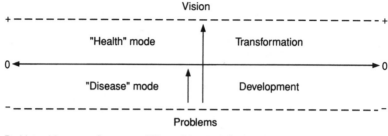

Problem-driven: confinement within problem/solution cycle,
                propensity of problemizing

Vision-driven: problems seen as opportunities,
                enlarging context/making limitations irrelevant,
                making adversity work for you

Figure 3.8   Revisioning (renewal/rebirth)

level the main forces that influence development are the ideologies prevailing in that society and its institutional framework. At the organizational level it is culture and structure that predetermines organizational development. Finally, at the individual level it is the totality of that person.

The approach we have adopted is basically a functional one. We have treated "self" as a "managing self." Through it you manage the various operating dimensions, or functional areas of your being, and through them your multiple roles in life. This enables you, in turn, to reach a higher level of consciousness. By operating at such a heightened level you should be able to enhance much of your hidden potential. As a result, not only can you grow and develop, to a much greater extent, as a human being, but you can also achieve the kind of success and the amount of satisfaction that you seek. Finally, you should create, in your immediate environment, a kind of "vibration around your self," which has a positive and powerful impact on those with whom you interact.

In essence, "managing your self" is about being vision driven rather than problem driven. In other words, managing your self is about re-visioning, implying renewal and a process of "rebirth," as shown in figure 3.8. At an ordinary level of consciousness, you would be conditioned to living and working in a "disease mode," or in a problem-driven mode, because your basic approach would involve identifying problems, as success consists of solving problems. In

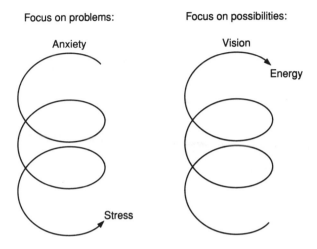

Figure 3.9 Problems versus possibilities

other words, you would remain within the problem–solution cycle. Therefore, development or success would be marked by the absence of problems. In fact, with such a focus on problems, you would experience the anxiety which generates negative stress; whereas if the focus is on "possibilities" with a clear vision, you will experience more positive energy, as shown in figure 3.9.

Individual transformation

As we have emphasized right from the start, the new-paradigm manager's reference point is not absence of problems, nor absence of illness. Rather, it is the presence of wellness and the experience of an invigorating joy. Such joyful experience is possible only if you have a very clear vision before you, and thereby operate in the "health mode." It is in this mode that peak performance happens, concomitantly with peak experience.

To ensure such a level of peak performance then, you need to have, firstly, a vision that is a very clear image of what your work and life is about. It is a kind of dream: without a dream there cannot be any lasting excitement. This is becoming even more relevant and important in the context of accelerating change, complexity, uncertainty, and conflict. It is through a clear vision that you will be able

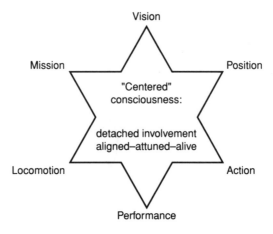

Figure 3.10   From vision to action

to experience a "quantum leap" (instead of just an incremental improvement) and acquire the necessary strengths: what Ilya Prigogine might call an "escape to a higher order."

Secondly (see figure 3.10), to enable you to convert such a vision into reality, you have to verbalize it in a statement, a mission – a statement about your own life. Thirdly, you have to take a very clear stand or position on this mission. In other words, you have to commit yourself totally to the achievement of that mission, giving to it whatever it takes.

Once you have determined the vision, mission, and position you need, to align all your resources – human and otherwise – you provide the locomotive power to finally move the entire organization's energies, single-mindedly and wholeheartedly, toward creative tension. This ensures remaining "grounded" (but not "stuck in the mud") as well as "up in the sky" (but not "lost in the clouds"): becoming a "visionary pragmatist" or a "pragmatic visionary."

Peak performance and peak experience will then happen to you. You create the context in which what shows up is performance. You become transparent. You become the performance – you identify your consciousness with performance. You and your performance become the stuff of which creativity and excellence are made. You remain involved with performance and yet are detached from the results. This facilitates peak performance and its consequential upward spiral.

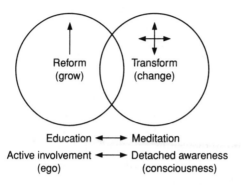

Education ←——→ Meditation
Active involvement ←——→ Detached awareness
(ego) (consciousness)

Figure 3.11 Self-development through detached involvement
(revisioning renewal)

Organizational transformation

The ultimate impact of self-management with detached involvement is on the organization, leading to its progressive transformation. Having developed your self along the lines illustrated above, you should be able to synthesize the individual and organizational roles and goals, processes and results. If you want to transform anything or anyone, including any organization, you have to begin with your self. You need to reform and transform your self, through relevant education and meditation (outer space and inner space), as indicated in figure 3.11.

When working in or with a typical organization, you will find that the prevailing culture is usually a "reactive" culture which will need to be transformed into a "creative" one if peak performance is to result. To achieve this, you will have to go carefully and patiently through a series of steps. In fact, you need to start by changing the reactive culture into a "proactive" one. To enable this to happen you have, initially, to turn the entire organization into a "responsive" one. You can facilitate this by opening up discussions on the "purpose" and functioning of the organization:

- why it exists – its philosophy
- what it is supposed to do – its ideology
- how it is going to achieve it – its strategy

Through engendering such a learning process you can move the organization to a "responsive" stage.

Over a period of time there is more "listening", and a climate of deeper understanding of the individual, group, and organizational roles begins to pervade. Such goal congruence leads to more personal interaction, to an intensification of team spirit, and to a greater sense of "belonging" and "commitment." This sets the stage for a proactive culture, which forms the essential precondition for the development of a more interactive and "creative" culture, when the organization becomes "vision driven" – leading to organizational peak performance on a sustained basis.

In order to evolve from proactivity to creativity at the individual, group, and organization levels, you need the qualities and competencies of a master manager, which are the natural consequences of management by detached involvement. This, then, is how you achieve an effective synthesis between your individual and organizational roles and goals, through a synergistic blend of personal and organizational transformation.

At this stage the individual, the groups, and the organization are fully aligned, attuned, and alive. Individual and organization have advanced beyond the Peter principle and the job, career, or life plateaux. This is what "managing your self" and detached involvement are all about. Figure 3.12 captures this idea by showing that the center of your being is a constant, strong, and stable pivot of consciousness, a base which liberates you into greater activity: "doing more" and at the same time feeling steady and secure and therefore "feeling better." This in turn facilitates and triggers even more activity and higher performance. The centered consciousness, or central pivot, is life avoidance. Detached involvement offers the courage to move with stillness in the world, instead of freezing into stillness in the face of accelerating change, uncertainty, and risk.

The paradox of happiness

The key to success is for you to align your expectations (of results) in a manner such that your basic experience, at any given point of time, is one of satisfaction. In other words, satisfaction or happiness consists of "striving to get what you want, but at the same time experiencing the wanting of whatever you get." Getting what you

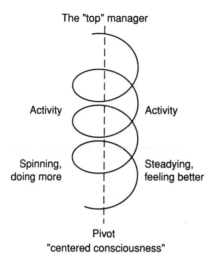

Figure 3.12 Management by "detached involvement" (MBDI)

want is success: wanting what you get is happiness. This is apparently a paradox, but if you have understood the basic approach outlined in this chapter, and got in touch with your deeper level of consciousness, you will have resolved the apparent contradiction.

You will be able to experience joy and satisfaction then, while functioning in your daily activities, because you are drawing your basic satisfaction from the inner source of joy, and not from the results or rewards for which you strive in your external environment. The essence of new-paradigm management, for the individual, therefore, is "management by detached involvement" (MBDI) – involved but not imprisoned, interested but not addicted. In essence, you are involved in the activities of your work and life, in your efforts to be successful, but you remain detached from the rewards themselves.

The missing link

The crucial dilemma for managers today is to resolve the continuing significant gap between the torrent of new management models they are exposed to in the contemporary literature and at seminars (and which they are expected to actualize), and their personal ability to do so: the gap between what they like to do and what they have to do. Management by detached involvement provides this missing link by raising the awareness and experience of, and identification with, a higher level of consciousness or self. This means becoming detached from the barriers and blocks of the ego-self, which is responsible for the above-mentioned "gap." Moreover, this also results in greater empowerment and freedom, which are enhanced by the gradual change, maturation, and eventual disappearance of self-limiting ego-consciousness or ego-sense. Symbolically, this could be expressed as follows:

LET
G
O

With a constant awareness, psychic involvement, and identification with the deeper consciousness – the pure and perpetual self – and detachment from or "de-identification" with the changing, ageing, and mortal ego-self, you will be able to conquer even the fear of the ultimate loss – that of death. If you experience your ego-death, you do not feel death when the body dies: your attitude becomes "the world dies, but I go on" rather than "I am dying and the world goes on." Death is seen as a transformational experience – not a point of termination. The essential elements of water do not die even when they change their form into ice or vapor. In this sense there is no death – only change in our cosmic address!

It is only when you operate from such a detached consciousness that you can bring about authentic organizational transformation. In the process you will be transforming organizational cultures from hierarchical structures into mutual support networks; from management styles based on control and aggression to those oriented toward "caring and connection." Moreover, in the final analysis, you will be transforming your role from that of either "innocent" or "professional" to that of master manager – a visionary pragmatist.

In the next three chapters, we consider, in more detail, the nature of visionary leadership, what the process of envisioning involves, and how you turn vision into action.

4

Visionary Leadership
Warren Bennis

Alfred Sloan and Martin Luther King, although from very different walks of life, both possessed one thing in common. They had attained self-mastery, and they had developed a vision. The same applied to William Paley.

When William Paley took over at America's CBS in 1928, at the age of 27, it had no stations of its own, was losing money, and was insignificant in an industry completely dominated by NBC. Within ten years, CBS had 114 stations and was earning $27.7 million. More than 40 years later, with Paley still at the helm, CBS was a dominant force in the broadcasting industry. David Halberstam has described Paley's ability like this:

> The critical years were the early ones. What he had from the start was a sense of vision, a sense of what might be. It was as if he could sit in New York in this tiny office with his almost bankrupt company and see not just his own desk, or the row of potential advertisers outside along Madison Avenue, but millions of the American people out in the hinterlands, so many of them out there, almost alone, many of them in homes as yet unconnected to electricity, people alone with almost no form of entertainment other than radio. It was his sense, his confidence that he could reach the masses, that he had something for them, that made him different. He could envision the audience at a time when there was in fact no audience. He not only had the vision, he knew how to harness it, he could see that the larger the audience, the greater the benefit to the network, because it would mean that many more advertisers would want to participate ... The larger the audience, the more time he could sell. To achieve that goal, he had something to offer – indeed to give away – by making his programs available to affiliate stations.

Over and over again, the senior managers we spoke to told us that they did the same things when they took charge of their organizations – they paid attention to what was going on, they determined what part of the events at hand would be important for the future of the organization, they set a new direction, and they concentrated the attention of everyone in the organization on it. We soon found that this was a universal principle of management, as true for orchestra conductors, army generals, football coaches, and school superintendents as for corporate executives. But if it all seems too easy, there is a catch. How do leaders know what is important for the future of their organizations, and how do they choose the new directions? That is what we must examine; but first we need to discuss why the principle works and why it is so fundamental to effective management.

Vision and Organizations

To choose a direction, an executive must first have developed (as indicated in chapter 3), a mental image of a possible and desirable future state of the organization. This image, which we call a vision, may be as vague as a dream or as precise as a goal or mission statement. The critical point is that a vision articulates a view of a realistic, credible, attractive future for the organization, a condition that is better in some important ways than what now exists.

A vision is a target that beckons. When John Kennedy set a goal of putting a man on the moon by 1970 or Stanford Weill aimed to make American Express the world's leading investment banking company in five years, they were focusing attention on worthwhile and attainable achievements. Note also that a vision always refers to a future state, a condition that does not presently exist and never existed before. With a vision, the executive provides the all-important bridge from the present to the future of the organization.

To understand why vision is so central to managerial success, we only need reflect on why organizations are formed in the first place. An organization is a group of people engaged in a common enterprise. Individuals join the enterprise in the hope of receiving rewards for their participation. Depending upon the organization and the individuals involved, the rewards might be largely economic, or they might be dominated by psycho-social considerations – status, self-esteem, a sense of accomplishment, a meaningful existence. Just as the individual derives rewards from his or her role in the organization, so too does the organization derive its rewards from finding an appropriate niche in the larger society. The organization's rewards might also be economic (profits, growth, access to resources) and/or psycho-social (prestige, legitimacy, power, and recognition).

So, on the one hand, an organization seeks to maximize its rewards from its position in the external environment and, on the other hand, individuals in the organization seek to maximize their rewards from their participation in the organization. When the organization has a clear sense of its purpose, direction, and desired future state, and when this image is widely shared, individuals are able to find their own roles both in the organization and in the larger society of which they are a part. This empowers individuals and confers status upon them because they can see themselves as part of a worthwhile enterprise. They gain a sense of importance, as they are transformed from robots blindly following instructions to human beings engaged in a creative and purposeful venture. When individuals feel that they can make a difference and that they can improve the society in which they are living through their participation in an organization, then it is much more likely that they will bring vigor and enthusiasm to their tasks and that the results of their work will be mutually reinforcing. Under these conditions, the human energies of the organization are aligned toward a common end, and a major precondition for success has been satisfied.

Consultants often report that they can feel this energy almost from the first moment they enter a corporation. It was present at America's Polaroid when Edwin Land led that firm into a new age of photography, and at Sears, Roebuck and Co. when the decision was made to become a financial services powerhouse. It takes the form of enthusiasm, commitment, pride, willingness to work hard and "go the extra mile." It is notably absent in some of the large conglomerates, where every month brings a new deal that proclaims to the employees that management is going into or out of a new business – or, more likely, is not really sure where it is going.

A shared vision of the future also suggests measures of effectiveness for the organization and for all its parts. It helps individuals distinguish between what is good and what is bad for the organization, and what it is worth while to want to achieve. And most important, it makes it possible to distribute decision-making widely. People can make difficult decisions without having to appeal to higher levels in the organization each time because they know what end results are desired. Thus, in a very real sense, individual behavior can be shaped, directed, and coordinated by a shared and empowering vision of the future. As John Young, head of America's Hewlett-Packard, said, "Successful companies have a consensus from top to bottom on a set of overall goals. The most brilliant management strategy will fail if that consensus is missing."

We have here one of the clearest distinctions between the new-paradigm and the old-paradigm manager. By focusing attention on a vision, the extraordinary manager operates on the emotional and spiritual resources of the organization, on its values, commitment, and aspirations. The ordinary manager, by contrast, operates on the physical resources of the organization, on its capital, human skills, raw materials, and technology. Any competent manager can make it possible for people in the organization to earn a living. An excellent manager can see to it that work is done productively and efficiently, on schedule, and with a high level of quality. It remains for the extraordinary one, however, to help people in the organization know pride and satisfaction in their work. Visionaries often inspire their followers to high levels of achievement by showing them how their work contributes to worthwhile ends. It is an emotional appeal to some of the most fundamental of human needs – the need to be important, to make a difference, to feel useful, to be a part of a successful and worthwhile enterprise.

With all of these benefits, one would think that organizations would take great care to develop a clear image of their desired future, but that does not seem to be the case. Instead, the visions of many organizations are out of focus and lack coherence. The reasons for this blurred focus are myriad. Some examples are as follows:

- within the past several decades, important new interpretations have been given to the role of the family, the quality of life, the work ethic, the social responsibility of business, the rights of minorities, and many other values and institutions that were once thought to be enduring and permanent
- telecommunications and rapid transportation have helped make the world increasingly interdependent for products, ideas, jobs, and resources
- the quickening pace of innovation has led to the specialization

of experts and massive problems of coordinating technical workers

- the general willingness to experiment with new social forms and norms has fractured society into a diversity of life-styles, each with its own product preferences
- workers are seeking and receiving a much greater voice in decisions that were once the exclusive territory of management

All of these forces and more contribute to the massive and growing complexity we see in today's world. This, in turn, creates great uncertainty and an overabundance of conflicting images in many organizations. The larger the organization, the greater the number of images is likely to be, the greater their complexity of interaction, and the quicker their shift in emphasis over time.

All of these things tend to cause organizational vertigo and lead to myopia. At the same time, they tend to make vision more imperative for the functional success of the organization, since without a coherent view of the future, these forces would conspire to shatter it in every direction. This explains, for example, why America's Thornton Bradshaw had to be hired away from ARCO to restore focus and a sense of purpose to the giant RCA corporation. Starting with a strong base in radio, television, and communications, RCA had drifted into such diverse fields as auto rental and financial services, under a succession of presidents, until it had become nearly paralyzed by conflicting images of where it should be headed. But where does the leader's vision come from?

Paying Attention: the Search for Vision

Historians tend to write about great personalities as if they possessed transcendent genius, as if they were capable of creating their visions and sense of destiny out of some mysterious inner resource. Perhaps some do, but upon closer examination it usually turns out that the vision did not originate with the personality but rather from others. For example, Harold Williams told us that, when he arrived at California's UCLA to take his new position as Dean of its Graduate School of Management, "it was really the faculty that brought together the concept of what it is we ought to do. They had the vision." Others looked elsewhere. John Kennedy spent a great deal of time reading history and studying the ideas of great thinkers. Martin Luther King Jr. found many of his ideas in the study of religious and ethical ideologies as well as in the traditions of his own and other peoples. Lenin was greatly influenced by the scholarship of Karl Marx, in much the same way as many contemporary business leaders are influenced by the works of leading economists and management scholars. Alfred P. Sloan's visions for the future of General Motors were greatly shaped by the prevailing cultural paradigm – the "American Dream" and the role of capitalism in it. Steve Jobs at Apple and Edwin Land at Polaroid were able to develop their visions from logical processes, mostly by seeking the technical limits of known technologies.

In all of these cases, the extraordinary person may have been the one who chose the image from those available at the moment, articulated it, gave it form and legitimacy, and focused attention on it, but only rarely was he or she the person who conceived the vision in the first place. Therefore, an extraordinary manager must be a superb listener, particularly to those advocating new or different images of the emerging reality. Many establish both formal and informal channels of communication in order to gain access to these ideas. Most also spend a substantial portion of their time interacting with advisers, consultants, other leaders, scholars, planners, and a wide variety of other people both inside and outside their own organizations in this search. Successful executives, we have found, are great askers, and they do pay attention.

Consider a typical example. Suppose you have been asked to take charge of a regional bank operating in the American state of California. The board of directors has turned to you for inspiration as a result of your success with a smaller bank in another state. How will you develop a sense of direction in your new circumstances? To whom will you pay attention, and how, to help you develop an appropriate vision of the future? Basically, there are three sources from which to seek guidance – the past, the present, and alternative images of future possibilities. We will consider each of these in turn.

The past

One obvious way to start is to reflect on your own experiences with other banks, to identify analogies and precedents that might apply to the new situation. Next, you talk to executives at other banks to collect their experiences with different approaches. You will surely want to learn about the history of the bank you are joining so you will be able to understand how it reached its current status and what qualities contributed to its past successes and failures. This you will get by talking to a wide variety of your new colleagues up and down the organization.

As you do this, you will be building a mental model of what worked and what did not work for this and similar banks in the past. You will be identifying some long-term trends – say, in deposits or loan experiences – that might be projected into the future as a first approximation of where the bank is heading if it continues as in the past. You collect thoughts about how the bank's performance has been linked to outside indicators – say, the state of the economy, interest rates, or development of the local community. And, of course, you pay attention to all the historical data you can get your hands on to increase your understanding of what this particular bank has been trying to do in the past, how successful it has been, and why.

The present

There is a lot to learn about the future from looking all around you at what is happening right now. For example, if you think about the year 1995, most of the buildings, roads, cities, people, corporations, and government agencies that will exist then are already here. The present provides a first approximation of the human, organizational, and material resources out of which the future will be formed. By studying these resources, it is possible to develop an understanding of the constraints and opportunities for their use and the conditions under which they may grow, decline, interact, or self-destruct. As a banker, you will pay a lot of attention to your current customer mix and the opportunities for expanding the services offered to them, to the locations of your branches, to your existing loan portfolios, and to what your competitors are doing.

There are early warning signals of impending change all around you. Your market researches, for example, should be able to identify growing markets at an early stage of development. The plans of politicians and business leaders are often widely reported. Public opinion polls document changing values and needs, and special surveys in your own field of financial services are often reported in the trade press. In fact, trend monitoring to provide early warning is a large and growing industry in the United States.

Finally, you can conduct small experiments in your own bank. Suppose that you are considering a major refocusing of the bank's attention in the direction of, say, loans for small businesses, or the professions, or particular industries. You can set up one branch or a small division with instructions to devote all its energies to the chosen area for some period of time, just as a chemical company develops a pilot plant before making a major commitment. You have, in effect, created a laboratory in which to experiment with your new vision.

The future

Your vision for the bank, as we have pointed out, will have to be set in some future time, so you need to study the conditions that may prevail at that time. Actually, although no one can predict what these conditions will be, there are many clues. Some sources and information have already been discussed – long-term trends, particularly in demography and resource usage; planning documents at the international, national, state, and corporate levels; the intentions and visions of policy-makers in all kinds of organizations; public opinion polls; and the leading edges of phenomena whose impact is expected to increase greatly in the future. But there are a few more sources of information.

You could look for structural clues to the future. For example, you might conclude that unless the government reverses its recent deregulation decisions, strong new competitors will continue to enter the banking business and a major restructuring of the industry will occur. You could then look at the kinds of structural changes and commitments being made by some of these potential competitors – Sears, Roebuck and Co., American Express, Prudential, and so on – and develop a scenario of what the market-place may look like if all these changes are made. You could then go on to examine the implications of such a scenario for specific customer groups, for the economy in general, for the investment community, and ultimately for the banking industry and your particular bank.

Beyond structural clues, you could obtain forecasts of all kinds to study: economic projections, demographic analyses, all kinds of industry forecasts, and the like. You could explore some of the intellectual ideas that may shape the future: philosophical works, science fiction novels, political party platforms, and books by leading sociologists, political scientists, and futurists. There are harbingers of future technologies, developments in research and development laboratories, technical papers presented at professional meetings, and government reports.

Thus, far from being devoid of information, you are likely to be inundated with information about the future, though only a small part may provide useful signposts in developing your vision for the bank. It is in the interpretation of this information that the real art of leadership lies. Just as the historian attempts to take piles of information about the past and construct an interpretation of the forces that may have been at work, so does the extraordinary manager select, organize, structure, and interpret information about the future in an attempt to construct a viable and credible vision. But the visionary leader has one distinctive advantage over the historian, in that much of the future can be invented or designed. By synthesizing an appropriate vision, he or she is influential in shaping the future itself.

Synthesizing Vision: Choice of Direction

All of the visionary leaders to whom we spoke seemed to have been masters at selecting, synthesizing, and articulating an appropriate vision of the future. Later, we learned that this was a common quality of such people down through the ages. Consider, for example, how a contemporary biographer of Napoleon, Louis Madelin, described him:

> He would deal with three or four alternatives at the same time and endeavor to conjure up every possible eventuality – preferably the worst. This foresight, the fruit of meditation, generally enabled him to be ready for any setback, nothing ever took him by surprise . . . His vision, as I have said, was capable of both breadth and depth. Perhaps the most astonishing characteristic of his intellect was the combination of idealism and realism which enabled him to face the most exalted visions at the same time as the most insignificant realities. And, indeed, he was in a sense a visionary, a dreamer of dreams.

The task of synthesizing an appropriate direction for the organization is complicated by the many dimensions of vision that may be required. Visionary leaders require foresight, so that they can judge how the vision fits into the way the environment of the organization may evolve; hindsight, so that the vision does not violate the traditions and culture of the organization; a world view, within which to interpret the impact of possible new developments and trends; depth perception, so that the whole picture can be seen in appropriate detail and perspective; peripheral vision, so that the possible responses of competitors and other stakeholders to the new direction can be comprehended; and a process of revision, so that all visions previously synthesized are constantly reviewed as the environment changes. Beyond this, decisions must be made about the appropriate time horizon to address, the simplicity or complexity of the image, the extent to which it will represent continuity with the past as opposed to a radical transformation, the degree of optimism or pessimism it will contain, its realism and credibility, and its potential impact on the organization.

If there is a spark of genius in the extraordinary manager at all, it must lie in this transcending ability, a kind of magic, to assemble – out of all the variety of images, signals, forecasts and alternatives – a clearly articulated vision of the future that is at once simple, easily understood, clearly desirable, and energizing.

Let us return to our banker example to see what might be involved. Up to this point, we have suggested how, you might collect all kinds of information that provides the raw material for a new vision of the future. Since vision cannot be limitless and still be credible to people in the organization, you will need to draw some boundaries. The vision should be projected in time and space beyond the boundaries of ordinary planning activities in the bank, but it should not be so far distant as to be beyond the ability of incumbents in the organization to realize. Perhaps you will decide to focus on a ten-year goal, far enough away to permit really dramatic change and yet within the comprehension and career aspirations of much of the current work force. Perhaps, too, you will want to move beyond the boundaries of current operations to include major new fields of activity such as personal financial planning or international banking, or to focus on a broad range of services to one or more specific target markets, such as high-technology industry.

The actual boundaries chosen will depend heavily on values as well. Your own values will determine which alternatives you seriously consider and the way they are evaluated. For example, America's Harold Williams now heads the country's J. Paul Getty Museum and Foundation, but his values were formed during a distinguished career in industry, academia, and public service. Thus, it is not surprising that he is steering the Getty Foundation in the direction of preservation and scholarship, and has promised not to allow the vast Getty fortune to be used to bid art prices up so high that other museums will be unable to acquire new works or serve their publics.

The values of the rest of the people in the bank, as reflected in the prevailing ideology, also suggest limits to the amount of change that might reasonably be expected. Values, for example, might dictate that whatever the new vision for the future of the bank is, it should emphasize quality and excellence of service rather than price or breadth of service.

With information and some boundary conditions in mind, you will try to understand the possible alternatives and weigh how attractive they are. Your most powerful tool for this purpose is the mental model you have built up over time of how the world works and how your bank operates in it. As a wise person, you will have tested this mental model many times in discussions with key executives, consultants, and others who have also thought deeply about the future of the bank. If you have access to a computer modeling facility and if the occasion justifies the cost, then a more formal, quantitative model can also be built.

Much of this analysis will have to be a series of "judgment calls," but it is possible to suggest some of the questions that should be addressed, including the following:

- What are the institutions that have a stake in the future of this bank, and what is it that they would like to see happen?
- What are the possible indicators of performance for the bank, and how can they be measured?
- What would happen to the bank if it continued on its present path without any major changes?
- What early warning signals might you detect if the external environment of the bank were in fact to change substantially?
- What could you do to alter the course of events, and what would the consequences of your actions be?

- What resources does your bank possess or can it obtain to act in the various futures that are possible?
- Of the alternative possible futures for the bank and its environments, which are more likely to be favorable to survival and success?

Through a series of questions such as these, patterns may appear that suggest viable alternative visions. You must then synthesize all this information into a single vision, and here is where the art form of the visionary really comes into play. The synthesis of a vision involves a great degree of judgement and, not infrequently, considerable intuition and creativity as well. Let us assume that in the banking example you have decided that the future of your bank, all things considered, would be most enhanced if it concentrated its attention on serving high-technology companies, particularly in newly emerging industries, with a wide range of financial services. It still remains to translate this vision into action.

Focusing Attention: Searching for Commitment

The visionary leader may generate new views of the future and may be a genius at synthesizing and articulating them, but this makes a difference only when the vision has been successfully communicated throughout the organization and effectively institutionalized as a guiding principle. Visionary leaders are only as powerful as the ideas they can communicate. His or her basic philosophy must be: "We have seen what this organization can be, we understand the consequences of that vision, and now we must act to make it so." A vision cannot be established in an organization by edict, or by the exercise of power or coercion. It is more an act of persuasion, of creating an enthusiastic and dedicated commitment to a vision because it is right for the times, right for the organization, and right for the people who are working in it.

We have found in our discussions with managers that visions can often be communicated best by metaphors, or models – as when a political leader promises "a chicken in every pot" or a phone company asks you to "reach out and touch someone." Perhaps in our banking example it might be something like "innovative banking for innovative companies," or "financial services at the leading edge." In any communication, some distortion takes place, but the extraordinary manager seems to be able to find just the right metaphor that clarifies the idea and minimizes distortion. In fact, the right metaphor often transcends verbal communication altogether; like a good poem or song, it is much more than mere words. It "feels right," it appeals at the gut level, it resonates with the listener's own emotional needs, it somehow "clicks."

A vision of the future is not offered once and for all and then allowed to fade away. It must be repeated time and again. It must be incorporated in the organization's culture and reinforced through the strategy and decision-making process. It must be constantly evaluated for possible change in the light of new circumstances.

Having now considered the "what" of envisioning, we need to turn more specifically towards the "how." Firstly, we consider how new-paradigm managers develop a vision and, secondly, how such vision is turned into action.

5

Developing a Vision

Jagdish Parikh, Fred Neubauer
and Alden G. Lank

Reflective, Intuitive, and Integrative Visioning

While Warren Bennis' approach to envisioning (chapter 4) draws on his American experience, this chapter is set full square within Europe, albeit with an eastern 'intuitive' influence.

The resulting model of 'corporate visioning' is captured in figure 5.1. As can be seen from that flow chart, the approach starts out with two strands, namely (1) **reflective visioning** and (2) **intuitive visioning**. Both streams are eventually combined to (3) **an integrative vision** which serves as a powerful basis for action. The model also implies that visioning is a continuing process.

Reflective Visioning

In order to explain the steps in the reflective visioning process (upper left-hand part of figure 5.1), we assume that the entity going through the process represents management of a corporation, of a division, or of a major (relatively independent) subsidiary. The process can, however, also be applied to functional areas in a company, for example an R & D or Human Resource Department.

Before entering the first step of the process, the group is familiarized with the concept of a vision and of visioning much along the lines we have discussed in the previous chapter. One of the main aims of this presentation is to impress on the group that it will have to avoid the temptation of falling back into some of the familiar routines of traditional (incremental) strategic planning. After this

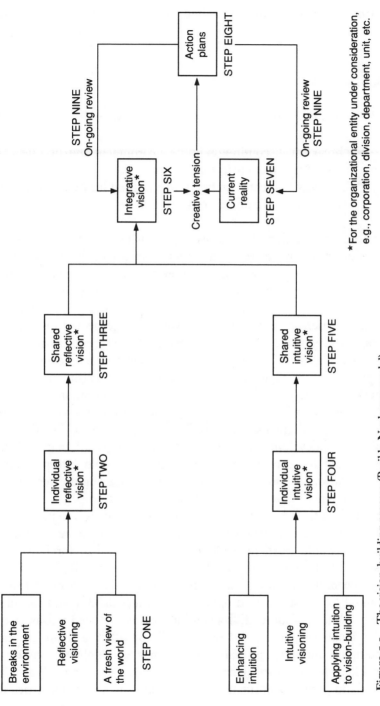

Figure 5.1 The vision-building process (Parikh–Neubauer model)

Boxes and labels in the diagram:

- Breaks in the environment
- Reflective visioning
- A fresh view of the world — STEP ONE
- Individual reflective vision* — STEP TWO
- Shared reflective vision* — STEP THREE
- Enhancing intuition
- Intuitive visioning
- Applying intuition to vision-building
- Individual intuitive vision* — STEP FOUR
- Shared intuitive vision* — STEP FIVE
- Integrative vision* — STEP SIX
- Current reality — STEP SEVEN
- Creative tension
- Action plans — STEP EIGHT
- STEP NINE — On-going review

*For the organizational entity under consideration, e.g., corporation, division, department, unit, etc.

introduction, the group is invited to begin the reflective visioning process itself.

Step one

The creation of a vision depends heavily on two major aspects:

- a break (or discontinuity) in the environment and/or a new way of "reading" that environment, and
- the ability to create "an image of a desired future organizational state" of the unit under consideration

In **step one** the first of these two aspects is dealt with.

In order to familiarize the managers with what is happening in the different environmental domains, they are exposed to short, pointed presentations by experts on the economic, technological, social, and political environments in which the company is living. The emphasis of these brief presentations is on observed or expected discontinuities, convergences, or undercurrents in the different environments. Examples of such developments in the environment could be the expected future regionalism in Europe, the globalization of capital markets, or the possible eclipse of the public corporation.

As we have pointed out earlier, the hallmark of the visionary, and the new-paradigm manager, is his or her ability to "read" these events and developments "differently from the pack," that is, differently from the way old-paradigm managers would interpret them. The following example illustrates this point. During the years of the independence movements in black Africa, Europeans who had established their business there in the colonial days became nervous about their future, fearing that the hotheads in the new administrations would push through threats to nationalize foreign-owned assets. In contrast, Tiny Rowland, the head of the British mining-finance house Lonrho, sensed that the new black African leaders wanted to reassure world opinion as to their stability and responsibility. While the other European businessmen moved out as fast as they could sell, he moved in forcefully by offering them low cash multiples, mopping up valuable earnings and debt-free assets at knocked-down prices (Channon and Robinson, 1973)! Was Tiny Rowland privy to information other businessmen in black Africa did not have? He was not. He just "read" the environment differently from the others. The essence of this part of the visioning exercise is well captured by the French writer, Marcel Proust, who said: "To go on a voyage of discovery you don't need new landscapes, you need fresh eyes."

In order to make it easier for managers to look at those environments with "fresh eyes," they are exposed to creativity-based techniques in the course of this step. In this context, you can for instance use techniques that Edward de Bono has introduced into the literature (and business practice) (see de Bono, 1985). The aim of this step is to come up with options for exciting and (hopefully) fresh business ideas.

Step two

In the second step of the process you are asked to do individual work. On the basis of the inputs provided in step one, you are requested to create your personal vision of the company, say, five years on. In order to give you some guidance on how to perform this task, we use a time-honored technique. We ask the participants to answer the question: "What would you like *Fortune* magazine to write about your company five years from now?" (If the company is not active internationally, we replace *Fortune* with any other prominent national business magazine that the participants know and appreciate.)

In our guidelines we ask you explicitly to write a lively, journalistic story, one you would use to lure the cream of the crop of graduating university students to your organization. This request forces managers, the participants, to abandon the terse outline with "bullets" that they typically use when they make presentations to peers and superiors (Tichy, 1984: 142). We urge you equally explicitly to jump ahead in this thinking and compose the story with no strings attached. (Later on, there will be ample opportunity to "pour water" into this "wine" of optimistic thinking.) Further on in the process we invite you to work "from your vision," i.e., to put yourself mentally in the future state described by the vision and ask what you would have to do today to arrive at that state.

Some of you resist this approach. We ask you to at least suspend your disbelief and to reserve your criticism for the outcome. This usually works. In the end, executives with whom we have interacted enjoyed visioning the desired future state of their organization.

Very similar to the "*Fortune*" approach is the "visioning the ideal" approach of which Tichy (1984: 140 ff) gives an example. In 1985, Clark Equipment and AB Volvo created a new company by merging Clark Michigan with Volvo's BM division. By doing so, they established one of the largest construction and mining equipment manufacturers in the world. On Clark's side of this transaction, we find an interesting illustration of this process in action.

Two years earlier, Clark found itself in great difficulties. In addition, there was no way to generate the resources to redirect its future in the time available. Rather than give up in despair, Clark Michigan took several unusual steps:

- They encouraged management to come up with an unconstrained design of an ideal competitor to the two giants in the industry, Caterpillar and Komatsu.
- Again without constraints, Clark Michigan's management considered which companies in the industry together with itself would most closely approximate the ideal company they had designed. Three organizations were identified as potential partners.
- Armed with this concept, they first approached Daimler-Benz and acquired their Euclid Truck subsidiary, a company specializing in off-road vehicles (used in open-pit mining, for instance). Furthermore, they opened discussion with Volvo BM, the construction equipment division of Volvo, suggesting a joint venture to them. The idea met with a friendly reception, but one manager insisted on some in-depth analyses to fully understand the merits of the case. Teams were formed who looked into the matter and discovered that the project would create advantages for both companies. In the fall of 1984 presentations were made to the Boards and the commitment to the joint venture was reached by the end of that year.

When the Clark managers looked back at the process and compared the outcome to the ideal they had envisioned, they had to admit to themselves that they had gotten most of what they had wanted. What happened at Clark would have been hardly achievable with conventional planning.

In our work with practitioners we find it helpful to combine the two approaches. When the participants write their *Fortune* article, we ask them to compose a story in which they envisage their company as an ideal competitor in their industry. As this task may awe some of the practitioners, we suggest that they break it up into more manageable sub-tasks.

One of the sub-tasks would be to answer the question: envisage the ideal version of your product – how would it look? Under normal circumstances, time allows us only to solicit your opinions. If the process were stretched out over a longer period, we might even confront key customers and distributors with this question and use their reactions when describing an ideal product. The same holds true, of course, for services that the company offers. Jan Carlzon's "Passenger Pleasing Plane" is an example. Carlzon's vision is a craft of unorthodox design with 75–80 percent of the interior volume of the fuselage allocated to passenger comfort and cabin baggage storage, compared to the 35 percent traditionally allocated. Here is his explanation of this dream: "For the 1990s our starting point is that we need an aircraft which the passenger wants. Then we can add on engines and the cockpit, not the other way around." In a news conference Carlzon picked up a model of a narrow-bodied plane, turned it aside and said: "This is what I see. The floor [of the Passenger Pleasing Plane] is lower; the roof higher. Seating would be no more than two seats abreast with an aisle. Belly space for the baggage would be reduced because there would be wardrobes for the traveler. Businessmen don't want to wait for their luggage." (Vandermerwe, 1989).

Another way to address an envisaged competitive advantage would be to ask: "What would be the ideal distribution system in your industry? If you could start all over again, how would you set it up?" A good example in this context would be the method Citicorp invented in 1986 to help Americans select their mortgage loans. In 1981 Citicorp was not even in the top 100 mortgage lenders in the US. To change the situation, they dreamed up a new distribution system:

Simply described, Citicorp has strung together three thousand real estate brokers, lawyers, and insurance agents into a thirty-seven-state referral network. To qualify for Mortgage Power (the name of the program) and receive a loan for an origination fee 1.5% below what one would get by going directly to Citicorp, the home buyer must go through a Citicorp agent. The agents, in turn, are paid by the home buyer a broker's fee of 0.5%. The positioning of the mortgage is not the lowest cost in the market, but a hassle-free one that will be approved (or not) within fifteen days, with very little paperwork. (Bandrowski, 1990).[1]

Further sub-tasks would include answering questions such as: "What would be the ideal organization structure for your company?" Or, "In your opinion, what would be the ideal management style?" (The answer to the last question would also express an opinion on a desirable culture and the basic values on which it rests.) Other sub-task questions which could be raised in this context are: "If we could start all over again, what would be the ideal business system for our company? What stage in the value chain should we concentrate on? Could we leave out stages that do not add value?"

A good example in this context would be IKEA, the international home furnishings retailer of Swedish origin. When enormous obstacles in Swedish furniture manufacturing and trade (e.g., a high degree of cartelization) hampered the growth of his budding company, Ingvar Kamprad, the founder of IKEA, dreamed up a modified form of the business system. IKEA eliminated or modified the activities that increased the delivery cost and did not add essential perceived value from the consumer point of view. Gilbert and Strebel describe Kamprad's concept in the following way:

Carefully monitoring sub-contracting of production to specialized manufacturers ensured quality at a lower cost. The furniture was no longer assembled, but flat-packed. It was not displayed in city-center stores but in hyper-stores outside cities. A trade-off was made between minimum inventories, to decrease delivered cost, and immediate availability. Furthermore, by doing its own product design, IKEA could insure a low delivered cost consistency throughout its business system. On the other hand, perceived value was added where this could be done for a low delivered cost. A very wide range of home products was offered under the same roof and could be looked at and tried by the consumer in the display section of the stores, rather than only seen in different stores or in catalogs. The furniture was normally available immediately and could be taken back home by car. Doing its own design IKEA could offer a homogeneous, modular product range. The desirable image of Scandinavian furniture was skilfully exploited to add perceived value. Last not least, by redesigning its entire business system, IKEA built an additional powerful competitive advantage: the know-how necessary to operate this formula. (Gilbert and Strebel, 1988).

Their unique approach made IKEA into the world's largest home furnishings retailer by the end of the 1980s.

The sub-tasks mentioned above are only meant to be indicative. Other aspects have to be added to round out the picture. These partial stories have to be combined and homogenized, so that they result in a cohesive story. We consider step two (which is done individually) an extremely important step in the process. As an artist always has an image of the work he wants to create in his mind, a visionary manager has to be able to create for himself his personal image of a desired future state of his organization. As Bennis has said: "If there is a spark of genius in the leadership function at all, it must lie in this transcending ability . . . to assemble – out of all the variety of images, signals, forecasts and alternatives – a clearly articulated vision of the future that is at once simple, easily understood, clearly desirable and energizing." (Bennis and Nanus, 1985)

Step three

In order to serve its purpose, a vision has to be a shared vision, as we said earlier. This sharing among yourselves is done, in step three, in a plenary session of the team. During this session, you jointly study the individual vision statements, discuss them in considerable depth, and identify areas which they have in common as well as outlying ideas. In this intensive session (in "sweatshirts, with flipcharts, cans of beer and sandwiches" to use John Harvey-Jones' words) and under the guidance of experienced process facilitators, a shared reflective vision is crafted in all the specificity needed to make it meaningful. A vision statement is, of course, never finished. Nevertheless, you have to push it to a certain completeness at this stage; otherwise, you have problems in the remaining steps of the exercise. (If the company happens to have several rather heterogeneous divisions, you might proceed in stages: first go through the process on the divisional level creating a shared divisional vision, and then convert these various visions into a shared corporate vision.)

As can be seen from this description of the first three steps, our process allows us to employ all the generic modes of visioning we have – individual approaches as well as interactive, sharing ways. The reflective visioning process has been made part of the exercise for a number of reasons. Although it breaks in several respects with the traditional planning approaches, it still is a rational way of proceeding. This means it offers you "a rod to hold on to"; that is, you yourselves are on a largely familiar terrain. This eases you into our visioning process. We feel that we have to provide this comfort before breaking even more radically with the traditional approaches by using non-rational – that is, intuitive – processes. These intuitive approaches are, however, needed to get the full benefit of the visioning process.

Intuitive Visioning

The basic difference between reflective visioning and intuitive visioning is that while pursuing reflective visioning, you are responding to the question "*What can I get?*" While this does not imply merely an incremental projection of growth and does enable a "jump" ahead of the conventional vision statement, it is still basically an intellectual or rational process. In other words, while it involves maximum possible stretching of your imagination into the future, it is inevitably tempered with realism. The process of intuitive visioning on the other hand implies responding to the question "*What do I really want?*" While responding to this question you do not keep the frame of reference of current reality or even what may be considered as realistic future possibility. It implies total resonance within yourself with whatever it is that you are doing in your life, with whatever are your basic urges and uncontaminated inner "dreams." In other words, after you intellectually, rationally, or realistically arrive at a maximum stretch of your imagination in the context of the real world possibilities – that is, developing the reflective vision – you should enter another level of mental activity; namely, the "intuitive" level. Therein you access your own "inner world" through some specific mental – intuitive – processes for creating an intuitive vision.

As mentioned above, at the intuitive level you are not either locked into linear thinking or blocked by any so-called rational constraints. Intuitive vision therefore would not only be a much bigger leap, a "quantum" leap from the current reality, but also qualitatively different from the reflective vision. In other words, in the process of reflective visioning you are still constrained by logical realism. In intuitive visioning, you have no such constraints. In other words, the intuitive visioning process facilitates the release of your innate creativity, duly unfettered by rational/analytical/linear thinking or by your existing mind-set. It enables you to break the connections with your conventional pattern of thinking, and experience a different kind or level of perception (or insight) about possibilities in the future. This enhances your ability to develop some totally new and different kinds of linkages. Finally, this process also helps to generate hitherto unthought of applications or innovative ideas.

The underlying assumption here is that while you have acquired certain kinds of knowledge and skills which enable you to intensify your depth of thinking, your education, experience, and expertise have tended to restrict the breadth or the width of your imagination and creativity. Modern education seems to have affected adversely our natural rounded sensibilities and narrowed them down into a "Cartesian" square hole. Moreover, being "realistic" also implies remaining linked with the existing, established paradigm or learnt viewpoint of what reality in the world of business is about. When we go deep inside us beyond this frame of reference, through intuitive processes, then we have no such limiting factors, which helps in "rounding the square." In other words, this process enables you to go beyond your ordinary conscious, logical, rational, somewhat simplistic mental state to the exploration of deeper and more complex patterns at subconscious levels (see chapter 3). This facilitates expansion or enlargement of the context in which you reflect, and leads to a more holistic, macroscopic, and a more synthesizing context in your thinking.

There are also suggestions that in such an intuitive process, when you are in a very relaxed and receptive state of mind, or as you begin to get in touch with a deeper and expanded state of consciousness, the constraints and barriers of your rational, egoistic skin-encapsulated thinking begin to soften and become dormant. Your consciousness in a sense gets connected and in tune with larger systems, and enables you to receive information from sources outside your own self. This phenomenon is also generally described as "extra-sensory perceptions."

These perceptions are basically supposed to be of three varieties. Firstly, our mind connects and taps other minds: this is described as "telepathy." Secondly, our mind interacts with matter: seeing, touching other objects, or articles and through them receiving some information. This is described as "clairvoyance." Thirdly, sometimes our minds also go beyond time and space coordinates and even supposedly tap into the future, which is described as "premonition."

Now from a business point of view, no matter what the processes are and what their descriptions, it is of immense value to develop a condition within yourself which enables you to expand the arena and sources of information. This would help in cultivating the ability, and therefore possibilities, of having some different kinds of insights and innovative connections which surface in your mind as intuition. However, it is important to ensure that you are able, over a period of time, to cultivate the sensitivity to distinguish between your instinctive drives or impulsive desires (what may be commonly described as wishful thinking) and authentic intuition. What happens ordinarily is that you experience these inner compulsive urges but you suppress them in the context of "realistic" life-styles. Therefore, these urges remain suppressed at a subconscious level, the level which can be described, among other things, as that of unarticulated dreams. Set within an old paradigm governed by rational, logical, analytical processes, you usually believe that you should not be carried away by your dreams, for fear of getting out of touch with reality. While this is basically correct there is a tendency to overdo it; to redress the balance, we need more systematically to explore our inner dynamics.

To put it in rather simplistic terms, keeping in mind the emerging scenarios in business – characterized by accelerating change, complexity, uncertainty, and conflict – we need to think not only from our heads, but also from our instincts and to develop the combination which reflects from our hearts.

While the essence and basis of your vision is intuition, the complete visioning process involves accessing. This implies a continuing interaction with your reasoning abilities as well as the energy of your emotions. It is a synthesis of all three (intuition, reason, and emotion) which leads to a virtuous spiral of analysis, imagination, and innovation. This is illustrated in figure 5.2.

It is through such an interaction triggered off by the intuitive processes that you can create an intuitive vision on an individual basis as well as a shared vision within an organization. The process of sharing your intuitive vision generates a deeper understanding within the organization and a sense of common belonging and bonding. This releases positive energy and on-going action to implement and actualize the shared vision. Work, in this way, is vision made visible.

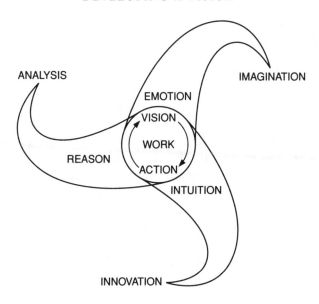

Figure 5.2 Work is vision made visible

Step four

A brief description of the sequence involved in this highly creative and exciting intuitive process is given below.

Relaxing

The first and the most important step is to be totally relaxed, in terms of body, mind, and emotion. There are specific relaxation processes which give you an experience of being "centered."

Imaging

Then go into the processes of imaging, and guiding yourself to a deeper inner level of awareness leading to an imaginary "retreat" detached and disconnected from the external environment.

Symbolizing

In your personal life, having reached such a state of being totally absorbed with your own inner self, begin to "dream" and create a picture about what you really "want" in your personal life, family life, life with your friends, and other social activities, allow the mind to think cognitively about your life and to create visual images intuitively about what you really want in your personal life. This is known as "**receiving**." Then **analyze** what you have received, by identifying the main elements that are dominant in these images or your personal dream scenarios.

In your professional life, **receiving** involves remaining in this state of deep relaxation and in a kind of twilight zone between your conscious and subconscious selves, while you begin to ask questions about what kind of activity or work you would like to be involved with. In other words, answer the question "What do I really want to do in my professional and public lives?" and develop a dream articulated into a vision: a visual picture or a symbol.

Analyze as you did with regard to your personal life, by identifying the elements of the dream scenario or picture for your professional life. Then, following the same sequence, articulate a **verbal** vision statement of your professional life.

This process, described above, leading to a picture or symbol, is useful and exciting in several ways. It enables you to become aware of your inner dynamics. Frequently it is most surprising to get in touch with your innermost urges and get an insight into what you are really up to in your life. The process also trains you to develop "total thinking," by learning the visual language of creating images, pictures, and symbols, and balancing and synthesizing the same with your conventional rational and analytical thinking. Above all, it is also a very enjoyable and energizing process. This process is described in figure 5.3.

However, the next stage is a crucial one: after having articulated a vision and a verbal statement about your personal life as well as about your professional life, you have to compare the two – the personal and the professional vision. On comparison, you would usually find some convergence as well as some discrepancies between the two visions. While you are generally aware of this situation, you have not

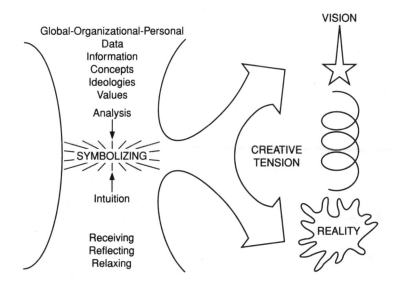

Figure 5.3 Intuitive vision-building

usually gone into a systematic process of identifying, crystalizing, and balancing in a conscious manner these complementaries and divergences, which therefore frequently become manifested in tension and even conflicts between your personal and family life on the one hand, and your professional and business life on the other.

While such tension and conflict cannot be totally avoided or resolved, you can certainly minimize them through a conscious and deliberate effort to bring about an **alignment** between the two visions and even convert such tension into a creative energy, thereby transforming your negative emotions into positive ones. At a deeper level, this also enables you to transform yourself from a reactive old-paradigm manager to a more proactive new-paradigm one. This transformation is of growing importance not only in your personal life but also in your business or corporate life. In summary, there are three distinct stages involved in step four, in the creation of an intuitive aligned vision that is a synthesized vision drawn from both your personal and professional contexts:

- developing an intuitive attuned personal vision
- developing your intuitive professional vision

- developing an aligned individual intuitive vision by balancing the above two

Step five

The next step is to develop a shared intuitive vision, and a corresponding verbal statement, through a group sharing and discussion process. This process is one of the most rewarding and powerful "bonding" experiences within an organization. It involves a multistage interaction and sharing of individual (personal and professional) visions in small groups. It can begin at any level, at the top or bottom, and percolate throughout the organization. There would rarely be a completely shared or totally identical vision throughout the organization. However, there could at least be a broad consensus about the major elements and direction in the vision. The really important thing in this step five is the process. While sharing the visual images or symbols, there is fun to be had as well as insight. In the process of "resonating" with colleagues at a deeper level, while articulating a verbal statement, a profound "fine tuning" takes place. This process of evolving a shared vision becomes a kind of common thread, or understanding, that brings all the diverse pulls and forces within an organization into a common track and direction.

In summary, for every vision – personal life vision, professional life vision, aligned individual intuitive vision and shared intuition vision – there are three aspects: (a) an image, picture or symbol, (b) the main "elements" in these visualizations, and (c) a verbal statement incorporating these elements.

Integrative Visioning

Step six

Having developed the shared reflections and intuitive visions we have now to go beyond this and develop an integration of these two by comparing and synthesizing or balancing them. The resulting vision is the integrative one. This then becomes the "new-paradigm" manager's driving force in life and also indicates the relevant activity and priorities for your immediate future. The entire process of developing an integrative vision is essentially a "learning process" which enables you to develop a "learning culture" (see Part IV) within your self and your family, as well as in any organization. While the process of developing a reflective vision stimulates your intellectual and imaginative faculties, it is still within the framework of a "responsible" view of reality and future possibilities. The intuitive processes "free" you from this state and facilitate a kind of creative or "quantum" leap. The real challenge is to engage, on a continuing basis, in the process of learning to integrate the two levels of visioning. As in the case of synthesizing your personal and professional intuitive visions there will be a continuing creative tension between the intuitive and reflective visions.

Step seven

Now we come to the most interesting part, namely step seven. This allows you to use the visioning and symbolizing process to influence the existing situation or the current reality in a manner that helps move that current reality toward the vision of the desired future state. This involves three stages of symbolization: (a) symbols of the desired future (which we call vision), (b) symbols of the current reality, and (c) symbols of the various intermediate stages, each one indicative of the shifts in each stage over the years, through which current reality could be pulled toward the envisioned state. There would also be a time frame for each stage. This is illustrated in the series of symbols shown in figure 5.4.

The ultimate objective is to take this entire process into the organization at all levels. At whatever level you are, you can enroll those teams or units or divisions or departments in the organization, so that ultimately there is a continuing shared vision at the corporate level. This becomes the real driving energy, a forceful thrust throughout the organization. In other words, basically two things happen:

- the corporation becomes positioned *vis-à-vis* its external environment differently from where you usually arrive through the old-paradigm planning processes
- it galvanizes the entire corporation into a single-purpose, single-minded, united drive toward actualizing the corporate vision

Figure 5.4

Current reality

Vision

Current reality

Vision

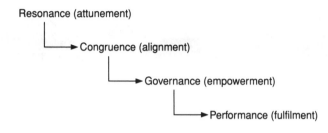

Figure 5.5

Keeping in mind the relevance, significance of, and even urgency of this process in new-paradigm management, we would like to coin a special term for this process and perhaps call it "visionance." It could become an organizing principle of business, or any organized activity. It brings a certain romance into management and is central to "arete," or virtue. In other words, it generates a resonance (attunement) with your self, a congruence (alignment) with your personal and professional life and a sharing with your colleagues and family. It also creates the basis for empowerment within the entire organization, ultimately leading to higher performance and a sense of fulfilment (see figure 5.5).

Step eight

The next step is to translate the shared integrated vision into a plan of action which should clearly indicate who should do what by what time and with what resources. This step is clearly the most crucial one and has to be processed with maximum possible participation and commitment at all levels. The process of converting vision into action is described in more detail, and from a somewhat different perspective, in chapter 6.

Step nine: a never-ending process

The real dynamics within the organization, the main 'theme' of the new-paradigm organization, therefore, would be a continuing review of the shared vision of the future, of the view of current reality from the perspective of that vision, and of the relevant plan of action.

Vision is not a solution to a problem. If it is seen in that light – how can the "problem" of low morale, or unclear strategic direction, go away? – the energy behind the vision also will go away. Building shared vision must be seen as a central element of the daily work of new-paradigm managers. It is on-going and never-ending. The continuous nature of this process is emphasized in figure 5.1 (page 63). A vision, this journey into an unknown, uncharted territory, has to be recalibrated again and again. This requires business acumen, strength of character, and courage. This has been true for pathfinders throughout the ages. As George Santayana, the Spanish-born American philosopher once said: "Columbus found a new world, and had no chart save one that Faith had deciphered in the skies."

Conclusion

Outlook, insight

All this may appear, at first sight, rather complex and may even overwhelm. However, after you have gone through a few rounds of this process, it becomes a very lucid, natural, and almost an automatic undertaking. It is just a question of learning how to learn. Like any other learning capability it takes a little time and effort, but if you pursue it with full faith and trust in the process, and with a sense of determination and commitment, it takes much less time and effort than you may imagine at the outset. Eventually it can become a natural way of thinking, a way of life.

The three processes – reflective, intuitive, and integrative visioning – in combination lead to a sustainable peak performance which is the goal of any new-paradigm manager (see figure 5.6). To put it differently, it involves:

- developing an understanding of whatever is in **sight** in the external environment
- looking inside your own internal "environment," or inner dynamics, and developing what we may call **insight**
- finally, integrating with this outlook your **insight** – the combination or synthesis will generate what we may call your unique "inlook"

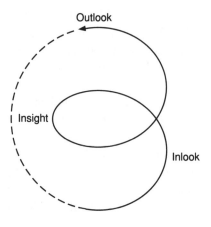

Figure 5.6

The interesting point is that such an "inlook," or the governing attitude with which you function, is not a reactive posture or an *ad hoc* approach, but a proactive one. It is a deep-rooted, connected, and integrated attitude based on a more creative (rather than reactive) perception, connection, and application of your desires and directions in life.

To repeat a well-known metaphor: an ordinary conventional stone-cutter would say "I am cutting stone"; a more intelligent, well-trained expert worker would say "I am converting stone into specific shapes," whereas a new-paradigm worker would say "I am building a cathedral." You can easily realize the significant difference that this vision-driven performance would make on the quality of the work as well as on the feeling of the worker during and after it. It is possible to have a vision of the cathedral even while pursuing a relatively dull activity, such as that of cutting stones, through the kinds of processes that are described so far. Even more powerful is the well-known illustration of Michelangelo and his David statue. On being questioned as to how he could create such a masterpiece out of an ordinary marble rock, he is supposed to have said that it was very simple. All that happened was that while looking at a marble rock he had a vision of David and after that all he did was merely cut or sculpt out from the marble rock all that was "not David!"

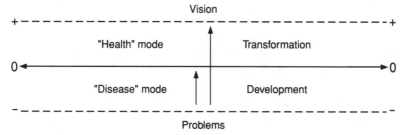

Figure 5.7

Becoming your vision

It is also important to note that this process of intuitive visioning, if pursued on a continuing basis, does lift you from the stage of "having" a vision to a level of intensely getting absorbed and identified with it or, shall we say, "becoming" your vision. In taking this further to the corporate level, you perceive your vision to be part of the corporate vision, and therefore perceive your self functioning in the corporation as a facilitative instrument for actualizing the corporate dream. This represents a significant shift from the posture of operating "toward" a vision to that of operating "from" a vision. Therein problems appear as opportunities through the enlargement of the context – in a sense, making limitations or adversity work for you. This is a shift from what we may call organization development to organizational transformation, from a problem-ridden "disease" mode to a vision-driven "health" mode, as shown in figure 5.7.

Reconceiving current reality

Another important issue is that your perception of the "current reality" itself changes if you are operating "from" a vision. From the optics of the vision of the future, the view of your current reality begins to appear different from the one which you ordinarily perceive through "problem-solving" lenses. Referring to the illustration of Michelangelo's David, described above, we can easily see the difference between the ordinary way of looking at a marble rock and viewing the same rock from the vision of seeing David in the rock. This is transformative in a true sense: in terms of your perception of the rock, the connection between your work (creating a David) and the current reality (ordinary rock) as well as the application and direction of one's energy (strategies and tools). Moreover, not only is the current reality viewed differently from an individual's viewpoint, but in a corporate setting, through this process, you can and should also develop a "consensus" or shared view of the current reality. Frequently, the frustrating problem faced by many managements today is that there are almost irreconcilable differences, even at the top management level, in the perception, interpretation, and judgement about it. What are the strengths and weaknesses, opportunities and threats in the current situation of the organization? With the process mentioned above, this is minimized. In fact, a constructive consensus arises over the perceived convergences as well as divergences in various viewpoints about the current reality. The attempt then with the vision-driven energy, which becomes a team effort, is to constantly enhance the convergence and overcome or minimize the divergence.

Going soft in the head?

It is not unlikely that you may face inner doubts or questions such as the following ones about this process, which while being interesting, appears to be not only unusual but in a sense also "far out." Is this process really relevant in the hard-nosed and hard-headed world of business? Can this sort of thing really work? Is it not too much dreaming or being rather too soft? Does it not also imply spending too much time on such processes? In business, and particularly in our fast-moving world, we have to make very quick decisions with very little data and is this process not too slow? Even if we may feel interested in it, is it not a kind of luxury which we can ill afford these days? Moreover, it does not seem to be grounded enough and perhaps it may take us too far out. We may even run the risk of being "spaced out" and not "have our nose to the ground," as they say.

Even if you brush aside all such doubts, you may even tell yourself: even if this thing works, so what? I have been successful so far with the way in which I have been thinking and functioning, so why go into anything which appears to be rather risky and may even endanger my success path, if I do something so different from what I have been used to so far? Therefore, you conclude, "this is not for me."

Making a difference

These are quite understandable thoughts, questions, and concerns that may arise in anyone's mind. But today we are talking about **making a difference**. This involves learning with a difference, and is it not true to say that if we want to make a real difference, then we have to think and function differently? Doing more of the same, and expecting different results, has been considered as another definition of insanity! In other words, unless we develop courage and the capacity of thinking differently, there are greater chances of our remaining stuck with a very limited perception in a fast-changing world. We will remain where we are but the world will move on. Therefore, perhaps the greatest risk today is not to take such a step.

If nothing else, this process of visioning at least creates a greater amount of clarity and direction within our own self, and a deeper understanding of our inner dynamics. At the next stage, in the process of shared vision-building within your own family, it creates a deeper feeling of caring and connection within the home. When this is extended to your arena of work in a corporate setting, then the process of shared visioning also helps generate a deeper rapport, a kind of bonding among the members of the organization, and a genuine feeling of mutual trust amongst people rather than a fear of each other. This process, therefore, results in the creation of shared meaning and purpose in your work life with colleagues, a kind of reassuring resonance with each other. This is the essence of authentic and durable team building. In other words, a shared vision develops a strong feeling of co-ownership of, and responsibility for, the purpose and the processes within the organization.

This is essential to the emerging concept of the new-paradigm manager in creating and facilitating success. This is also a most natural and organic way of converting what otherwise has been an arena of adversarial and conflicting cultures – which inevitably results in negative stress and frustrations – into an affectionate atmosphere, a healing climate of genuine partnership in progress. This is not only more authentic and durable, it is, above all, very pleasant and fulfilling. The least, therefore, that this process of visioning can contribute is to bring some enjoyment, some fun, some joy into the arena of work. In other words, it enables you to move from functioning with a fear of losing into a posture of performing with the joy of doing. We now need to focus, more explicitly, on the process whereby vision, once developed, can be converted into action.

Note

1   By 1988, Citicorp had become the nation's biggest mortgage lender.

References

Dandrowski, J. F. 1990: *Corporate Imagination Plus*. New York: Free Press, 34.

Bennis, W. and Nanus, B. 1985: *Leaders*. New York: Harper and Row, 103.

de Bono, E. 1985: *Six Thinking Hats*. Boston: Little, Brown.

Channon, D. F. and Robinson, D. 1973: The London and Rhodesian Mining Company Ltd. Case study, Manchester Business School.

Fritz, R. 1982: *The Path Of Least Resistance*. Self-published.

Gilbert, X. and Strebel, P. 1988: Developing competitive advantage, in J. B. Quinn, H. Mintzberg, and M. James (eds.), *The Strategy Process*. Englewood Cliffs, New Jersey: Prentice-Hall, 79.

Senge, P. M. 1990: *The Fifth Discipline: The Art and Practice of the Learning Organisation*. New York: Doubleday, 214.

Tichy, N. 1984: *Transformational Leadership*. New York: John Wiley.

Vandermerwe, S. 1989: *Scandinavian Airlines System SAS* (A). Case study, IMD, 10.

6

From Vision to Action
Ronnie Lessem

Introduction: The Functions of Myth

In the previous chapter we focused on reflection, intuition, and integration in developing vision. Here we wish to consider the journey (process) of transformation, including the role of myth and heroism.

It has always been a central function of mythology to supply the symbols that carry the human spirit forward, in counteraction to those other images that constantly hold us back. As Joseph Campbell says in *The Hero with a Thousand Faces*, "We remain fixated to the unexercized images of our infancy, and hence disinclined to the necessary passages of adulthood." This disinclination can apply just as much to organizations as to individuals (Campbell, 1949: 43).

It is with these individual and organizational passages that this chapter is concerned. The new-paradigm manager, in effect, is an agent of transformation, as opposed to development, a revolutionary as opposed to an evolutionary. As such he or she is engaged in a journey of truly heroic proportion, equal in dramatic impact to the mythological journey of antiquity.

The late Joseph Campbell describes the four primary functions of the myth – accompanying such heroic journeys – as follows:

- to awaken consciousness to the fascinating mystery of the existing universe
- to interpret that mystery in order to give meaning to life
- to sustain the moral order
- to foster the centering and unfolding of the individual

The role of the hero

The leading characters in the great myths, throughout the centuries and across the globe, are the heroes, engaged in their triumphant or tragic journeys. Peters and Waterman (1982) point out that heroes abound in excellent companies. Deal and Kennedy (1982) differentiate between the "born hero," the mainstay of the business, and the "compass hero," an important but lesser mortal.

Organisation heroes

> If values are the soul of the culture, then heroes personify values and epitomize the strength of the organisation. They create the role models for employees to follow. The hero is the great motivator, the magician, the person everyone will count on when things get tough. They have unshakeable character and style. Heroes are symbolic figures whose deeds are out of the ordinary but not far out. They show, often dramatically, that the ideal of success lies within human capacity.
>
> The success of the born hero lies in not only having built an organisation, but also in having established an institution that survived them and added their personal sense of values to the world. Their visions changed the way we do business and their influence is still pervasive.
>
> A second type of "made" hero is the compass hero. If a company is in a situation where things have to change and there are no role models for it, it is good management practice to find role models, plant them inside the company, and make them heroes. By doing so, management communicates that, in the future, business will be done either more "aggressively" or more "courteously", in any case, less as it was done and more as the new hero style conveys. (Deal and Kennedy, 1982)

Our concern here is with the born hero, although as new-paradigm managers, we all have a chance of becoming such heroes in the course of our maturation. This does necessarily involve, as we have indicated, a truly heroic journey.

The journey of the spirit

Harrison Owen, the American transformational thinker, like Joseph Campbell, is both interested in entering into the great mysteries of the universe and also in the centering and unfolding of the individual (Owen, 1987). Owen traces the hero's journey, as follows.

Through potential

- From out of the depths of the hero's subconscious motivation
- into his vision of individual and organizational potential
- via understanding of the context in which (s)he was operating
- through a special language that enabled him or her to communicate; including
- the information to accomplish his/her prospective task

By this point our hero has equipped him or herself with the motivation, imagination, understanding, language, and information to accomplish his historic mission. But he still has to cross that great divide between knowledge and action, between potential and its actualization. He journeys on, as follows.

Toward the actual

- He reacts first to the onset of circumstances
- before becoming more deliberately responsive to situations
- therefore growing truly purposeful or proactive
- becoming, at a later state, genuinely interactive; as well as
- ultimately, and wholly, inspired

Joseph Campbell, via his *Hero with a Thousand Faces* (Campbell, 1949: 64), presents us with a heroic journey which is more visual and dramatic. We want to become involved, with you, in Campbell's heroic journey before converting it into more accessibly analytical language. In the process, we shall journey with you from action toward vision – that is the way of learning; and from vision back to action – that is the way of transformation.

The heroic journey

Campbell's hero, and the passages he undergoes, reflect the flavor of a journey through life. The image of the eventful journey rather than that of the successful destination is the one that sticks in our minds. It begins with a call to adventure (action) and ends with the discovery of power (vision). The result of a successful journey is the unlocking and release of a flow of life into the body of the world.

Responding to the call

The call to adventure is the first stage of the mythological journey. Destiny summons the hero and transfers his center of gravity from within the pole of society to a zone unknown. In other words, our hero disregards social convention, and instead of going to university or landing a good job, he sets out toward an unfamiliar destination.

Often in actual life, and not infrequently in the myths and popular tales, we encounter cases of the call being unanswered. In business parlance, opportunities go unrecognized. Refusal to follow the call results in boredom, or disintegration of the individual or enterprise. All the person can do is create problems for himself and await the gradual approach of his demise: "His flowering world becomes a wasteland of dry stones and his life seems meaningless." The myths and folk tales of the whole world make clear that the refusal is essentially the rejection of one's own individual self-interest or social purpose or "dream."

Opening yourself to a protector

For those who have not refused the call, the first encounter on the heroic journey is with a protective figure. Such a person also provides the adventurer "with amulets against the dragon forces he is about to pass."

Having responded to his own call, and continuing courageously as both positive and negative consequences unfold, the hero finds the powerful forces of the unconscious on his side. In so far as the hero's actions coincide with that for which his society is ready, he seems to stride along to the great rhythm of the historic process.

Entering the road of trials

Having responded to the call, then, the hero crosses the threshold of the known into the world of the unknown. Armed with a protector, he moves into a dream landscape of curiously fluid, ambiguous forms, where he must survive a road of trials. These are well known, of course, to the risk-taking entrepreneur, to the proverbial adventurer, and to the business visionary.

Risking loss or gain

World mythology has produced a vast literature of miraculous tests and ordeals. The hero, however, is aided by the advice, resources, and even "secret agents" of the magical helper whom he met before entering into the unknown. But he still has to stand the ultimate test alone. Is he able to put his old self to death? Is he willing to put his own security, both physical and psychological, aside? "For many headed is the surrounding Hydra; one head cut off, two more appear." Dragons have now to be slain and surprising barriers to be passed, again and again. There will meanwhile be a multitude of preliminary victories and momentary glimpses of the promised land.

Engaging in a mystical union

The ultimate adventure, when all the barriers and ogres have been overcome, is commonly represented by a mystical marriage of the triumphant hero-soul with the queen goddess of the world. The "corporation" should be seen as the great receptacle for the heroic spirit. The "mystical union" to which we refer also involves a marriage of *yang* and *yin*, of active heroism and receptive appreciation, of power and love, of product and market.

Penetrating to the source

Subsequent to the mystical union, and further heroic accomplishments, the hero's quest is accomplished only when and if he succeeds in penetrating to the source. Within the source lies the true vision to be realized. In order to reach that vision our hero has to acquire supreme power.

Such power can only be gained by proceeding to the threshold of adventure. There the hero encounters the shadow presence of guards of the ultimate passage. If he overcomes them he enters into another new and unfamiliar world of strange and yet intimate forces, of which some challenge him and others give him magical aid.

Acquiring the power of vision

When the hero arrives at the nadir of his mythological round, he undergoes a supreme ordeal. If he survives he gains his reward, the power of vision.

The full round of departure and return requires that the hero now begins the labor of bringing the golden fleece, as it were, back into the kingdom of humanity. In other words, the vision has to be converted into action, whereby the individual, the corporation, the community, or planet can realize itself.

From Vision to Action

Learning: the departure

The hero with a thousand faces, with all his mythological overtones, may appear as somewhat fanciful to the hardened realists amongst you. For some 20 years now a British philosopher and psychologist, with strong Indian connections, Kevin Kingsland, has been developing an approach to business and to life which turns the mythologies of antiquity into everyday realities. While Kevin has worked with thousands of students in Britain, in India, and in America, running programs on personal communication, we have been applying this "vision to action" approach to businesses small and large in America, in Europe, in India, and in Southern Africa (Lessem, 1980).

The call to adventure: the first physical step

Kingland's vision-to-action approach, like Jacob's Ladder linking heaven with earth, spans the complete spectrum of human endeavor. We learn in business and in life by ascending, as it were, Jacob's Ladder step by step, thus following the path of the hero. That, if you like, is the heroic departure. The "call to adventure" represents the first and physical step. Without activity there is no learning. The newborn babe learns about life through physical challenge and response. When learning ceases to be an adventure it loses its primordial aspect.

The role of protector: making a social connection

The role of the protector symbolizes the supportive part to be played by a mother figure, a caring teacher, or "comrades in adversity." Without a social context into which learning can be placed it becomes depersonalized and sterile. If we fail to open ourselves to the supportive influence of teachers and of mentors, who inevitably cross our heroic path, our journey will be in vain. We shall remain insular and insulated.

The road of trials: learning from experience

The "road of trials" quite obviously represents the processes of trial and error, action and reflection, that the individual or enterprise undergoes in order to learn from experience. This is the period of mental alertness and of youthful discovery that is such an important part of growing up. It represents, built into the learning process, the period before we settle down in an adult way. Any task we tackle, then, should involve some degree of exploration and experimentation before we commit ourselves to a particular line of thought or action.

Taking a risk: committing yourself

"Risking the loss of your old self" is the inward equivalent of the outward risk-taking that accompanies business and personal enterprise. Whatever ideas you pick up intellectually you have to develop the emotional commitment to put both them and yourself to the test. In the process you may become a different person, disassembled and reassembled, as a result of the emotional wrangles you have undergone.

The marriage of interest: defining your role

As your new self fully emerges, or a new business comes into its own, a further learning step is required if there is to be continued development. A "marriage of interest" between the thrusting force of the newly formed ego (the hero soul) and the receptive force of an existing organization (the mother goddess) is needed for both individual and enterprise to outgrow narrowly based self-interest. The combined result is a rounded business concept, an individual with role integrity, or an organization with a coherent philosophy.

Penetrating to the source: developing insight

You may have role integrity or a business may have a clearly defined mission, but neither will ensure that you or your organization has "penetrated to its source." That degree of understanding of the source and destination of your personal or organizational being requires a particular brand of personal and social insight. Such insight is developed through a capacity to listen, a power to observe, a willingness to be overawed, and an ability and inclination to link like with unlike, actual with potential, visible energy with invisible spirit, whether in the person or in the business.

The power of vision: engaging in creative action

The "acquisition of visionary power," finally, only comes when the insight developed through penetrating the source of your own or your company's being is tested out in practice. You only learn about the power of vision when you engage in the kind of creative action that serves to bring it about. There is much of the chicken and the egg about it, and it is always difficult to tell which came first. But when you have acquired the power of vision, nothing will hold you back.

> When you have found your vision you do not ask yourself whether you have one. You inform the world about it. If you're wondering whether you have a vision, then you haven't got one.
> When you've discovered your vision you abound with inspiration. Your eyes sparkle. You can see it in the atmosphere. It is pulsing with life.
> When you have a vision everything you plan and do stems from it. Its all-consuming nature makes all previous attitudes and ideas seem like a training ground for the ultimate vision.
> When you feel part of an overall vision you don't think of rest and reward. Total absorption removes all sense of personal effort. You cannot help but pursue the vision.
> When you have a vision that is all you want to talk about. Everything people say or do is a readout of that vision. The world becomes a theater for your visionary script.
> When the vision is present in you everyone around gets included or ignored, depending on whether or not they feel associated with it. In other words, people become actors in your production, or else they remain off stage.
> When you find your vision nothing will be permitted to stand in its way. Obstacles must be overcome or else life won't be worth living for you. (Kevin Kingsland, "Attributes of Vision")

Innovation: the return

Learning reflects the mythological hero's outward journey, from the call to adventure on to the acquisition of power. Innovation represents his or her return. In other words, having ascended Jacob's Ladder, rising from action up to vision, he now descends the ladder, this time turning vision into action. This descent constitutes the process and substance of innovation. The highest point on the ladder, the one most filled with spiritual substance, emerging from out of the subconscious depths, is personal imagination and corporate vision.

Developing vision

- What is your personal mission?
- How is it going to change the world around you?
- How will its fulfillment change your life, work and vocation?
- What universal problem will your unique idea solve?
- Where does your imagination lead you?

Vision will be stillborn unless it is united with insight and understanding, and thereby with social need.

Recognizing market need

- Does your idea have market potential?
- How is technology and society evolving and where does your vision fit in with such developments?
- What particular market trends pertain to your idea?
- What underlying need will you serve?
- What business partnerships and alliances will arise?

If vision is father to the innovation, and need is mother, the resultant offspring is the business concept and organization, expressed in a unique language, and both yielding and drawn from particular information.

Structuring a business and organization

- What product or service is being designed for what market?
- How is the product created, developed, produced, and sold?
- How do the different business functions interact with one another and with the outside world?
- How is a balance maintained between freedom and order?
- How are physical and human resources procured and channeled?

The product and organization, once designed as a "mystical marriage" of vision and need, are brought to life through the commitment of inner will and outer resources, resulting in a defensive/aggressive reaction to adverse circumstances.

Asserting your will/acquiring resources

- What is in it for you personally and financially?
- What is your competitive advantage?
- Who will champion your product's cause?
- What financial resources need to be committed?
- What is the risk and what is the likely return?
- How do you sell yourself?

Once the commitment is made, and business is under way, progress needs to be planned and monitored, so both individual and organization can respond purposefully to change.

Adapting to change

- How are targets and programs established and monitored?
- How are tasks planned and implemented, step by step?
- What systems have been installed to process information?
- What experimental forms enable you and your organization to adapt to change?
- How does the organization provide scope for free expression?

Envisioning (acquiring creative power), unraveling (penetrating to the source), integrating (entering the mystical union), committing (risking yourself) and learning (engaging in the road of trials), take the innovator almost all the way along his or her chosen path. The interactive and inspired steps still remaining lead him closer to the social and physical end points of his journey.

Involving people

The next step involves people, that is, symbolically, the protector and magic helpers, and literally all those employees, customers, suppliers, shareholders, and other allies that comprise the human body of the organization.

- How do you effect shared values, so that people feel they belong?
- What myths and rituals bind people together?
- How do you bring about a family atmosphere, and a sense of community?
- How do you maintain closeness to the customer?
- How do you achieve productivity through people?

Finally, and ultimately, the complex and ethereal vision needs to be embodied in simple tangible form, to inspire effort.

Taking action

- How do you keep the energy level up?
- What is physically produced, at the end of the day?
- How do you ensure that the product remains constantly and physically visible both inside and outside the business?
- How do you impose a sense of urgency?
- How do you maintain a bias for action?

Having responded to all these questions, you as a heroic innovator, or your innovative organization, will have completed both departure and return. Of the steps along the journey's way it is the extraction of vision which is probably the most difficult for you to perceive, largely because the unconscious spirit has been well concealed from us, like the night is from the day.

We now want to investigate, with you, how personal and corporate vision can be both inhibited and acquired.

Acquiring the Power of Vision

What inhibits vision?

The first question we have to ask ourselves is what stops us embarking on, and returning from, the heroic journey, the combination of which ultimately results in the extraction of vision. Why do we fail to grow up? Why do our organizations fail to mature? Why do our visions fail to come out?

Personal transformation

All the life potentialities that we never managed to bring to adult realization, those other portions of oneself are there; for such golden seeds do not die. If only a portion of that lost totality could be dredged up into the light of day we should experience a marvelous expansion of our powers, a vivid renewal of life.

Moreover, if we could dredge up something forgotten not only by ourselves but also by our whole generation or our entire civilization we should become the heroes of the day. (Campbell, 1949: 17)

What specifically, then, blocks your vision, what are the consequences of such inhibition, and how can you become unblocked?

Blocks to vision

1 To begin with, we block our vision by seeing ourselves as "down to earth and feet on the ground." (See also chapter 5.) We get stuck, therefore, on the first rung of the ladder of learning. A desire to work hard and "go for it" overwhelms any desire for reflection. The call to adventure leads you nowhere rather than somewhere. You are too busy getting on with life to take time out to contemplate the future. Companies are too busy "getting the stuff out of the door" to plan ahead. There is too much "real work" to be done for us to bother about "fancy stuff dreamed up by people with their heads in the stars."

2 The second stumbling block on the ladder arises when we see ourselves as "just one of the boys (or girls)." It is comfortable and comforting to allow ourselves to have undemanding expectations. Our protectors then shield us from experience rather than guiding us through it. Being like everyone else is much easier going than becoming distinctive. Being just another cornerstore is much simpler than becoming a department store.

3 We get stuck on the third rung of the ladder when we flit from

one activity and experience to another just for the fun of it. The road of trials then becomes a distraction rather than an intention. How better to distract ourselves from our real vision and purpose than by the fascination of novelty? How quickly time goes by when we are busy doing one thing, or project, after another. There are so many things to be done that we, individually or in our organizations, seem to have to run merely to keep still.

4 The fourth step along the way becomes a stumbling block rather than a stepping stone because we take a risk "just for the hell of it." So we manage to command everyone's attention except that of the people who really count. We surround our lives with drama but become a tragic hero rather than a triumphant one. We lose our old selves and never find a new one, as an individual or organization. Shaking everything up is an excellent way to avoid making real headway.

5 We cling to established principles to avoid having to deal with uncertainty, ambiguity, or conflict. Instead of effecting a union amongst opposites we divide and rule. Anything that fails to fit in with preset personal or institutional attitudes we dismiss as diversionary, divisive, improper, or unnecessary.

6 The next block occurs when open-mindedness leads not to empathy and sensitivity but to confusion and indecision. Everything becomes a kind of haze. Different issues, problems, or opportunities are all lumped together into the same pot, adding to its insubstantial contents. Floating along in a haze or getting lost in the fog is a way of cushioning yourself from the real world.

7 We slip and fall at the seventh and last rung when we feel we already have all the answers. Nobody can tell us anything that can improve on what already is. Other options are inevitably suspect rather than enriching, dangerous rather than enticing. Such total suppression of possibility is a perfect way to sustain ignorance rather than empower both ourselves and other people.

The consequences of inhibited vision

To the extent that vision is blocked, in the individual or in the organization, there are the inevitable adverse consequences. The development of vision is then inhibited through the following:

Lack of purpose

Without purpose there is a lack of direction of life. You lack spiritual substance. Your activity lacks luster or intrinsic worth. Life is hollow. There is no ultimate vision of the future. The sole purpose of it all is survival.

Lack of meaning

Your activity lacks a meaningful context. There is no penetrating source of demand for what you are doing. You are lacking in foundations. Other people's work is not respected because you fail to respect your own. The atmosphere becomes soured. The physical environment deteriorates. Depression scts in. Who cares anyway!

Lack of planning

To what ends can any plans be directed? There seems little point in planning for the ephemeral. Why plan when disorder will nevertheless follow? How can you build on the past when there is no foreseeable future? Nothing makes sense.

Lack of motivation

Drive is reduced. Going around in circles is unrewarding. Energy may be filled digging holes and filling them up again. Effort does not seem to get us anywhere.

Lack of priorities

There is nothing to distinguish one task from another. How can priorities be set when so many things demand attention? How can time be found for anything when there is no energy?

Lack of pride

Why bother to put up a front when you feel down and out? Keeping up appearances or maintaining good relationships seems futile when there are no priorities set.

Lack of activity

Procrastination is natural when you have nothing special to do. Tomorrow will probably be like today, so what is the hurry? When we feel we have nothing to offer we may as well sit back and see what others have to offer us.

Jacob's Ladder, then – from vision to action and vice versa – can function as a negative or a positive cascade. It becomes positive when the higher step nourishes the lower one. You are active (rung one) in order to be attractive (rung two). You take pride in what you do (rung two) because you know or have been told what is worth doing (rung three). You have bothered to sort out your priorities (rung three), because either you are self-motivated or else someone is motivating you (rung four). You are committed to taking risks (rung four), because there is an overall structure (rung five), such as a formal religion, scientific order or bureaucracy, which provides overriding stability. It is worth planning ahead (rung five), because there is a wider context (rung six), for which to plan. Finally, there is meaning to life and work (rung six), because there is an ulterior purpose (rung seven), that surpasses the mere fulfilment of personal or customer need. That ultimate purpose, which is true vision, is something other than shared values. It requires the full extent of the heroic departure and return to acquire it.

Extracting a personal vision

There are specific methods, in fact, of overcoming both personal and corporate blocks to vision, removing the inhibitors in the process. We were already exposed to some of those in chapter 5. Here are some others. These methods are not simple, once-and-for-all techniques, but are more like continuing and iterative processes. We shall begin with the personal approaches and then move on to some corporate applications.

Recognizing a vision

Before we embark on our vision-building exercises, though, let me reveal to you an example of one, drawing on the experience of Mary Quant, the British designer:

Black and white image

> As a child I didn't like stiffness or artificiality. I didn't want to grow up. I wanted people around me to move, run, dance. The image came to me first when I was eight. A tap dancer with a bullet haircut, wearing black tights, black shirt, black patent leather shoes, and white socks. This black and white image branded my mind. It has stuck with me forever. (Quant, 1987)

A vision, then, arises out of the imagination, and infuses the rest of your life with purpose. Naturally the original image will be less focused than the ultimate manifestation, should we realize our dreams. Mary Quant has since built up an international business in cosmetics, fabrics, soft furnishing, and stationery products, all drawing on that original image, and manifested today in bold colors and designs.

Developing a vision

The practical necessity for developing a vision arises for people like Mary Quant when the already described symptoms of lack of vision reach an intolerable stage. The tolerance level of different people varies enormously. Generally speaking, the more sensitive you are, the more intolerant you will be of lack of vision. Quant was appalled by the dowdy fashions in the 1950s. Terence Conran, also in Britain, was deeply offended by the ugly furniture he saw in the high street. Both were sufficiently incensed to pursue their emergent visions.

Discovering your natural inclinations

By the time you feel the urge to seek after your vision it is probably close at hand. It is perhaps working its way through your awareness, but has not yet actually been perceived. So how can you extract it from the realms of semi-darkness?

Start by looking at your life, and see what is actually going on. Look particularly at what you are doing at your own discretion. Most of your obligatory work may be taken up with activities that are a relic of your past. The momentum remains but you may be beginning to question their value. So note down what you do. Now think about what you like doing. Distinguish between those things that are done only because they have to be, and those things which you enjoy doing. Treat those things which you get no satisfaction out of as red herrings.

Then begin to enliven, enlarge, and invigorate those realms of activity which you naturally want to do. In sum, they will comprise your vision.

Discerning what enhances you

A variation on the above theme is to ask yourself, for a start, what really enhances you. What do you love doing? What captivates your imagination in the context of what you do? Now write down, as a list, the most enjoyable, fulfilling, and creative aspects of your existence. It would be nice to think that you could now take all those things and make them your life's work. But, in practice, that is too simplistic an approach. Negativity gets in the way.

So write down a list of all the things that go on in your life which are incompatible with the first list. Form two lists, on the left-hand side those things that enhance you, and on the right-hand side those which cancel out each of the items on the left. Reflect on this list from time to time and resolve to remove the items on the right-hand side.

Both of the above approaches to developing a vision require relatively modest effort. Now we come to three approaches that require more thought.

Unraveling your vision

In order to unravel your vision, you need to project yourself into your desired future:

- What will you physically look like? What energy level will you be operating at? How will you be physically occupied? What kind of sporting activity will you be undertaking and when?
- What will be your social standing? Will you have a reputation to be proud of, and of what sort? What kinds of organization will you be closely associated with, and how will they affect your self-image? What social groupings will be represented in your work and life and how will you meet them?
- How educated and informed will you be? What degree of knowledge and skill will you require and how, specifically, will it be different from now? What kind of communications will you have with others? What kind of training will you be undergoing? How will you keep in touch with artistic and technological developments? How will you develop your ability to learn?
- What will your economic standing be? What sorts and value of assets will you have acquired? How will your assets be apportioned as fixtures and fittings, land and buildings, and investments? Will your assets all be owned outright or rented or leased? How acquisitive will you be in your approach, and in what way? What return on your investment will you be seeking?
- How much authority will you have? To what extent will your opinion matter and to whom? What titles, awards, and accreditations will you acquire? What role will you be playing in your local, national, and international communities? How will you structure your activities to achieve efficiency and effectiveness?
- How will you develop yourself and others? Will you become more sensitive and caring, and in what way? How will you have improved the quality of your physical and social environment? How will people's minds and hearts have become elevated?
- What will be your original and long-lasting creation? What will you have contributed uniquely to the world that will give you a deep sense of fulfillment? At what will you be able to point, and say, 'That is the reason for my being?'

Bringing your vision to life

The previous exercise was future-oriented, whereas this one begins with the past and the present. You are invited to consider, first of all, where you are most alive:

- Physically, do you relish your strength, endurance, and versatility? In what way? Do you love being physically close to other people, playing contact sport, undertaking exercise, working hard and playing hard?
- Socially, do you really enjoy being with others? Do you happily rely on one another? Is there a strong family feeling? Are you pleased when someone drops unexpectedly into the house or office? Do you go to lots of parties and outings, just for the fun of it?
- Intellectually, do you have insatiable curiosity? Do you eagerly anticipate the next book or computer program that you come across? Do you eagerly scan the television and radio pages for programs that will expand your mind? Are ideas common currency in your conversations? Do you make sure that you are up to date with the latest concepts and techniques in your field?
- Entrepreneurially, do you thrill in anticipation of challenge? Do you love a good fight for justice, good service or market share? Are you irrepressible in spirit? Do you champion your pet product or favored cause? Do you ever give up championing something you believe in? Can you be beaten off? Are you a risk-taker?
- Organizationally, are you fanatical about order, including filing, record-keeping, budgeting, systems? Are things habitually straightened out, systematized, and organized? Do you derive pleasure out of creating systems and devising procedures? Do you find putting order into chaos deeply satisfying?
- Esthetically, do you look in awe upon beautiful settings, elegant buildings, and well-designed products. Are quiet moments of contemplation greatly valued? Does the sense of fulfilled potential excite you? Conversely, does unfulfilled potential cause you despair?
- Creatively, do you suffer greatly when you go a day without making something beautiful, making a breakthrough, or trans-

forming some aspect of your life? Do you ascend to seventh heaven as brilliant ideas enter your mind, and flow out verbally, pictorially, physically, or organizationally? Is the world your stage, canvas, or magic garden?

Now determine those areas with which you could identify. Did you find yourself alive to all realms, to some of them, or to none? Write down one new area of emphasis for each of the weeks that follow. You may find yourself dismissing some areas as inapplicable. These may be areas where you are blocked; in other words, they lie underdeveloped. By getting to grips with those neglected areas you will be removing the shroud that covers your vision up. As you allow yourself to enjoy your total being, then the intensity of your vision will be raised. In fact it will become brilliant and unmistakable.

Going back to your roots

So much for vision, plucked out of the ground, as it were. For a more thoroughgoing and enduring attempt to extract vision we have to go back to your roots. To start with, then:

1 List on the left-hand side of a page the key events in your life history.
2 Then identify, alongside, your emotional reactions to these events, as and when they happened.
3 Now list, alongside these, actions that you took, or you think should have been taken, as a result.

You will now have three columns containing histories of activities and events in your life, emotional reactions, and resulting behavior. The combined result of your uncovering of the past and of the roots of your identity, should provide you with the raw material for your vision. You now need to summarize and condense your personal history. That will take a little time and effort. You should be in a position, after paying particular attention to the experiences and actions uncovered on your historical journey, to do the following:

- create a name for your vision
- create a logo that represents it

- create a suitable motto
- compose a new statement of your personal mission, one that will capture the imaginations of all that matter around you

Criteria for visionary evaluation

In the final analysis, then, how can you tell whether you have tapped the real depths of your personal vision? The sorts of criteria for evaluation are laid out in the panel that follows.

Vision Criteria

Consciousness

You need to become obsessed by your vision. If this does not happen there is no way in which it can become all pervading

Internal consistency

Various elements of the vision may be incompatible. It may be manifested differently in one part of you as compared with another. It may be reflected in your outer image but not in the inner behavior. This will detract from your vision.

Clarity

Your vision may be confused. It may not yet have penetrated the minds of people. The message may still not have got across. Such lack of clarity will get in the visionary way.

Intensity

Visions need to be brilliant to show up against the background of images and attitudes that get in the way. They need to be impactful, colorful, captivating, and energizing.

Confidence

Acceptance of your vision can be delayed by your concentrating too much on its alternatives, and too little on itself; too much on the negative and too little on the positive.

Recognition

Without the outside world to encourage you, your vision will be devalued. You need people around you who can recognize your creative potential.

Faith

To manifest a vision, you must increasingly·act as if it were a reality. Without the conviction to do this the vision remains a fantasy.

The same criteria can be applied to the assessment of the power of a corporate vision, as to the evaluation of the strength of a personal one.

In fact, all five of the methods we have revealed for extracting a personal vision are equally applicable to the extraction of a corporate one. In each case you will be substituting either part or the whole of an organization, collectively, for yourself, individually. Obviously that increases the layers of complexity, but it can nevertheless be done. For example, you can just as well assess the 'aliveness' of a corporation – physically, socially, or intellectually – as an individual. Equally, you can just as well assess the most fulfilling and creative aspects of your organization's being, as your own. However, a vision, once extracted, has still to be actualized. This is indeed what the heroic journey is ultimately about, converting vision into action. In the concluding part of this chapter we shall illustrate how a corporate visionary may go about it.

Conclusion: From Corporate Vision to Action

We come now to the extraction of vision from the depths of the organizational subconscious (similar principles apply to the individual), and to its subsequent and cumulative conversion into action.

- Uncover the historically based vision of the company, as reflected in: (a) the origins of its natural culture and economy; (b) the historical roots of the product and technology; (c) the founder's underlying motives and psychology.

    - What powerful and captivating vision has emerged out of your company's unique cultural, economic, technological, and personal heritage? How can it be stated and visually represented in the word and picture language of uplift and idealism? How might it serve as a 'meta-vision' to embrace each of your people's own personal visions?

- Relate the acquired vision to an underlying context, thereby discovering its meaning or significance.

    - What unique cultural and economic context, in the pattern of geographical space and historical time, marks your evolving enterprise?

- Structure and conceptualize the union between vision and context, thereby defining the product and organization in practical terms.

    - What particularly appropriate principles and structures of management and organization have you developed in your company?

- Harness the will and motivations of your people to drive the company forward, committed to profitable growth, so that the resources can be acquired to put its principles into practice, to fulfil the needs of its people, and to serve its mission.

- How have you tapped the egotistical drives of your people while providing means of channelling these self-centered motives into the common cause, organizationally, contextually, and spiritually?

• Establish a family atmosphere whereby values are shared and people feel they belong together, even though individual flexibility and enterprise is encouraged, and individuals can dream their own dreams within the context of the whole.

- How do you cultivate a family atmosphere in your company with a common identity and culture, reinforced by social ties and binding myths and rituals?

• Ensure that vision is continuously manifested in action, through which the dream ultimately becomes a reality; the true power of vision is realized, and the resources of the earth are transformed.

- How are you deploying energy to transform energy so that, in turn, your vision can be refuelled, reformed and renewed?

Vision and adventure

Unlike the purely technological inventor or the artistic creator, the visionary new-paradigm manager immersed in his or her heroic journey is both innovator and adventurer. Be he an Alfred Nobel or a Henry Ford from the 19th century, an Alfred Sloan or a Luther King from the 20th, an Anita Roddick or a Bill Gates in the 21st, he harnesses spirit and transforms energy on his heroic journey.

We now need to turn from the new-paradigm manager, as an individual, to the synergetic group, of which the new-paradigm manager is an integral part.

References

Campbell, J. 1949: *The Hero with a Thousand Faces*. Princeton, New Jersey: Princeton University Press.

Deal, T. and Kennedy, A. 1982: *Corporate Cultures*. Reading, Massachusetts: Addison Wesley, 43.

Lessem, R. 1980: Linking ancient wisdom and modern business practice. *Journal of Enterprise Management* (Autumn).

Owen, H. 1987: *Spirit, Transformation and Development*. Abbott Publishing, 62.

Peters, T. and Waterman, B. 1982: *In Search of Excellence*. New York: Harper and Row, 11.

Quant, M., *ex* Lessem, R. 1987: *Intrapreneurship*. London: Wildwood House, 84.

PART III

As a Group – From Conflict to Synergy

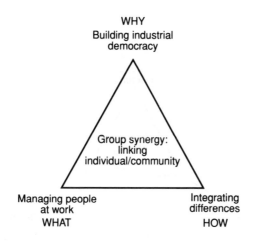

WHY
Building industrial
democracy

Group synergy:
linking
individual/community

Managing people
at work
WHAT

Integrating
differences
HOW

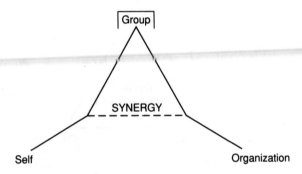

From conflict to synergy

7

Managing People At Work: Spiral Integration

Don Beck and Chris Cowan

Organizations are constructions of the mind. Words printed on wall charts, symbols of rank worn around the neck, and spaces occupied as manifestations of power are but artifacts and icons. The real connections are within the ᵛMEME profiles (part of our psychological "DNA") of people, those invisible webs that order society and snare relationships. We carry them with us in our heads every waking moment. Each location along the Spiral has its own mental configuration like a radar scope on which the contours of its ideal life form are painted. Which blips are most important varies depending on which ᵛMEMEs are active. The screen appears to . . .

PURPLE . . . as a magic circle that makes all inside feel safe.

RED . . . as a self-centered empire where one feels powerful and in control or weak and submissive.

BLUE . . . as a fixed pyramid that gives stability, permanence, and assigns one's place.

ORANGE . . . as a game-board matrix that promotes opportunity and rewards skill.

GREEN . . . as a warm, supportive community of equals that cares for its own.

YELLOW . . . as flowing networks that shift functions up, down, and across natural layers.

TURQUOISE . . . as a living organism that brings order from within chaos.

The Wonderful World of Virtual Reality

"Red Right, Double Post, Left Cross 10, Swing Right – on TWO" barks the quarterback of the Dallas Cowboys in the huddle of a National Football League game against the Washington Redskins. That coded message sends precise instructions to each of the eleven players as to what he should do. The play, which has been designed to exploit the weakness of the Redskins' defensive formation and specific personnel, was diagrammed on paper and "run through" many times in practice.

Good football plays have alternative scenarios built into their designs. The quarterback and pass receivers will have worked out a series of flexible options to be exercised based on the initial moves of the defensive backs. The Redskins might suddenly change formation, causing the Cowboys' quarterback to call an audible in response. Sometimes he will even ask for a "time out" to think when the *Life Conditions* (consisting of historic times, physical place, problems of existence and social circumstances) are too confusing and seek assistance from his consultants on the sideline. These are called strategic retreats in contemporary corporate lingo; saving your ass in football.

As the players approach the line of scrimmage, they have been taught to visualize exactly what they plan to do when the quarterback yells "hut – HUT." The team executes the play mentally before it runs the play physically. This model in their minds connects them in a sequence of well thought out, well coordinated movements in what we will call a "Template." (We use "Template" metaphorically to describe an adjustable overlay, an expanding and contracting map, and a graphic image for the flow of organizational energy, relationships among processes, decision time-lines, and work streams.) This ability of the team to pre-create the play, to feel themselves moving across that mental screen, and then to adapt the visualization to the reality confronting them, is a form of virtual reality.

There are more technical ways. Meld a brain with a good computer and Virtual Reality (VR) is the best connection between human and machine yet devised. By attaching fingers, ears, eyes, voice, and brain waves directly with the microprocessors, one can move around in simulated 3–D space and do things in an electronic domain that seem quite "real" but only exist in the cyberspace between mind and chip. Soon, football players will conduct drills wearing VR helmets, gloves, and suits designed to let them feel the action as various scenarios are played out. There may even be silicon-based cheerleaders to go with the binary socks and jocks.

Many "virtual corporations" will be formed and sustained in a similar joint electronic-human domain. As Second Tier (influenced by yellow (systemic) turquoise (holistic) and further elaborated 'MEMEs) thinking takes off and post-Information Age work becomes even more cerebral and less muscular, members of the virtual company will work at home or in a shared neighborhood facility. Already cellular phones, computers, and fax machines have become so portable that many people carry their offices in a brief case. Pocket-sized world-wide electronic access is only a couple of years away.

Fancy atrium headquarters to entertain clients, elaborate power desks to show workers their places, and even face-to-face meetings to compare shoes and executive cologne become unimportant in managing the virtual corporation. Buildings exist to hold useful and necessary things, not as temples to the manipulation of others. Offices, if they exist at all, are functional gathering points or quiet places to reflect, not status-rich turf to protect. Second Tier clients are impressed by excellence of function, not superfluous forms they ultimately pay for. The organization exists in the individual and collective minds of stakeholders and in the information systems that connect them. In the past we saw "the company" as the mill, the office suite, on the organization chart, or at a display of products or services. For a Spiral company such as we are describing, you might have to log onto a network to "see" the staff. Its head-quarters, if one is even needed, will resemble a healthy small town more than a monument. Once again, people will not so much go to work as simply begin to work at their cottages in the information village or the factory downstairs. Drive-time radio will be scrounging for listeners again and airlines' computer nets will be far greater assets than their aluminum cans stuffed with revenue passenger miles.

The Need for Templates: An Illustration in the Air

By the twenty-first century the US Federal Aviation Administration had hoped a $32 billion plan to reform air travel, dubbed AERA (Automated En-Route Air Traffic Control) would be up and running. Optimal spacing of airplanes, voice recognition computers, navigation via GPS (global positioning satellites) and direct links between ground and cockpit computers were to be commonplace. This would be a far cry from the FAA that the now-forgiven PATCO air traffic controllers struck during the first Reagan administration, or even the upgraded but still very much First Tier, industrial, FAA of today. For the system to work, the FAA will have to put this new, high-tech wine into fresh Second Tier wineskins instead of just rinsing out the old, musty organizational forms of the past. Frankly, the odds are not good.

The FAA's World War II vintage, First Tier model – Washington's National Airport, for example, still depends on vacuum tubes links together a series of Civil Servants ranked in boxes, separated into geographic regions, through a vast **BLUE** governmental pyramid with a few **ORANGE** perks. The twenty-first century FAA must shift into a flow-state design that can facilitate the movement of many kinds of traffic – both air and ground – through information-rich conduits where territoriality does not fit. Its thinking has to become global instead of regional or even national. The FAA must cut some new Templates. If it is unable to adapt, the functions will simply be privatized into the hands of some new kind of entity which can.

The FAA is not at-risk alone. IBM, Digital Equipment Company, and other high-tech monoliths have almost met their Waterloos because they were structured around a nineteenth-century machine-age template. Engineers decided what could, should, and would be done. The customer had to take what the engineer-priests decided to give them. IBM held onto its proprietary control, trying to make the mainframe customer dependent on Big Blue's whims and peculiarities. Even as the computer business grew, supposedly user-friendly Apple, by shrinking, would be guilty of this archaic view.

Technical advances are shaking out the thinking machine industry. Restructured IBM and Apple are holding hands with Motorola while Big Blue reassesses the lucrative mainframe niche and Apple tries to survive by redefining itself. The PC has become a commodity that practically anyone can turn out. Young and successful entrepreneurs, intimately connected to the needs of the user and peripheral developer, now construct interactive template formulas that bring suppliers and the marketplace into their rapid-response decision streams. The same can be said for Southwest Airlines, Federal Express, Wal-Mart, United Parcel Service and others who were awakened by alarms years before their **BLUE** brothers sensed the danger. As cited above, even Eastman Kodak, "the great yellow father" of chemical photography, has begun to realign its templates for the pixel age.

How Templates Work on the Spiral

Templates outline the most natural designs for people, technology, and work flow to accomplish specific outcomes. Each Template must be cut to fit a specific circumstance, the indigenous *life conditions* and ᵛMEME systems. Such issues as rank, ideology, territory, interpersonal relations, and tradition are initially set aside. This is Second Tier work. The rigid, pre-cut First Tier shapes of **PURPLE** through **GREEN** are temporarily shelved, too. For now, they are contaminants. Awaken, instead, the **YELLOW** and **turquoise** ᵛMEMEs, rouse Second Tier models and follow closely.

Visualize the motherboard of a PC with its synergistic blend of modules, components, channels, and processors all connected in a grand design. The ten-element sequence of *Streams* (see Figure 1) is the leader's diagnostic that identifies which ᵛMEMEs to plug where in the organizational circuits because they are congruent with the work and life conditions in that space. The three **Templates** (see below) give Spiral managers the tool to customize, tweak, integrate, and upgrade the corporate machine's operation by applying principles of Second Tier thinking.

Instead of being rigid, permanent cutouts, Spiral Templates are alive, like the interdependent layers that fuse together, stretch, and adjust in our skin. For now we will artificially separate the three Templates to explain their different functions, though they actually mesh together so that what happens in one instantly impacts the others. In fact, a person's job may well include functions on all three Spiral Templates.

THE THREE SPIRAL TEMPLATES

- The "Z" Template: Command Intelligences
- The "Y" Template: Supporting People, Technology, and Systems.
- The "X" Template: Most Natural Forms and Flows of the Critical Functions

Note: These templates are not updated versions of the old power pyramid that separated the workers from mid-manager and then both from executives. They mesh together into a single, over-laid organism based on functional jobs to be done instead of rank, privilege, or power (unless those components are necessary in getting the mission accomplished).

Spiral Templates can be designed under two conditions. First, they may be drawn from scratch for a start-up company using the *Streams* process (especially Element 4 – *Establish Set-Points* and Element 6 – *Connect Everything to Everything Else*). Or second, they can be created in the midst of reengineering an entity fluctuating in the throes of chaos and change. Under those circumstances, you may want to design two organizational models. One will be the standard First Tier form that shows traditional reporting bases and budgetary responsibilities to satisfy here-and-now needs of anxious directors and financial backers. The other, your Second Tier approach, will be Templates-based and oriented toward the specific Strategic Vision you develop in *Streams'* Element 5 and the encompassing Grand Vision you outlined in Element 2. Both designs will be useful in the uncertainty of transformation from the present toward the future entity.

Back at the turn of the century, merchants and military men envisioned a short-cut for shipping through the Americas. France attempted to build a canal by just digging a huge ditch, a First Tier approach which was a malarial disaster. Learning from the French mistakes, the Americans took it on. Their strategy was to drain the swamps and build housing and long-term support facilities that fit the *Life Conditions* of construction in a Central American jungle. The job was still terribly difficult, but it was successfully accomplished and marked an early step toward Second Tier thinking.

Today, far too many quality programs and OD interventions try to dig right through mosquito-infested swamps without building the necessary support system of **P–O–A** (three components of spiral-based management – Politeness, Openness, and responsive Autoc-

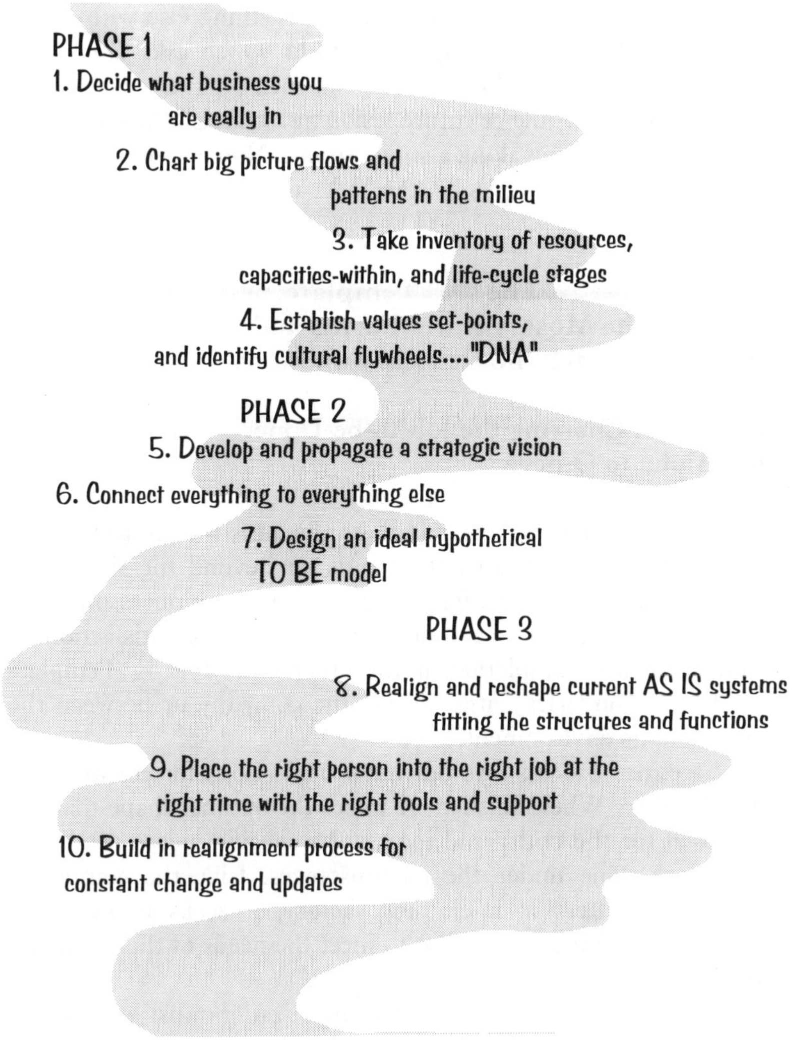

PHASE 1

1. Decide what business you
   are really in

2. Chart big picture flows and
   patterns in the milieu

3. Take inventory of resources,
   capacities-within, and life-cycle stages

4. Establish values set-points,
   and identify cultural flywheels...."DNA"

PHASE 2

5. Develop and propagate a strategic vision

6. Connect everything to everything else

7. Design an ideal hypothetical
   TO BE model

PHASE 3

8. Realign and reshape current AS IS systems
   fitting the structures and functions

9. Place the right person into the right job at the
   right time with the right tools and support

10. Build in realignment process for
    constant change and updates

Figure 1   The Ten Element Sequence of *Streams*

racy), congruent leadership packages, or appropriate forms of compensation for the 'MEMEs doing the digging. They assault mountains "full speed ahead" rather than following natural contours which are already there. The efforts fail because the planners do not first align their Templates.

In the previous chapter we added three tools for engineering the flow of work: (1) the **Plumb Line Process** which establishes the highest priority of the entity then aligns everything else with it, (2) Graves' elegantly simple **Design Formula** which asks *How Who* should manage *Whom* in doing *What*, and then (3) the ten-elements of **Streams** which sequence future visioning, strategic thinking, long and short-term planning along a single strand. Now for the next tools in your Second Tier Wizard's kit, the **X**, **Y**, and **Z** Templates.

The "X" Template:
The Most Natural Forms and Flows
for the Critical Functions

Scripting and Charting the Job-to-be-Done
"From Alpha to Omega"

On the **X** Template every variable that influences the job to be done is included in the work flow. It extends far beyond the shop floor and traditional company limits to include initial suppliers of information and raw materials at one end, the ultimate satisfaction of customers on task completion at the other end. The **X** Template has no fixed boundaries, either inside the company or between the company and its environment.

The **Streams** process lays out the specifications for constructing the **X** Template. When finished, **X** traces the optimal shape that has been chosen for the entity and locates the specific pieces needed to get the work done under the circumstances. Like the computer-guided fabric cutters in a clothing factory, it seeks to minimize waste, maximize utility, and tailor to meet the needs of the particular customer.

To be successful, every piece of the organization must be involved at the beginning. Traditionally, layout decisions of this nature have either been made by "the authorities" or "those experts" and handed off for implementation. Maybe others at lower echelons were invited to fine-tune, make adjustments, or look for ways to reduce costs, but they were not involved in pattern making at the start. One of the revelations in the participatory management upsurge has been that those who plan the party have the best time.

In Second Tier Spiral thinking, everybody involved in the process must have direct input into the design of the **X** Template at the front end. Engineers, production people, salespeople, personnel specialists, even custodians join in the process. This certainly extends to "outsiders" – suppliers, regulators, and end users – since they are also integral to the job to be done. This value engineering technique takes a scalpel to cut away waste at the design stage instead of relying on shears downstream when major errors may not be correctable or, if they are, cost a fortune or a career. A good illustration of this kind of approach is the designing of Boeing's 777 aircraft, the first plane to fly directly from ideas in global networks to machine tools.

Such terms as Value Analysis, Value Chain, Simultaneous Distributed Work, Work Mechanics, Enterprise Networking, Concurrent Engineering, and Horizontal Management have been used to describe this aspect of the process. Here are some other transport industry illustrations:

- When Toyota designed the Lexus motor car, the company first began with the cost to the consumer, and then worked backward. They centered the Plumb Bob over the price point. Then every stage and function in the traditional design and production stream was involved at the front end. The journey covered five years; involved 2,300 technicians, 1,400 engineers, 450 prototypes, millions of test kilometers and 300 patent applications. It produced a fine new family of autos.
- Ford's Team Taurus project used a similar value chain. Purchasing, design, quality assurance, marketing, sales, distribution, repair, personnel, environmental relations, legal and even insurance company inputs were integrated in the simultaneous design process. The project was brought in for $250 million less than budget. Not only was the quality good enough for the model to be exported to Japan and Germany, but the design cycle had been reduced from 5–6 to 2–3 years. The venture deserves credit for helping turn Detroit's fortunes around.
- The United Auto Workers joined with General Motors management in a "Committee of 99" (2/5 management, 3/5 union) to design the new Saturn Division from the ground up. The joint venture created the product, located the plant, and produces a world-class car at a highly competitive price. A uniquely involved and service-oriented dealer net completes the package. Though **RED**, **BLUE**, and **ORANGE** contami-

nation from both GM and the UAW keep Saturn chasing after **GREEN**-er Japanese-managed competitors, it continues to be a remarkable case study.

- When British Airways decided to do a major overhaul of its entire customer service and marketing function, it relied on a number of problem-solving groups to redesign the system. Michele Heyworth of their Market Research team discovered a company that specializes in bringing passengers and providers together to talk about the key needs and services that would make a vital difference.

  Forty managers from Sales, Cabin Services, Brands and Brands Development, Overseas Marketing and Sales, and Catering and Design got together with ninety frequent fliers from all over the world. David Charlton, Group Brands Manager, noted: "The idea was to find out where our products and services fit into their lives, rather than the other way round." Very sensibly, the Plumb Line was centered over the air traveller. British Airways makes extensive use of project teams that engage all elements impacted by a decision in its marketing and full implementation.

- In 1992 New York Telephone commissioned an eight-person commando team and charged them with rethinking how the telephone company should go about "provisioning" customers with one of its most advanced products. They were then to restructure how the work gets done. The commando team was staffed jointly by "craft" (union) workers and first-line managers and told to get on with it. They sought after input from a Science and Technology expert, a systems laboratory, and an anthropologist. They consulted with customers and users.

  By looking at the process "from A to Z," reported 22-year veteran and union member Leroy Gilchrist, "it was the first time that anybody had an idea of what the whole process looked like." Filling an order, the group discovered, involved 126 steps and more than 40 people. No wonder customers were frustrated: the process was costly and things continued to fall between the cracks.

Motorola, Federal Express, American Express, Glaxo, Merck, Nike, Apple Computer, Honda, Boeing Aircraft and Intel have intuitively made extensive use of **X** Template technology. Advanced information systems make possible the tracking, continuous monitoring and improvement, and fine-tuning of work flows. These natural structures and scripts are replacing traditional organizational charts and their inevitable bottle-necks.

The visualized X Template may resemble a network, a cluster, a clover leaf, a neuronet, interlocking Olympic rings, a starburst a constellation, a game board, a story line, a time sequence, the passage of people through stages, or any other pattern that accurately describes the flow of work. The form will be dictated by the function. You may or may not be able to find this Template if you visit the company to observe its activity since the X Template can exist quite well only in the minds of people and their computer links.

Earlier in this section we cited evidence that the quality movement has lost some of its luster because it appears not to be producing the results that were either expected or promised. Much of what is done in the name of the Total Product Quality (TPQ) initiative has elements of the X Template. Among these are flowcharts, statistical measures, decision-trees, and time-lines. However, many TPQ projects have caused more problems than they have solved because the client company cultures were simply not ready for the technology, and the implementation was incomplete. The supportive ᵛMEMEs were not yet awakened and the other two essential Templates were not committed to the process.

Managers bought promises of increased productivity and cost efficiencies without understanding how and why the entire culture had to be altered first. They could not bring themselves to embrace all of the philosophical assumptions that Deming's way requires, especially the need to remove fear and eliminate appraisal-type ratings of people.

There is a great deal of the Second Tier in Deming's point of view, but it is rarely carried through to implementation. Arrested **BLUE** is put off because it breaks set. Overly **ORANGE** executives want to pick-and-choose from Deming's points while overlooking the essential human factors. Closed **GREEN** sometimes thinks "competitive advantage" is a dirty word and "progress" is a threat to harmony. Deep-seated ᵛMEMEs permeate every aspect of corporate life. Unless you recognize the Spiral and align it properly, expensive and time consuming TPQ and TQM (Total Quality Management) initiatives, as well as noble reengineering efforts, sink in the bog of tradition, blame, and excuses.

Linking of Customers, Clients, Stakeholders, and Functions in Strategic Alliances on the X Template

The term "strategic alliance" has entered the mainstream of managerial thought. It describes mutually beneficial relationships among a company and its customers, regulators, suppliers, competitors, and other stakeholders. If you belong to American Airlines' frequent flier program, you can also qualify for award mileage by flying British Airways, TWA, Singapore Airlines, staying in Sheraton hotels, renting your care from Avis, and charging it all up on a special Master Card that reconnects with American.

We have already said that involved outsiders may be asked to supply their input on matters of common interest when laying out the X Template. In a strategic alliance, those entities play an even more vital role in the success of the enterprise. This is not to say the alliance is always sweetness and light. Often it is as troublesome as a shotgun wedding and produces strange bedfellows, indeed. The partners may be in need, not in love. If the 'MEMEs never mesh, the alliance will surely break up.

Another form of alliance is outsourcing. In this case, a specific internal function is actually turned over, lock, stock, and personnel, to an external entity. EDS (Electronic Data Systems) was built on the premise that it would take over the entire information processing function in a client company and do the job better, even for one as fine as Xerox. EDS must be able to morph itself to client 'MEMEs or it will trigger antibodies and the relationship will become toxic. Today, everything from management training to custodial services to running national parks is handled on an "outsourcing" basis. You really have to trust outsource partners because you may literally give them the keys to your building.

Value is potentially added through an alliance by sharing competencies. Personal relationships, always including Openness and Politeness, may be enhanced. Information is distributed throughout, based on the functional need to know and carefully regulated by healthy Autocracy. More can be done with greater efficiency.

But good things generally have an opposite. In such cases a naive alliance partner becomes vulnerable to rip-off's, industrial espionage, and spin-off competition because of the very Openness that gives the venture strength. Again, for outsourcing it is critical that you pay close attention to the dominant 'MEMEs and ethical systems of a potential partner. Be especially wary of the guiltless side of **RED** and the deceptive, "whatever you want to hear," angle of **ORANGE**.

Assign people whose 'MEME profiles are complementary to each entity but who also recognize the common Set Points to complete the link. To close the deal you must identify what each potential ally needs from you to connect psychologically, as well as economically. Some strategic partners need to sense **RED** power before they can link comfortably; others are more drawn by an **ORANGE** high-tech, high-potential display; yet others would like to feel an expression of sensitive and socially-conscious **GREEN**. Think of the initial connections as a FAX-like handshake between 'MEMEs. The secret is to think like networking software to hook up diverse individual profiles, organization flywheels, and cultural 'MEMEs because these are the real bonds that ultimately make or break the arrangement.

Design of Job Models and Work Modules Within the X Template

Competency models and the careful matching of people with jobs are replacing "warm body" hiring practices. In the Design Formula we discussed how you constitute effective matches. An expansion joint should be built into every job model so a person can grow either in the function or by changing roles. That is the simplest way to build a continuous improvement feature into an organization.

Some entities may choose to define jobs more generically. They prefer to assemble teams who are virtually interchangeable in doing several tasks. Members can rotate through the jobs to avoid boredom. They might both operate machines and fix them, reducing the amount of time any particular unit is off-line. In many cases, the team actually can self-manage, thus sharing the pay that once would have gone to a non-producing supervisor. A good **X** Template will delineate the selection of people who have that kind of flexibility.

Whether narrow or broad based, job models require a sensitivity to the unique characteristics of persons. An understanding of 'MEME profiles and Patterns of Thinking becomes essential from two perspectives. First, the total culture or "capability based environment" (CBE) must be fully understood before attempting to "dig the Panama Canal." Second, understanding human differences assists in the alignment of people with technology and work flows. This critical matching of job functions with minds and ᵛMEMEs has been long in coming in organizational life. Grenier and Metes say it clearly in *Enterprise Networking*:

> Besides the obvious language differences, personal likes and dislikes, ideologies, prejudices, and traditions that separate people, certain emotional as well as cognitive traits are particularly inhibiting to produce information sharing in distributed environments. Suspicion, protection of territory (conceptual and physical ownership), conventional beliefs in the supremacy of one's own creativity, vision, methods, and tools create key psychological and social barriers. (p. 55)

Their terms "emotional as well as cognitive traits" match our ᵛMEME profiles and Patterns of Thinking. Organizations have been reluctant to fully acknowledge these differences in the recent past because of BLUE and GREEN blinders. Good intentions did not allow us to recognize individual uniqueness or differentiate competencies. Now, better intentions expect no less.

ᵛMEME Profiles and Levels of Complexity

Because they reflect layers of complexity, ᵛMEME profiles impact the way individuals filter, interpret, and respond to the entire *gestalt* of issues. The particular *Life Conditions* of a job require that certain ᵛMEMEs be active and that others be turned down. A description of the essential thinking, whether in ᵛMEME colors or some other language, should be included in the job profile to match people with various areas of the X Template. Then, job applicants from either inside or outside can be evaluated fairly in terms of their access to these processing patterns.

For example, when selecting a high performance team, its overall composition of ᵛMEMES should be crafted and stacked in the direction of the essential outputs. If the team is to be involved in a critical strategic issue, it should have a heavy **ORANGE** cast to enable it to find the "best solution," and then deploy assets in a quick and efficient manner. You would also need some **YELLOW** thinking to inject long-term implications and someone leaning toward **BLUE** to determine what is proper and in line with standards.

Applying Patterns of Thinking and Natural Intelligences

Our thinking about people in general, their nature and potentials, has shifted from "empty brains" and "anybody can do anything" to an acceptance of unique and innate differences and capacities. Mind/ brain research, gene mapping, and even analysis of identical twins who were reared separately have heightened our awareness of both differences and similarities. The nature *vs.* nurture dial is shifting from "mostly nurture" to synergy between the two. In Spiral language, we are slowly draining the **GREEN**, egalitarian swamp and revealing natural differences in complexity of thinking. We are uncovering **YELLOW** and awaiting what **TURQUOISE** will bring.

For example, what kinds of minds were needed to work as air traffic controllers in high density airports in the days before powerful computers? The ability to visualize airspace three-dimensionally was crucial to sorting out and aligning blips on a flat radar screen. Quick decisiveness was also important since each green dot represented a different kind of aircraft, at a different altitude, speed, and trajectory. The controller was called upon to sequence airplanes for landing by integrating a large amount of data. Even though they were highly "intelligent," up to 90 per cent of applicants washed out during training because the X Template was ill-defined and it was not until several weeks into the course that the 3-D thinking capacity was called upon.

Job models, however, do change. Now the FAA must select different kinds of people who are more adept with information management tools than sorting out airplanes in their minds. Some current employees will make the transition easily; others will not. Certainly, the X Template must be re-cut if the agency intends to implement AERA, much less a Second Tier initiative.

Thinking back to the last chapter, you want to look at similar patterns of thinking in selecting visionary thinkers and good scouts for your *Streams* team. The best candidates are most often Chaotic-Conceptual in focus. They perform well in open, free-wheeling, and highly creative activities. Abstractions play to their strength. Their weakness is that strength pushed to excess. Do not expect them necessarily to be good with details, precise lineups, or repetitive pages. You will need to select other minds, with different kinds of thinking, to do those things.

In summary, the X Template is designed to link together all of the variables that impinge upon the job to be done so that they are handled in a sequential and logical manner. The three sub-Spirals of technology, human factors, and business systems are in sync. The payoff is that the ultimate output will be clean, focused, strategic, and lean.

The Y Template: People Factors and Management Systems

While we wrap the Y Template around the X Template, that does not imply "better than," or "superior to," only "different from." Those performing X template functions are focused on getting the job done. People and resources operating on behalf of the Y Template support, facilitate, assist, enhance, and improve the X Template's performance and procedures. In Second Tier entities they are not bosses *per se*; they do not pull rank; they do not play games. Their primary purpose is to add value, make repairs, and fine-tune while the work is being done. Many people function on both X and Y Templates at once.

As we have pointed out, many TPQ, TQM, and Reengineering initiatives run aground because they have been unable to reshape the total culture and specific leadership behaviors on the Y Template to match X Template's needs. For example, in the past, mid- and top-level executives have gotten perks and bonuses at the obvious expense of "the line" or "first level" employees. They have been riding the backs of the X Template. That must change for the Templates process to work. The X template, where the jobs are actually performed, must be enriched before any cream is skimmed at the top.

The X Template must be laid out first since it is where the Plumb Line points. Once those decisions are made, you are ready to do Y Template things like the design of management systems, motivation packages, dispatch of human and other resources, and engineering maintenance. As the Y Template goes into place you can begin to think more broadly and start putting together the kinds of Command Intelligences (Z Template) necessary to deal with your specific X and Y Templates.

The tasks, people, and technology mix of each particular X Template function will dictate what needs to happen when and by whom on Y and even Z Templates. By hanging the Plumb Bob so it points to a given job (or assemblage of people) on the X Template, one can then determine what needs to happen at Y level to support that job to be done and foster synergy among that group. If a **RED** empire is necessary to get the job done, the capability to manage and motivate **RED** Empires must exist on Y. It will be legitimized and kept healthy from the Z Template for the good of the organization's whole Spiral, as well.

Templates end the debate as to the "right" or "best" way to manage people. The issue, rather, is how to manage or facilitate those people doing those jobs in those *Life Conditions*. Looking through the Y Template, you assess the ᵛMEMEs and Patterns of Thinking of those people who naturally perform the work laid out on the X Template. Then you align Y accordingly. Repeat the Design Formula – "*How* should *Who* manage *Whom* to do *What When?*" Arguments over contrasting managerial theories, competing gurus, or trendy training packages are fruitless. You simply lower the Plumb Bob and then lay on the packages and protocols that will both serve the immediate needs of the people at that place on the X Template and the interests of the entire company as well.

There is no standard form for Templates, period. Companies, particularly those who are global in scope, must be sure that in shaping the X Template they do not force a single prescription over their many diverse sub-cultures. Rather, each version of the X Template must be indigenous to its *milieu* and to the kinds of ᵛMEMEs and Patterns that *milieu* presents. Beware of simply importing the latest managerial fad into your company until you have sorted out your own Design Formula, Plumb Line Process, and *Streams* sequence for your X and Y Templates. You may have the best solutions already in hand.

Using the Y Templates for Selection, Alignment, and Integration of People and Processes

The function of the Y Template is managing, facilitating, leading, and expediting the human factors within the X flow. This Second Tier process should be operationalized through Spiral Wizardry since there must be heavy involvement and consultation with the X Template people directly involved in production because it is they who are the most knowing about the job(s) being done, but they are also the most likely to represent widely diverse 'MEME profiles.

Grenier and Metes (p. 119) list the following competencies which fit the Y Template:

- Network fault analysis and resolution management [finding faults and fixing them]
- Configuration management [arranging people, technology, and facilities in functional streams]
- Performance management [effective supervision of people and systems]
- Security management [Keeping things and people safe]
- Accounting management [taking care of the books]
- Applications management [dispensing new ideas through the template]

Let us add knowing how to support and coordinate multiple 'MEME systems since the Y Template is concerned with the health of the entire work stream – individuals, the organization, and the community-at-large. You create this healthy climate by a multi-colored strategy of embellishing, strengthening, and enhancing all of the 'MEMEs that exist within the entity. Think of this as preventive maintenance for human beings. To illustrate . . .

- **PURPLE** is nurtured through observing seasonal rituals, honoring individual's rites of passage (weddings, graduations, funerals) and expressing a sense of enchantment and magic in life's mystery. Let the groups have their special time together.
- **RED** is nurtured by preserving the stories of company heroes, or by celebrating the great feats of conquest when the company, figuratively at least, "slew the dragon." Positive outlets for energy like sports and constructive activities that get out and build something keep it fit.
- **BLUE** is reinforced through appeals to traditions, by respecting the past, by honoring length of service and loyalty. Various forms of patriotic appeals and charitable sacrifice accompany

observances of national, religious, or secular holidays and commemorative events.

- **ORANGE** is exercised by displaying symbols of progress, success, growth, and accomplishment. Individuals or groups who excel should be recognized for their achievements. They like a piece-of-the-action but also enjoy getting good things done.
- **GREEN** is enhanced by stressing the importance of human beings and the warmth that exudes from a feeling of a caring community. Socially responsible activities should become tastefully visible as everyone in the group contributes.
- **YELLOW** is enhanced by conveying a sense of personal freedom with emphasis on getting an important job done without specifying how it must be done. Here, especially, flex-time, alternative working hours, remote working, and job interchange are ways to avoid over-managing.

While every set of Templates will be different, one basic Second Tier principle runs throughout: Decisions are made by the people most competent to make them and as close to the X Template as possible, not by some large class of "managers" or "executives." The nature of the problem to be solved, decision to be reached, or issue to be resolved will determine who is involved and where the buck stops. Furthermore, compensation of all kinds should be calibrated with levels of competency, implications of ideas, consequences of contributions, and the extent to which people add to the life of the organization's Spiral throughout the Seven Variations of Change.

Y Template Management of Technology, Resources, and Facilities

These functions involve hardware, maintenance, house-keeping, up-keeps and up-dates, and other tasks often assigned to engineering, facilities and personnel departments. If you are using Templates there is a difference since the corporate Plumb Line now hovers over X outputs, not titles on office doors or pay grades. Support functions now become integrated across the input-throughput-output flow as the Y Template shifts them to where they are most needed rather than to where they fall on charts. Training and selection functions become so closely integrated with X Template requirements that the so-called "line" *vs.* "staff" conflict cannot happen because everyone is now in the same business.

The healthy Y Template is lean, flexible, apolitical, and demands P–O–A. It morphs, changes, and reconstitutes itself as new needs arise from X. Interpersonal squabbles and "us" *vs.* "them" conflicts are nipped in the bud. Enhanced information systems provide the same knowledge base to all three Templates so rumors and allegations of injustice or mismanagement can be quickly resolved.

After his stint on the General Motors Board, computer magnate Ross Perot contrasted the way his former company, EDS, operated as opposed to GM's culture. He said that if EDS people saw a snake, they would kill it. Whereas traditional GM management, after going through the time-honored committee investigation, would dance around while trying to find the proper person somewhere in their vast hierarchy who was the authorized "snake killer." They might even hire a search firm to do the looking. In the meantime, the snake would probably get away, especially if it was Japanese. (Perot has never been charged with political, much less "animal rights," correctness.)

Day-by-Day Monitoring of Events, Issues, and Performance from the Y Template

The functional differences between the X and Y Templates are more of degree and scope than type. People in the Y Template need to exercise a broader perspective than X operatives who concentrate on getting the work out. They should be able to call up more resources to sort out problems and bring more knowledge to bear on the situation. They may be expert workers who also can act as facilitators, supervisors, or managers as needed. Y Template personnel have to see the value chain from start to finish, from supplier to customer. In Second Tier entities they operate more in *ad hoc* decision teams than permanent structures. The lines of authority between X and Y layers are kept deliberately fuzzy, making it difficult to start territorial battles and keeping good outputs part of everybody's job.

Unlike traditional "up the organization" models, a pro-motion does not mean having to move from the X Template to Y responsibilities in Second Tier entities; that is only one option. Each job in the company will have its own benchmarks and a built-in advancement track. A healthy Y Template makes it possible for a satisfied X Template person to climb a horizontal competency ladder by learning more, doing more things, accessing more knowledge about the entire value-chain, or acquiring new skill bundles for future use. Through Change of the first or second Variation the person has become more valuable to the X Template and thereby has enhanced the Spiral. An entire, satisfying career might be spent on the X Template. If Change of a higher Variation is underway, then the Templates can make room for that option as more complex thinking appears.

In summary, the Y Template is responsible for fine-tuning the flow of work, monitoring all of the vital signs, enhancing the competencies of people doing the work, and providing the integration necessary to produce a seamless company. The Y layer is not the filter or intermediary between Z and X. Its role is to unburden the X Template from ancillary tasks and extraneous duties that divert it from the job to be done. If you want a graphic of Y, turn a typical organization chart up-side-down like SAS (Scandinavian Airlines) did. Now, the mechanics and customer contact people – "where the rubber meets the road" – have priority. The executive level supports, rather than "lords over," the people performing the critical jobs of the airline. This form comes naturally to Spiral Wizards because it involves integrating ᵛMEME Profiles and diverse Thinking Patterns in complex systems, not mastering a few Traits of a Leader or demonstrating the habits of success.

Z Template: Command Intelligences

Many organizations are trying to become thin, lean, and efficient. Some simply lay off mid-managers. Others crack the whip harder at the lowest echelons while the top layer prospers. In entities managed by Spiral Wizards, more power, responsibility, and resources flow into production/service streams while executive trappings and expensive perks go away. Be not mistaken; this does not mean the company is being given away to the employees, or that quick **ORANGE** minds are now surplus property, or that **GREEN** relativistic impulses are replacing **BLUE** heritage. Something else, something more profound, something downright **YELLOW** is happening. People on both X and Y Templates have more power because of access to information and fundamental shifts in the human ʼMEME stack.

The role and scope of the executive function is shifting. Fewer entities are relying on quasi-military chain-of-command structures where power is vested in single persons or elitist groups up and down a power pyramid. Rather, they are now forming task-specific brain syndicates, a new decision-team approach that relies on competency, trust, cooperation, independence, and consensus combined.

Business issues are more complex and multidimensional today. The environment in which critical decisions are now being made is more chaotic, faster paced, and less forgiving. More CEOs and senior level managers are aware of the incompleteness of their own knowledge and insight base, particularly where human dynamics are concerned. What they learned in MBA programs or executive seminars is no longer sufficient or even particularly relevant. New priorities far beyond bottom line performance such as social and environmental citizenship are being imposed. In response, many executives, through interactive planning and visioning activities, are broadening the base of participation in decision making. Companies, today, are more high-tech, information rich, global in scope, and integrated in operation. Diversity is appreciated and flexibility is essential.

Fewer and fewer stakeholders are willing to put up with the extravagant, flamboyant egos that have existed at the top of corporate and governmental **ORANGE**. When President George Bush escorted American CEOs to Japan with hats in hand in 1992, it dramatized the differences between executives in the two societies, framing America's version as over-paid, over-egoed, and out-foxed. No wonder the President got ill.

The Z Template is not home to red carpet VIP's but to Command Intelligences. By this we mean the collective wisdom, knowledge, and judgment that is focused on specific problems and issues, both long and short term. In the traditional pyramid, the only opinions that count are housed at the top; in spite of their intelligences, everyone else is essentially "along for the ride." In a Second Tier organization, all knowledge is important. The unique insight and wisdom of the Z Template comes in two forms – the Executive Core and Focused Intelligences.

First, **Z** houses the Executive Core (EC) which monitors the whole process like the CPU in a computer. The EC will be small, consisting of the CEO and others to have been chosen because of their scope of vision, necessary experiences, maturity of judgment, abilities with **P–O–A**, and competency. It is accountable for the whole entity – (fiduciary, legal, ethical, productivity, and financial). This Core represents the microcosm of thinking required to (a) coordinate **X** and **Y** Template functions and (b) maintain a lookout to enable the organization to thrive in the *milieu*-at-large.

The *Executive Core* looks and behaves more like a creative and inclusive "skunk works" than a top-level, exclusive club. It functions as a complex, high-order **Streams** team for the whole entity (as opposed to issue-specific teams taken from **X** and **Y** Templates). A natural tendency of any organism is to explore outside, then change inside. The EC constantly reshapes the company to fit the *Life Conditions*. Of course that disturbs the vMEME stack. The EC, having worked on the outside, then has to fix the inside. Once the inside has been rearranged, it must again focus on the outside. The EC is a busy place requiring persons of high energy, interest, scruples, and abilities. Organizationally, the Executive Core floats in the midst of the three Templates. If the Templates are a three-ring circus, then the EC is ring-master.

The second function of the **Z** Template is to bring *Focused Intelligences* to specific problems. Under the direction of the EC, intelligences from throughout the three templates are assigned to a given task. The Value Engineering discipline or similar collaborative models are used to tap the talents and insights of everybody involved in an objective, clean, non-political, and non-territorial fashion. Persons from the Executive Core participate directly with those from the **X** and **Y** Templates. Knowledge, know-how, and informed perspectives transcend position and rank in making decisions. The Executive Core sees to it that the best decisions are being made. "What is right" is always more important than "who is right."

Continuous Scanning of Present and Future From the Z Template

Just as the **Y** Template monitors all aspects of operations, the organization's **Z** Template tunes into the kinds of exotic messages from the future such as those needed for **Streams** Element 10. Visit an organizational grave yard and look at all the tombstones of airlines, steel companies, computer vendors, and banks. Most died because they failed to keep their eyes open to what was coming at them from upstream, got blind-sided while looking at the bottom-line, or lost touch with their moral anchors and went adrift. Many were weakened by the diseases of greed and arrogance, final state blindness, Quick-Fixitis, and Do-or-Die quarterly reports.

The Command Intelligences, coordinated from **Z** but dispersed throughout all three Templates, should include an early warning device that identifies potential flash points like these before they ignite and sensors that constantly sweep both the internal and external environments for what is coming 'round the bend. These include forces of the marketplace, emerging technologies, shifting population trends, strange behavior from competitors, and the first signs of political turbulence. Usually, "bad" news is more valuable than good.

The Z-Template: Macro-Managing the Total Organism

Every organization has vital signs, indicators of its health. Some of these are seen in the usual spreadsheet numbers – from productivity measurements and quality statistics to return on investment. Most of the cultural life signs are more intangible, elusive, and harder to figure.

Everybody's eyes and ears are needed to recognize signs of distress or sighs of satisfaction. This is also Command Intelligences at work. Every company will, at some time or another, encounter the stresses of BETA conditions. The sooner those are recognized the better lest a GAMMA Trap be sprung. Denial, political gamesmanship, or self-serving gatekeepers often isolate executives from knowing what is going on until it is too late to avoid the jaws of disaster.

As former Southwest and Braniff Airlines CEO Howard Putnam points out, "you should get mad at situations, not people." If workers fear for their professional lives every time they make a mistake, two things will happen, both bad. (1) They will not risk, take a chance, or venture into the unknown. (2) They will hide their mistakes or pass them off to others, perhaps causing a more serious foul-up in the future. Under such terms, Change Condition 6 (consolidation in a supportive environment) is unattainable and anything beyond the first or second Variation is out.

The Templates approach gives people more freedom and more safety. It allows for the design and deployment of a wide range of unique cubbyholes, niches, and microsystems which function independently of the traditional lines of authority or bottom-line accountability. Thus, key people from all over the organization can be brought together in an emergency or assigned on a temporary basis – Focused Intelligences where it counts, when it counts.

Some clusters drawn from all the Templates might include . . .

- **Wild Duck Pond:** a place where bright, nonconformist individuals can "swim alone" to explore off-the-wall ideas without getting punished or threatening more traditional structures.
- **Nursery:** a developmental track where neophytes can be nurtured through a series of training experiences and simulations before they are exposed to mainline functions in any of the three templates. They can "learn the ropes" without imposing on people engaged in serious X Template activities or mess up Y Template operations during their learning curves. All too often secretaries have to train their new bosses who are simply paying dues enroute up the organization while the much lower pay grade "executive assistant" actually holds down the fort.
- **War Room:** either a physical space or an information network that displays the vital signs of the company, models of the environment, profiles of competitors, and other antagonists. The War Room can simulate alternative responses to particular scenarios before they are implemented in the "real" world.
- **Play Pen:** a loose and creative environment where teams can attack very serious problems through playful brainstorming, model building, and scenario construction, forcibly liberating their "right brain" capacities and scanning potentials.
- **Crisis Team:** a rapid response "A Team" of experts from the X, Y, and Z Templates that can be deployed quickly anywhere in the environment to fend off danger, stabilize functions, and repair damage to keep the organization functioning.
- **Rescue Squad:** a source of nurturance and support that dispenses "chicken soup" to ailing parts of the organism after a crisis is over. It could mobilize in case of work-related

accidents – either physical or emotional – to get things stabilized, personal problems dealt with, and the entity back to a new state of normal. All major air carriers have what American Airlines calls "the care team," a group of experts that rallies to action in case of disasters.

• **Wizard's Tree House:** a periodic convocation of Spiral Wizards who scan far out into the future searching for new trends, new opportunities, and new dangers. It feeds ideas to both the **Z** Command Intelligences and *ad hoc* Streams Teams.

Shaping Large-Scale Change and Strategic Interventions

The **X** and **Y** Templates monitor and support the day-to-day operations of the entity. Compared to **Z** their view is more linear and focused on the nature of the job to be done. The **Z** Template's Command Intelligences really take hold when the organization goes into DELTA because it needs a major overhaul, a significant change in direction, or to be reconstituted following a merger or acquisition. The intelligences to do these things permeate all three Templates; everyone in the organization is potentially a **Z** agent. The Executive Core which coordinates this is also headquartered in **Z** and functions as the unified command and control center for the enterprise, mobilizing the Command Intelligences as needed. It behaves very much in the fashion of General Schwartzkopf and his staff during operation Desert Storm.

Since a Template company has a built-in change capacity dispersed throughout its operating units, it automatically morphs itself, adjusts quickly to new shapes, forms, networks, and tasks, and fuses itself with new entities as need be. Empowerment is disseminated throughout the organism. That appropriate Autocracy – remember, it is vital – connects with competency to allow quick decisions to be made and judgments to be exercised without having to ask permission or look to one's backside.

Jobs are defined differently in a Template arrangement. Instead of the traditional one-person-assigned-to-one-job-in-one-place mentality, each contributor may have pieces of a number of functions all along the value-chain. If you look in anyone's locker, you may find a cap with a "**Z**" on it. Traditional models encourage competition between engineering and production, line and staff, and regions and home office. The Spiral Wizard's Templates weave a seamless process, one that focuses on systemic outputs, not narrow functions. Cooperation and synergy among separate components are stitched into the design. Everybody is rewarded for pulling together, but also for excelling alone. This instills a unique flexibility in the culture; namely, the ability for individuals to adjust quickly to new assignments and responsibilities. Nobody needs a course in managing change; it is already part of the process. Barriers and boundaries never become permanent in virtual reality.

To summarize the Z Template and end this chapter, consider six intelligences. We identified these in development research for the BrainSCAN Assessment, now part of the Quantum Mind research package. These capacities are:

- **World sensing:** Like an absorbent sponge, sweeping radar, and early warning detector. It is high in non-quantitative market research and public relations professionals and others who rely on "sensing" information and guided intuitions.
- **Sequential plan construction:** The capacity to locate entities in space, in sequence, and in order. Often high in planning departments, layout functions, and orderly bureaucratic jobs. NASA's planners who have the patience to specify the essential activities at every second of a projected space flight must be high in this competence. It is crucial for logistics operations.
- **Complex plan execution:** Ability to suppress competing stimuli, block out distracting events, and integrate complex ideas and flows. High in good emergency room physicians and nurses, sales professionals who must negotiate deals under pressure, and others who must select among options, orchestrate plans of action, and mesh a number of tributaries while on the go. This capacity is imperative for successful military leaders and event managers.

Included in our studies were chief executive officers and managing directors from around the world. They demonstrated these three distinct "Executive Intelligence" patterns:

- **Entrepreneurial intelligence:** The impulse to start something new, to peer into the future, a fierce determination to succeed, a penchant for high risk, unconventional freedom, a creative resourcefulness, the ability to integrate complexity, focus to obtain a pragmatic outcome, the ego strength to stand alone, a demand for total control, and a practical visionary. High in CEOs who built their own companies or in innovative leaders who cut their own pathways. Excels at managing start-ups, either within or outside of larger companies. This intelligence could be utilized in new product sponsorship; sent to inaugurate a new outpost; or assigned to head up new ventures.

- **Translational intelligence:** Essential in the maintenance of systems, continual monitoring and fine-tuning, and the guarantee of consistent standards and quality. Shows patience and tolerance of sameness and regimentation, satisfied with small victories or incremental improvements, and able to reduce uncertainty, tension, and internal conflict. Excels at looking after large systems, adapting and implementing new ideas into a steady state. Adept at taking over as Chief Operating Officer after start-up entrepreneurs have reached their levels of incompetence.

- **Transformational intelligence:** Essential in navigating through changing chaotic environments while using sketchy blue-prints to literally morph a system, company, or society from one world to the next. Excels during periods of profound and rapid change. Transformational intelligence is high in Change Wizards who rescue a company from failure, or merge several entities into a new organization. This element is necessary in managing a company through its inevitable life cycles on the S-curve.

The intelligence core of an organization should have all six of these patterns at its disposal, along with representatives who speak for all the ᵛMEMEs. Otherwise, there will be serious gaps in both perspectives and action. Put them all together, though, and add them to the Wizard's Tool Kit and Spiral Dynamics is yours.

It is not all that difficult to do. The twenty-first century company, like the twenty-first century country, is still a work in progress; but its outlines are beginning to jell. Leaders everywhere are attempting to design and manage revolutions of great magnitude – geopolitical, technological, and human – all at the same time. New markets, extraordinary advances in communications, and global sources of brain power and skilled labor will herald an explosion in business opportunities.

The New Company, one that can function and thrive in such a rapidly evolving environment, will require new leadership, no matter how the old approaches have been repackaged or reengineered. This emerging executive intelligence will stand in striking contrast to the gray flannel "organization man" of the 1950s or even the smartly-suited Harvard MBAer from the 1980s.

Such leaders must mesh global markets with local operations and vice versa. They must be open to new ideas, tactics, and technologies. Leaders of the New Company must encourage information-sharing and innovation throughout organizations which are continually in process of being aligned and integrated. Perhaps above all, they must value ethical behavior, integrity, and fair play. At the same time, they must be irreverent about hierarchy and office politics, tolerating, even enjoying, some unruliness. They must reward those who work smartly, produce high-quality goods and services, and thrive on the challenges of the times with personalized recognition, continuous training, and a good living.

But even this will not be enough. New Company leaders must also be responsible human beings who enrich families, neighborhoods, communities, nations, and life itself. They will hear the faint beat of ancient drums while they also sense the electronic pulses of worlds yet to be. Human society's crucibles are beginning to forge beings of just such intelligences in significant numbers.

We now turn from the practice of social synergy, through 'spiral integration', to its application in managing joint ventures.

Reference

Grenier and Metes, *Enterprise Networking: Working Together Apart*

8

Managing Joint Ventures
Bernard Lievegoed

Mergers and Reorganization

At the present time mergers, and other less complete collaborative arrangements, are the order of the day. The reasons for such joint ventures are manifold.

Ideally, a joint venture or merger should come about as a free decision on the part of two healthy expanding enterprises who see integration as a means of strengthening both their positions. In practice, however, the freedom of decision of the partners varies according to whether both are healthy or both are undergoing difficulties, or whether one is strong and one weak. In the latter case a merger is a cover-up for a takeover.

Whenever such a joint venture takes place, two enterprises, two systems with their own often different policies, have to grow together to form a new, larger enterprise, a single system with new policies and new organizational principles. A merger is therefore always a process of intensive social change; and in practice it is usually unplanned social change.

Whether the process of integration is carried out horizontally, vertically, laterally, or in the form of a chain merger, the expectation is always that the whole result of such a combining of forces will be greater than the sum of the parts. Mergers are made according to the formula "2 + 2 = 5;" but this does not become reality unless the merger is carried out as a planned revolution. On the morning after the night before, when the ceremonial pen has been laid aside and the champagne glasses have been cleared away, the new combination faces the task of realizing the expectations.

A merger shows everything in a clearer light: the unviability (see chapter 12) of marginal enterprises, the over-ripe pioneer phase, the rigid phase of differentiation – all these are highlighted by the need to develop into a new and larger entity. In addition, it becomes painfully obvious that the forward vision, the horizon and the time-span of the management, which may already have been too small for the separate firms, are unquestionably too small for the much larger new entity.

A joint venture or merger often means a jump not only to a quantitatively larger totality but, more importantly, to a qualitatively different market and to different technology, financing, and infor-mation-processing. This means that a new kind of human resource is needed in the new situation. Some people are made redundant by duplication; for many of the new positions there will be a need for at least some retraining and very often for a considerable change of attitude; and for some positions new people will have to be taken on who have knowledge and experience of a kind not available in the merging enterprises. Most important of all, however, is the concept of the new organization structure and the new policy.

In the normal course of events we have been concerned with planned change and organizational development taking place in an evolutionary manner. But in the case of a merger, organizational development takes place in a revolutionary manner. Within a short period of time a series of coordinated reorganizations have to be achieved within the framework of a well-thought-out plan, if the advantage of the merger is not to be lost. If the new internal and external policies have been insufficiently worked through in advance, this is where failure will occur. It is obvious, moreover, that classical organization theory cannot meet this situation.

An answer to the situation can be found, however, in a new kind of organization and in the path from the differentiated phase of organization to an integrated one.

Planning and Implementing a Merger

Forming a board of directors

First of all, the place and task of the top management must be clearly defined in a merger. This gives rise to a number of practical difficulties. Taken together, the merging enterprises have too many directors. Also, particularly in the early years, the new top management must be able to make quick decisions and carry out policies without disagreement. A board of three directors working as colleagues, as described below, or a chairman and three directors, is appropriate for the task.

Experience shows that it is not effective to leave the boards of the partners as they are, simply letting them meet from time to time as the new joint board. The clash of roles is so great that conflicts cannot be avoided. Important decisions, which could "hurt" one or other of the partners, are often not made. Whether it is necessary to engage anyone from outside at director level depends on the talents of the two former boards. But it is no use appointing a chairman from outside if the existing directors are split because:

- within the new combination the partners adhere to their former policies
- there is a power struggle between persons or groups or
- one of the partners feels superior to the other

This is why it is so important that the partners should establish more precisely than usual, before the merger, who will be the new directors, how the tasks will be divided, and what policy will be introduced. If agreement is not reached about these things beforehand, it is better not to go ahead with the merger.

New commercial policy

The founder entrepreneur had as his or her commercial objective the selling of products to known customers within a familiar market. In the growth phase this objective often changes to selling for turnover to an anonymous market. In the phase of renewal (see chapter 12) the goal must become marketing development, where account is taken not only of existing products and known or conquerable markets but also of the needs of existing or potential consumers. These could be solved by the enterprise with the help of current know-how, relations, or technology.

The moment the merger takes place can be the moment to start in principle with this form of marketing, by formulating new commercial objectives and reshaping the commercial organization. At the same time, there must be an overall analysis of the situation of the two merging partners and a general investigation of the personnel position, including an estimate of training requirements and of the need for new personnel.

Integrated processes

The next step will be the investigation of the technical processes with the two companies. In the case of a horizontal merger these will be almost identical. In a vertical merger the two will join within a larger process flow. With a lateral merger, many techniques will be the same although the companies are making different products.

Here again an overall joint opinion pertaining to the new through-put of the merged companies must be reached. A decision will also have to be made on the separation of units with their own technical objectives, or even on the departmentalization of the new organization according to products, geographical location, or market areas.

Integrated resources

The resources brought in by each partner have usually been esti-mated and assessed at the time of the merger. The financial resources are often the only ones that have been explicitly allocated. In addition, there are various properties, the buildings, and machines. What approximately will be the position and function of these in the new situation?

The human resources are a problem on their own. Any merger, as a form of accelerated growth, leads to uncertainty about being able to keep up with the new situation. What degree of uncertainty is morally justified? To give categorical assurances that no one will become redundant is a form of deception. And even if the total number of employees does not decrease, the increase in scale and the acceleration of development will still mean a significant change in all management positions. Now all unsuitable appointments made in the past, all merely nominal functions, all those who have been shunted into sidings or "kicked upstairs" into harmless positions will be revealed. For this reason a training program and a rough estimate of critical positions must be made beforehand. You may offer all the help you can, but no promises should be made which cannot later be fulfilled.

Much will depend on a realistic and yet inspiring personnel policy, supported by a united top management which sets an example in that it comprises new skills. The new commercial policy may need new technical processes and resources. How can the enterprise achieve a rapid expansion of the know-how required for uninterrupted development? A general estimate will have to be made of this too. It will be necessary to know what working groups to establish and what tasks to give them.

In this way, once the merger has taken place, workers and management will notice that the new board knows what it wants. This gives them the motivation they need if they are to put their hearts into their work. Conversely, uncertainty at the top about all these problems will lead to a resistance to change at the lower levels.

Integrating information

The increase in scale of the new combination will result in great changes in internal communication channels. Many of these will grow longer as the distance from decision centers increases, and information will begin to travel along different paths. For example, the merger may show up the need for a central data-processing service. The correct place of the information center in the organization must have been broadly agreed upon, otherwise there may be a tug-of-war later.

The geographical location of the new board must also be decided in advance. It is definitely undesirable to compromise by selecting a meeting-place for the board half way between the original centers, while the members remain in their former offices for day-to-day work. This problem is important because the psychological status of the company near the board is higher than that of the other companies further away. For the period immediately following the merger it is important for the board to be located where it can have real contact with the largest possible part of the future enterprise.

All these matters are reviewed and discussed in advance, and then, as soon as possible after the merger is announced, the management must be shown the general plan of the new organization structure, including the approximate timing of its realization.

This brings us to a model of planned development which differs somewhat from incremental development. This developmental model (see figure 9.1) shows us the following.

(1) Before the merger takes place there is a general concept of the future. This can be created by the partners at board level, possibly with the participation of a few trusted managers or with the help of an external consultant.

(2) When the merger is announced, the steering committee, which has the task of effecting the merger in practice, is introduced to personnel.

With the general concept of the future as a basis, the committee begins to set up a number of operational objectives (e.g. commercial concentration; in the technical sphere, provisional exchange and improvement of work methods; unification of administration; establishment of an information-processing center). This is followed immediately by an operational analysis of the extent of changes, staffing, critical areas, where change is likely to be easier, and so on. These two investigations lead to a still quite general plan of implementation, showing priorities and approximate timing.

It is important that already at this stage a broad network should emerge, showing sequences and interdependencies. Then comes the approximate assessment of timing, which shows the probable critical path. Particular attention should be paid to the latter. It is likely that at this point the steering committee will wish to call in an external (independent) consultant to help with the elaboration of the first network.

Thus the general plan of implementation is made visible on a chart for all concerned, and can be seen and understood in its totality. This last point is most important: people accept the necessary change in their own area more readily when it is seen as part of an overall plan rather than as a disaster befalling only themselves.

(3) A number of projects emerge from the overall plan. It is useful to set up a smaller steering committee for each project, to plan its execution in attainable steps. At the same time, the main steering committee considers the training requirements for effective functioning in the new situation, and the training departments are mobilized to tackle the task of adapting training activities to the organizational changes, either internally or with outside help.

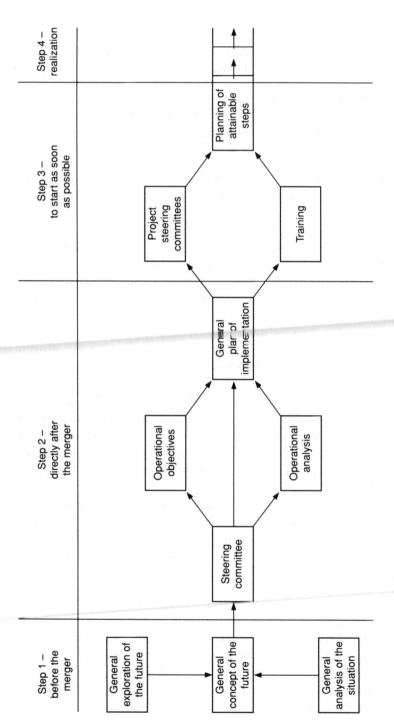

Figure 9.1 Mergers and the clover-leaf organization

The main steering committee then withdraws and retains only the function of supervising progress. For this purpose it receives sumaries of the monthly plans for the various projects, and progress reports evaluating what has actually happened. This main steering committee can, if possible, be installed at the level directly below the board.

If, at the time of the merger, a top management team is formed, representing the merger board and the directors or assistant directors of the departments in the fields of commerce, processes, resources, and central services (e.g. information-processing, personnel, training), then the board itself will be free for its proper tasks and yet will be sufficiently informed about the progress of the merger.

Organization structure

Most of the literature on mergers deals only briefly with the concretization of mergers as described above, and for this reason we have gone more deeply into this aspect. We conclude with a few remarks about the organization structure once the merger is completed.

Each of the original enterprises had, for better or worse, a complete board with a complete management task. As a result of the merger, the tasks and areas of competence unavoidably overlap, and there are too many directors for the future board. This means that a merger always leads to a form of group structure. Large companies that already have a group structure have, therefore, far fewer difficulties with a merger. They are already used to a layered structure at the top, and divisional management within the group policy. However, when medium-sized enterprises merge, the situation is rather different. Here the level below the board can hardly be called general management; the tasks are really functional.

When companies merge, the board members should understand that it is not a disgrace in the new structure to be the director of a division of the merged group, having a general management task within the group policy. Indeed, it is a new and invigorating experience to contribute as much as possible to the total result within the framework of the general policy. The members of an efficiently functioning top management team in a group that has area directors are certainly less likely to die of heart attacks than are members of an over-populated board with duplication of positions, poor delineation of tasks, and power struggles.

The merger board is therefore well-advised to organize itself as a group board. This means that at the top there is no longer room for a technical, a commercial, and a financial director, each with well-defined tasks not to be infringed by others. The members of a group board are colleagues in their responsibility for the totality of management. However, each of the directors does have a main area to which he acts as a point of entry for the rest of the board, so that they know who they must turn to in the first instance in respect of any area. Depending on the complexity of the tasks, the board must be supported by its own specialists accommodated in a large secretariat or a number of small staff departments. These staff give assistance on the more technical problems arising from the establishment of the new objectives and the new policies. Communication with the area directors takes place via a top management team which meets regularly to discuss both the information from the top and the information from the various areas.

A merger is a planned revolution. The unfortunate thing is that usually everybody imagines he or she can achieve a compromise by pouring water into someone else's wine. But the revolution is either complete or it fails. A failed merger brings about a maximum of human suffering. A successful merger can bring a new lease of life.

Apart from a complete merger, collaboration in certain areas is also possible. There can be formal collaboration in purchasing, in personnel administration, medical services, exports, imports, personnel policy, advertising, and building activities. The advantage of these forms of cooperation and association is that each enterprise retains its individuality but at the same time reaps the benefit of an increase of scale in the relevant areas. These examples apply mainly to small and medium-sized enterprises. A merger is final and means that the individuality of an enterprise is absorbed into the spirit of the larger entity. An association leaves an enterprise much freer, so that collaboration can be terminated if it is no longer advantageous.

Conclusion: Functions of the Group Board

The chief functions of the group board consist of: **initiating** (objectives), **integrating** (policies), and **evaluating**.

In carrying out its functions, the group board is supported by a number of small staff departments with highly qualified staff whose task it is to share the board's work in policy-making (but not to provide services for the companies). These staff departments cover (as necessary):

- commercial matters – sales policy, market research
- technical matters – product development policy and production allocation
- economic and financial matters and internal accountancy
- social matters – management development
- communication policy, including information-processing policy
- (possibly) legal matters, public relations, etc.

The four main tasks of the group board are:

- strengthening and developing the commercial basis of the group
- management development (development of the human resources in the group)
- financing of commercial and technical developments
- long-term development policy (internal and external)

Organization

- If possible there should be collective management (but in times of extensive reorganization it can be desirable to have a chairman).
- The top should be as small as possible in relation to the extent of the task.
- There should be no "super" specialists at the top.
- Three kinds of task can be distinguished:
  (a) A number of tasks are the joint responsibility of the whole board (see below).
  (b) Other tasks are the concern of a particular group director who acts as a point of entry to them for the group top (see below). This director also deals with the appropriate functionaries on behalf of the board as a whole.
  (c) Each director maintains special personal contact with the company or companies allotted to him. The company

problems with which he is primarily involved are commercial, personnel, and financial-economic matters pertaining to the development policy.

Joint tasks of the group board

Policy questions

These include the following:

- long-term planning of commerce, personnel, technology
- political relations, annual report, etc.
- group organization (among other things, appointment of directors, top-category salaries, etc.)
- market allocation, products, and manufacturing technology
- expansion plans and mergers
- communication policy, including information-processing

Communicative functions

There are four of these.

1 **Meetings of the group board** should be frequent (e.g., weekly); in the case of a collective body the function of chairman should rotate. Participants are the group board, the board secretary, and the directors of the staff departments. The members of the group board can meet together as often as they think necessary.

2 **Meetings of individual members of the group board** with the directors of the companies will be less frequent.

- Form I: a member of the group board discusses the general situation with "his" company.
- Form II: a member of the group board discusses his "special attention" area with a number of company directors responsible in the same area (e.g., commercial, technical, financial, social issues).

3 **Group conferences** should take place several times a year. Participants are the group board and all the directors of all the companies.

4 As required, **working groups** and **policy groups** can be formed: they can be anything from *ad hoc* committees for the solution of temporary problems to permanent committees meeting regularly and joined when necessary by board members, directors, and staff.

Separate task areas of board members

As a rule, in group boards, with or without a chairman, each member is allotted a number of special areas of attention. These areas are distributed according to the main functions of the clover-leaf organization:

- supervision of commercial functions (marketing up to and including selling)
- supervision of process flows, the throughput (product development, production grouping, technological policy)
- supervision of resources organization (finance, capital goods, personnel)
- supervision of communication and information policy

Each member of the group board has his most important supervisory task within one of these four areas. In order to prevent one-sidedness, however, he also has a number of ancillary tasks in other areas. These include the following:

- observing external developments in the area in question, with the help of the staff department
- pursuing the group's internal answers to these external developments
- asking stimulating questions to promote investigations and the submission of proposals to the board
- together with the staff department, assimilating proposals and integrating these with personal points of view, thus providing policy information for the whole group board

We now turn from the group within an organization, and from the group as joint ventures, to the group-oriented society at large. In this respect we shift from the First World to the Third, from developed country to developing one.

9

Linking Individualism to Communalism

Albert Koopman

Defining the First and Third Worlds is not an easy task. You may feel that it lies in the difference between rich and poor. You may also have an understanding that, generally, the industrialized west is the First World, while the developing countries are Third World. Both these views place the two worlds within a context in which you have old-style communism at the one end as a political system, and maybe capitalism/liberalism at the other. Looking at it simplistically, the continuum from left to right softens with socialism moving to mixed and then to free markets.

Since the industrial age, during the period 1900 to the present day, the world has advanced incredibly. With the advent of computer technology, biotechnology, advances in TV and video technology – all of which impacted on people – there has been a dissemination of information which humankind has never experienced before. People are in touch with the whole world and, indirectly, information has shrunk the world into a "global village." There is, therefore, an increased awareness amongst individuals of each other's aspirations, belief systems, and expectations. People are changing through information but the "isms" are not coping. Surely it is wrong to continue viewing the left/right debate in the old-fashioned unidimensional way? Given the global state of affairs it has become an anachronism. New-paradigm managers simply have to take new cognizance of people, their behavior, their culture, and their way of doing things because at the end of the day it is not *countries* which export a lot, it is the *people* inside those countries. At the end of the day it is people who will dictate the ultimate outcome, so unless our world matches the strategic elements on the politico-economic axis with the behavioral drives of the psycho-sociological axis, we will not do mankind any favors.

The Advent of Information

The key issue seems to be not what happens within industrial society, but what will happen in the conflict between industrial society and the new information society which is rising to challenge it. The struggles for political freedom within typical Third World countries are small compared to the super-struggle which we will have to face in the evolution of our industrial order.

In the face of incredible population increases and ever-growing technology-induced complexities, how long will it take before all the highly centralized command states collapse? Information flows within a strong central structure, as we saw in the former Soviet Union, cannot be fed back rapidly enough to satisfy the aspirations of normal people. How long can closed socialist systems survive, given the liberation of man through information, the very information which highly centralized governments surely want to withhold from people?

The apparent fear of a highly centralized government was the onslaught of their arch enemy, capitalism. They said it poisoned the people's minds, and then they responded accordingly, by developing a "new socialism," whatever that might be. They simply wanted more of the same. The real enemy, which they did not want to recognize, was information. As became apparent throughout Eastern Europe, if highly centralized command states do not recognize this as the real cause of pressure on their systems none of the scientific socialist ideals will help in the face of the super-struggle. They were blown out of the sky simply because their old "ism" could no longer cope with the psycho-sociological needs of the people at large.

Thus, with knowledge and information spreading world-wide, people themselves will be demanding more freedom to do what they want to, whether at a national level or within the confines of a business enterprise.

Take, for example, a story drawn from a "Cash and Carry" in South Africa. The top management appointed a typical "First World Child" as their local manager, a man who, with his police training and background, could be described as a right-winger. His overt need to control other people was evidenced daily, in the form of demeaning statements, violation of individual rights, and coercive practices when it came to his interaction with blacks. Now, the town of Vryburg, where the incident occurred, was well removed from the urban center. One might have assumed that the local black populace was not as well informed about the freedom struggle as their counterparts in the cities. Therefore, they might have been expected to be more compliant when it came to a violation of their dignity. Not on your life! The local underground press and structures made sure that all people everywhere remained informed. Before long management noticed the sales dipping drastically and upon asking the manager what the problem was he merely responded that it was the drought.

So insensitive to people was the manager, that he did not even realize what was happening to his business. Eventually the problem came to a head over the issue of the cleanliness of toilets. The manager's instruction, which he bellowed in his best autocratic manner, was: "If you can't keep the toilets clean you do not deserve to use them, therefore I'm locking them." "But where do we go and relieve ourselves?" asked the shop steward, to which he replied, "In the veld" (the field or open area). Well, that was it: suddenly, instead of doing a turnover of some $140,000 per week, the business slid right back to about $80,000 per week. Consultation with their employees led to top management firing this manager, and when asked how they managed to pull it off, one shop steward replied, "We told our customers (80 percent black) that if they supported this store they would be petrol-bombed and that was it." Those shopkeepers just had to be informed and reminded of what happened to their shops during the 1985 riots and they responded by withholding their business.

Although this incident took place in a racially divided country, it nevertheless illustrates that the collective information with regard to enforcing change was carried through, and used as an effective tool to make top management change their view. It was a mini-revolution against the governance of that organization.

Freedom to be Enterprising

Looking at First World and Third World in a unidimensional manner, we would associate the First World with freedom-seeking and the Third World with power-seeking as they remove the shackles of the old colonialist past. The First World country will possess typical multiparty political structures, while the Third World one will confine itself to one-party states. The First World is more open, while the Third World is more closed. Third Worlders typically talk about redistribution, the seizure of government, and the control over other people. First Worlders want to live and let live. Authoritarianism and rigid control is the hallmark of Third Worlders, and democracy and tolerance that of the First World. However, on a psycho-sociological axis, things might well look different.

During a trip to Dakar in Senegal, we could not help but watch the freedom to be enterprising at work. There were hawkers, taxi drivers, and backyard shoe manufacturers, all pursuing their self-interest and putting in efforts for desired rewards. But the economy at large was sick. Banks and factories had all been nationalized once freedom from France was achieved, and the country subsequently chose to move into poverty. Those hawkers and small entrepreneurs were First World people operating in a Third World country!

Mauritius, an island which suffered under socialist rule for too long, decided to liberalize its economy. It lowered foreign-owned company tax to 5 percent and individual tax to 15 percent. Every entrepreneur jumped on the bandwagon and established a textile factory. Their erstwhile Third World economy had previously hinged around sugar, which represented 80 percent of their income in 1970. The mills were then state-owned. When the mills were privatized in the early 1980s sugar production doubled, yet by 1989 it only represented 52 percent of GNP, the balance literally being made up of textile exports. At last the people were allowed the freedom to be enterprising. As a result Mauritius rose to third position as a world exporter of textiles. It began entering the First World.

In the First World one would observe unlimited trading hours. Cafes and shops open seven days a week trading around the clock. In the Third World there is some bureaucrat in charge of Customer Service who closes the counter window promptly at one o'clock, and proceeds to eat his lunch in front of the remaining queue of people.

In the First World you are on your own, and can trade without restriction with whom you like, based on your endeavors and competitiveness. In the Third World you seek government protection against imports.

The First World will typically display free trade and unrestricted investment. The Third World will subsidize farmers, the bread price, the meat price, and anything that is perceived to be in the public interest, just in order to secure votes.

The next debate is whether culture and the ethos come into play within the First World/Third World debate. The answer is clearly no. Compare the ethos of Japan with the ethos of Africa over the past few decades. After the Second World War Japan had immense illiteracy problems and anything that came from Japan was regarded as inferior. Although their ethos of authoritarianism was rather more marked than the African version, they did not let it become their Achilles' heel. They broke away from the shackles of their past – the Samurai and the peasants. In fact, the group-cooperative nature of Japanese people showed great similarities with the ethos of Africa. The difference is that Japan harnessed the collective nature of her peoples by designing a master shared value for the survival of Japan while maintaining the freedom to be enterprising. Consensus management became the order of the day and communication (information-sharing) was rapid in the organic structures.

Africa did the opposite. It clung to authoritarianism, coerced the collective, and destroyed the freedom to be enterprising through strong centralization. It had an obsession with fighting for a freedom from oppression, without a visionary shared value of a freedom to move toward a survival package. Its mechanistic rigidity stopped communication and information-sharing and the people became pawns of the system.

Compare Romania, a typical Third World country with, until 1989, a communist dictatorship to boot. While the culture of people there showed no direct similarity to that of either Africa or Japan, it was still caught up under the banner of coercive communism. A collective egalitarianism was imposed on the people – mismatch between the "ism" and the culture of the people.

Clearly, it is "isms" which determine the state of affairs between the First and Third Worlds, and not necessarily the cultures of people. If an "ism" and a culture are mismatched the incompatibility between the two will eventually break down that particular society. Therefore, if we are to have a greater understanding of the First World/Third World debate, we now need to juxtapose the politico-economic axis with the psycho-sociological axis. This is shown in figure 10.1.

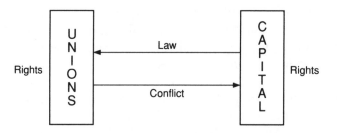

Figure 10.1

Industrialism began with the efforts of individual people. Before long, however, mergers, acquisitions, and the like served to build up faceless corporations, such as the oil, steel, and gold monopolies. Many of these huge corporations, with their dehumanized methods of work, cling on to the past with a vengeance, through a myriad of bureaucratic and mechanistic organizational designs. These have all but killed the work ethic and the spirit of enterprise within those organizations. Decision-making is centralized and top-down whilst the employees at large are not allowed to participate, let alone exercise the freedom to be enterprising.

In a South African gold mine an artisan refused to repair a particular water pump because he felt that it would endanger the lives of miners further down the mine. The case he put to his foreman (one level up in this bureaucratic organization) was that he had actually repaired this pump 17 times previously and that it was time to replace it. The foreman made the typical remark, "Repair it when I say so! You shouldn't be the one concerned about other people's lives." By this time the artisan was so disgusted that he reported the matter to the mine overseer (one level up from the foreman). Now here was an artisan who was proud of his work. Here was a man who cared for his job and business but was confronted by a foreman who cared naught for dignity and personal worth. Here was an artisan who wanted nothing more than the freedom to be enterprising. Upon putting his case to the mine overseer he eventually managed to get a new pump, but the ramifications! Suddenly the foreman started victimizing this artisan for having gone over his head to the mine overseer. So violent did the conflict become between artisan, foreman and mine overseer, that the General Manager of this 2,000-people organization came up with the following memo:

From tomorrow, no level of employee may communicate with any other level besides the level immediately above him/her and/or immediately below him/her.

Signed ....

It does not take a wise man to see what the result of this capitalist technocrat's decision would be. By writing that memo he dealt a death blow to his organization and killed the spirit of enterprise within it. His average quarterly profit of $3.2 million diminished to $0.8 million over the next three quarters, and we call such a general manager a capitalist?

What makes this type of capitalist function any better (from a human perspective) than the nationalized state functionaries of the socialist? Are they not in fact similar? Both believe in mass distribution. Both are built on large cities, and nation-states. Both consume fossil fuels. Both believe in the same system of centralization, standardization, and maximization. Both are products of industrialism and both face extinction unless radical organizational change takes place in tandem with the broader new civilization which is emerging alongside the information society. So, at the organizational level, we have to consider the components shown in figure 10.2 when matching culture/social values with strategy or form of governance.

We are sure that you will now share our confusion as to the world order of things, specifically if we had to overlay figure 10.1 and figure 10.2. For ease of reference and better understanding we can draw up a short table (table 10.1) to simplify the comparison between the group cooperative/communal ethos and that of the individualist/competitive ethos.

In looking at figures 10.1 and 10.2, a few questions and statements come to our mind.

1 If the US is supposed to be the epitome of libertarian capitalism why did she kill the spirit of enterprise by designing such centralized, mechanistic organizational structures for ostensibly an individualist competitive ethos? If US organizations were more organic, surely a participative style would emerge as a natural way of doing things, thereby increasing productive capability immensely. Instead, the bureaucratic focus resulted in an anarchic management, where the organization no longer has a coherent purpose, but where individuals compete for power through back-biting. The competition for who

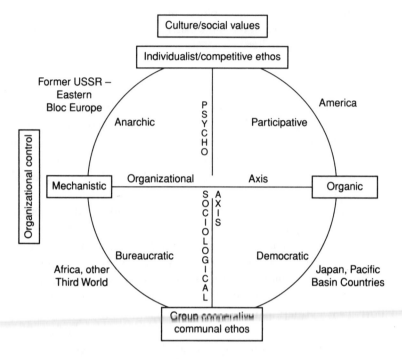

Figure 10.2 Organizational and psycho-sociological axes

produced what model car at Ford was exemplified by Lee Iacocca. In fact, there were few people at Ford who actually worked in the interest of Ford Motor Company.

2 If Marxist egalitarianism was imposed on the intrinsically individualist/competitive ethos of Russia, is that not the reason why anarchy and uprising was a constant threat to the state, which in turn has had to use coercive methods to ensure that it does not rear its head? Now that it has collapsed because of this mismatch, will the new governments be able to handle the transition?

3 Did the bureaucratic style of colonial, mechanistic organizational structure not perhaps cause the African power-seeking authoritarianism to flourish and destroy the continent? We simply should not impose mechanistic structures on to an ethos which is consensus-seeking and conflict-avoiding such as in Africa.

4 Is Japan perhaps not the only country in the world which has managed to match its organizational control with the ethos of its people, thereby becoming a "winning" nation? It discarded the

Table 10.1   A comparison of a competitive ethos with a group ethos

Individual competitive	Group communal
● Profit for me is derived from self-interest	● Profit to me is a vote of confidence my society gives me for service rendered to that society
● I am mutually exclusive from my fellow-man	● I am mutually inclusive
● I prefer to be a self-actualized person	● I prefer to be a social person
● The more I have the more I am	● I am, therefore the more I am prepared to share and give
● I demand productivity from people	● I prefer to create a climate in which people will be willingly more productive
● I am actually an aggressive kind of person	● I am actually a receptive kind of person
● I look you in the eye and challenge you	● I bow my head and show you respect
● My concern is for production	● My concern is for people

militarist, authoritarian trait of the group/mass and harnessed the strength of the collective/team through open organic structures.

5 If we now focus on the circle in figure 10.2, to the left at the mechanistic level, and to the right at the organic level, which "ism" applies in each case? Is the "ism" debate of the left not based on "the people will decide" – which is supposed to be organic and democratic, and the "ism" debated of the right-wing not "we need more control"? How and why did the converse happen? Mismatch?

6 In the context of the new and emerging information civilization, which side (mechanistic or organic) of the circle would show a greater propensity for information-sharing through whatever means? Are the Quality Circles, statistical control by workers, frequent group discussions, and small group activities of the Japanese factory not at the very heart of the information-sharing society? Has Zen perhaps transcended industrialism and the "ism" debate?

These points are by no means exhaustive, and should not serve to promote a philosophical discussion. Rather, our intention is to make you, as a new-paradigm manager, more concerned about matching strategy with culture and understanding our new, emerging civilization. We simply have to start looking at the world in a multidimensional way because the information society is forcing us that way. Moreover, it is the deluge of information which will spur civilization to change, reorganize, and restructure. If we do not respond now we might find that our valuable capitalist organization will become nothing more than the dinosaur of enterprise.

Matching Culture and Strategy

We are sure that by now you have realized that our personal viewpoint in the First World/Third World debate stands diametrically opposed to the traditional unidimensional "ism"-based viewpoint of old. Rather, we view the matter from a cross-cultural standpoint, taking into account either an individualist competitive ethos, or a strong cooperative ethos, arising out of the local society. Our viewpoint therefore hinges around the matching of culture and strategy, in the broader sense, and around its appropriateness to a particular world.

For example, the strategic control system of a particular South African bottling company was highly centralized and mechanistic. Reporting layers were rigid with people waiting for "dead man's shoes" in order to advance. When a vacancy arose for a foreman on a particular line – bottling some 54,945 gallons per month – management thought it prudent, and in keeping with the so-called "Black Advancement" policy, to seek the most competent black worker from amongst the ranks to fill the vacancy. The man was given the appointment. Some three weeks later, however, the bottling line did not manage to cork more than 10,989 gallons. At that point the General Manager wondered what to do. In his view his workers were lazy. Instinctively, his consultant knew that it was not laziness but mismatching that was causing the problem. He promptly went to consult on-site and found that the workers were highly upset that they were not asked whether or not they wanted to work for this new black foreman, and were proclaiming the injustice done by going slow. Once we had a letter from management in place, giving a democratic right to choose whether they wished to continue working for this foreman, production reverted to 54,945 gallons. What, then, were the elements at play?

The management said (individualist competitive ethos), "We have a right to appoint whomever we wish and whomsoever we see fit for the job. Why should we seek an opinion from the workers? Sure, we have rigid boxes, and it's been like that for 80-odd years, why change now? Yes, we are driven top-down, but it's always worked for us in the past, why not now?" Control, control, control.

The workers said (group cooperative ethos), "You must not divide us with your boxes. We are communal people and we would like to have a say as to whether we want to work with the foreman. Debate the issue with us. We need to know why you're doing it." Information, information, information.

Guess who won? The majority. You see, the design (mechanistic) of the organization was out of step with the democratic need to be involved, of people driven by the group cooperative ethos (organic). This resulted in a mismatch which in turn destroyed the wealth-creating capacity of the company. This anecdote serves further to illustrate a compatibility between the way many Africans would like to see things being done and the way in which the Japanese are doing it already.

Here is another example of such a mismatch in thought and behavior. A particular mine had implemented an extremely mechanistic grievance and disciplinary procedure within the context of its recognition agreement between management and labor. By virtue of this countervailing document there existed a tremendous rift between capital and labor, between "us" and "them."

On a particular day an artisan, with the assistance of two other workers, was busy lowering an impeller, six yards in diameter, into its casing. The two workers were controlling the chain pulleys from platforms five yards high. The artisan was gently guiding the impeller with shouts of "Yebo, Yebo" (Yes, Yes), indicating that they should continue lowering the impeller slowly. However, to the ears of the workers on the scaffold, one set of Yebos sounded like the final Yebo and they let go while the impeller was still some six inches from its position. The impeller dropped and you can imagine what the weight of the impeller did to the casing – it cracked it in half. Promptly the frustrated artisan arose and shouted off the top of his head "I could kill you," which to him was a way in which to vent his anger. The two workers did not see it that way. They took the literal term to heart, and saw it as a threat to their lives. Immediately they reported the incident to their union, who insisted on an inquiry as to whether this man actually intended killing them. The rest of the workers downed tools and the mine lost $1,000,000 in production, while the lawyers from the union, and the lawyers of management, argued their case over a period of five days. Was this really necessary? If the pursuit of the capitalist is to create wealth, why does he continuously insist on dealing with intrinsically human issues through such mechanistic, rigid ways which in effect destroy his wealth-creating capacity? What would have happened if there were forums for debate in this case, or a method of casting a vote of no confidence against the accused by the aggrieved? What would have happened if humans were in fact allowed to solve human problems, not in an adversarial situation but in one of mutuality and openness?

Consider also some of these possibilities.

- What would the result be in Japan if you replaced all the top Japanese management, who are intrinsically organic and holistic in outlook, with American individualists?
- Old-paradigm American managers love rigid hierarchies and somehow they appear to be less effective operating within the Japanese society than the other way around. Why?
- Why were the Utopian nationalized companies of the eastern bloc so inefficient and nonproductive within their imposed egalitarian states? Was it not because the inherent individualist competitive ethos of their societies was violated by this imposition – which killed the will to work?

Conclusion

In conclusion, we maintain that political systems, governmental structures, and forms of management, as we know them today, were constructed long ago in societies which were far simpler than our current complex information-based world. As new-paradigm managers, therefore, the challenges facing us are exciting ones, for we are going to be charged with helping to design organizations to cope with changing expectations in the future. We will have to be preemptive in all our dealings within the communities we serve, and carefully balance values with governance.

With reference to culture, we are being forced to take account of the aspirations, expectations, and relationships amongst people within a particular society rooted in its own value systems, rather than simply superimpose our value system on to theirs. We are also being forced to recognize the difference between free enterprise, as an ideology, and the freedom to be enterprising, as a spiritual human value manifested in the nature of work within communities.

We will have to review our basis of reward systems within our enterprise and ask whether it is compatible with the expectations of local communities. In other words, should it be individual reward for individual effort, or group reward for group effort? We will have to reevaluate the use of power and authority within the organization, and its acceptability by the local ethos, and maybe change the way that we do things inside our organizations.

The challenge facing us as business leaders is to search energetically for compatible alternatives between all the above components. The degree to which we manage to evolve new organisms will determine the degree to which we will create conditions for their effectiveness and development. In the next chapter, in fact, we focus on one such "new organism" – an industrial democracy born and bred in communal Southern Africa.

10

Building Industrial Democracy
Albert Koopman

The ultimate expression of social synergy, within an enterprise as a whole, might arguably be an industrial democracy. A definition of **industrial democracy**, taken from the 1971 Congress of the Swedish Trade Union Conferences reads:

> Industrial Democracy is part of the effort made by the labor movement to extend democracy throughout society. Life away from the workplace has developed in one way and life at the workplace has developed in another. The difference constantly grows and is at the root of the increasing need which employees feel to exert an influence on conditions of work and on management. If arbitrary situations are allowed to persist in one sector of society, they are an obstacle to the progress of democracy in other sectors. Industrial Democracy should be regarded as part of the general process of democratization.

We, as new-paradigm managers, will have to evolve ways of building up interdependence between capital and labor, in order to play our vital role in the design and implementation of economic strategies for our companies as a whole.

As we have already said, business cannot exist in a socio-politico-economic vacuum, and it is unrealistic to say that we have no role to play in an ever changing world. We are intrinsic to that process of change and not an adjunct to it. As such, we should adopt a far more preemptive role in the democratization process, by addressing the redistribution of power within our businesses. That having been said, we have to acknowledge that industrial democracy is a political issue from which no business can escape. For it is aimed at shaping and changing the society in which we live and, as such, plays a pivotal role in the process of worker participation/democracy, so vital throughout the world.

Having addressed these main issues, it is important to determine how we can best achieve this democratization process within our companies. In other words, what can we do to establish greater interdependence between labor and capital within and between our companies and the greater community at large? We shall answer this question under three main headings: commonality of purpose, tools for democratization, and structures to be considered.

Commonality of Purpose

It is true to say that for a long time now, with the gap widening between labor and capital, we have been talking past, rather than listening to, one another. So the time has come to brush aside the misconceptions and rhetoric and start debating and discussing our common purposes. To this end, a place of work can be likened to a fountain of water from which both parties drink. If one party puts in poison or drinks too much, the other party may die or do without. It is a prerequisite to both parties' survival that the water fountain continues to produce clean and pure water, and therefore that we start focusing on our commonality of interests, albeit from different perspectives. These common interests are highlighted in the following sections.

Scrapping discrimination at the work-place

Surely it stands to reason that if in a freer Second or Third World human rights and dignity of the individual are restored, we have to reject any system which discriminates on that basis. No democracy can exist in a system which is coercive or dictatorial, and we have to renounce the exploitation of advantages as provided for under antiquated laws. This applies to all other forms of discrimination, sexual or racial, structural or political. All people within an enterprise should be treated equally, and promotions based on competence, merit, and capability. Any employee who feels uncomfortable with such an approach will either have to change or look for another employer. Favoritism will not find a home under such a system and no protection of the color of a person's skin can be allowed to exist.

Human rights, dignity, and self-worth

The time has come for both capital and labor to reassess their ethical and moral objectives, and consider an industrial democracy which acknowledges the rights of all people to be respected for their own worth, and which is not based on some authoritarian premise. This should form the cornerstone of any industrial democracy. It is opportune, at this time, to reevaluate the concepts of human dignity and the needs of all population groups, whether in South Africa or across the globe. The clause on human rights within the context of the Freedom Charter in South Africa, for example, exemplifies these aspects:

- The law shall guarantee to all their right to speak, to organize, to meet together, to publish, to preach, to worship, and to educate their children.
- The privacy of the house from police and riots shall be protected by law.
- All shall be free to travel without restriction from countryside to town, from province to province, and from South Africa to abroad.
- Pass laws, permits, and all other laws restricting these freedoms shall be abolished.
- Only a democratic state, based on the will of the people, can secure to all their birthright without distinction of color, sex, or belief.

All over the world we have tended to overlook these important human elements within the context of business and economic development. Now we need to acknowledge the fact that it is humans who run a business as an economic unit and not only the management. Unless all people are focused in the same direction, both capital and labor, a business has very little chance of succeeding in any turbulent environment.

Training and information-sharing

Knowledge and understanding builds trust, ignorance creates distrust, and therefore the company must ensure that information is disclosed as far down the line as possible. It is every employee's democratic right to know what is happening to that "fountain which produces the water." Both labor and capital must accept obligations of disclosure of information from one another in order to build interdependence and achieve mutual objectives.

Distribution of wealth and security of work

A business can only offer work and security in so far as it fulfills its prime function of remaining in business through the creation of wealth. However, such creation of wealth will not be achievable unless the work force is free from the fear of destitution. This fear can only be removed once a form of democratic structure is in place which will ensure that the work force has the necessary power and democratic rights to influence the decision-making processes which affect their lives. Many experiences have illustrated the fact that once workers are given real access to power and decision-making, they respond with high levels of maturity, responsibility, and ethical conduct. It is only when people are assumed to be irresponsible and unethical that they behave in that way and put limitations on their true creative potential.

This having been said, one of the major challenges facing us is to close the gap between capital and labor, through broader-based negotiations and consultation on how to optimize both the generation and just distribution of wealth, not only the creation of profit. This can only be done by accepting each other as interdependent peers rather than as perpetual adversaries.

Any participation through industrial democracy will at some stage have to address the question of the distribution of wealth, in the context of a collective bargaining process. With pressures on business – climbing out of recession and descending back into recession – it will not be an easily resolvable matter, particularly in poorly performing economies. Neither can we found our vision on outmoded capitalist/socialist notions from the old order of industrialization.

While we as management are still advocating a strict capitalist approach, and labor rhetoric in some parts of the world promotes a socialist one, representatives from both sides will have to at least investigate alternatives, such as creating learning organizations.

The balance of power

Labor has an inalienable right to strike and the right to withhold labor, but likewise, capital has an inalienable right and obligation to generate wealth in any system. A power balance between these two forces has to be established. We can illustrate a power imbalance as follows. Management has gained and earned positional power in the organization through the acquisition of skills and knowledge and therefore has due authority to command the enterprise on behalf of its constituency, the stockholders and directors (capital). Workers have gained and earned personal power which they acquired through their interaction and interpersonal relationships with their fellow-men. Elected shop stewards and the unions therefore have due power to command the enterprise on behalf of its constituency, the workers (labor).

Authority therefore lies in the hands of management with no real personal power, and personal power lies in the hands of labor with no real authority. This imbalance can play havoc with the wealth-creating capacity of the firm. Inasmuch as labor and capital serve opposite interests and do not serve the common interest, the survival of the business entity as a whole, from which both participants can benefit economically, is threatened. The business entity will therefore never be able to optimize its wealth-creating ability, and will always perform at less than its productive capacity.

The devolution of decision-making power to the lowest level of authority, and the building up of management's personal power base through active involvement with labor at an interpersonal and consultative level, is of paramount importance. Therefore it stands to reason that the interdependent way forward is the new-paradigm one, and that management per se has to be redefined. It should no longer be a position within the organization, but a function between capital and labor.

This democratic coordinating process, and its implied total involvement in the wealth-creating process, offers a value far greater than the price which we would have to pay by abstaining and resisting cooperation and involvement. An entrepreneur or capitalist finds the idea of socialism irksome and the chances are that socialism could kill off the endeavors of these individuals, leaving one pillar of the wealth-creating process in a weakened state. If that pillar weakens, the equitable distribution of wealth could become a myth as there simply will not be wealth to distribute. Likewise, socialists find the idea of capitalism exploitative and threatening because of its class distinction. If the worker pillar of the wealth-creating process serves to undermine the enterprise, there would be no wealth to distribute either in wages or in dividends.

So, instead, democratic structures have to be forged between labor and capital, to ensure that a new pragmatism evolves, enhancing both the wealth generation capacity of the firm and social justice. Only in this manner can greater and more productive wealth be created for the benefit of both, with management now as a function (not a position) between labor and capital. Interdependence will ensure a reduction of the fear of destitution on the part of the worker and minimize the fear of bankruptcy on the part of the entrepreneur. Allow the capitalist his free-enterprise objectives, but simultaneously allow the workers the freedom to be enterprising, along with human dignity and justice. Allow the socialist his demand for equal distriution of wealth, but simultaneously allow the capitalist a fair return on his investment.

This interdependence can only be achieved if we can come to some agreement on a common economic and social purpose. No better time exists than now in the wake of the next millenium to discuss the aspirations of workers and management in the pursuit of the evolution of democratic processes at the work-place.

Tools for Democratization

Conditions in many parts of the world are ripe for some form of industrial democracy. If we, as managers, miss this opportunity, then polarization between management and workers can and will cause us ever greater harm. I believe that if we are not prepared to openly challenge the present political system, then the least we can do is to vigorously pursue active participation in the promotion of a pragmatic industrial democracy by using some of the tools for democratization listed below.

Consultation and information-sharing

The process of forging understanding of what our businesses are all about is of paramount importance. Not only do we have a need to communicate with our employees, we have an obligation to do so, and our unions should recognize this. No better way exists to build trust and respect than through consultation and communication. If we make no attempt to promote the concepts of industrial democracy, we have not even tried to change the climate of distrust with its accompanying apathy. Respect can only be earned if, in our deliberations, we allow the other man to save face by asking him or her for an opinion rather than simply giving him an order to execute.

Harnessing the collective talent in our companies will only be achievable if we have frequent problem-solving meetings and workshops, focusing on specific issues of the day, for example, improvement of sales, customer service, or increases in profitability. No longer can these aspects be the sole domain of management and we have to concede that the work force has changed from that of five or ten years ago. The collective cry for dignity and respect is far greater than our ability, as managers, to force authoritarianism on to them. Not only has the autocratic style become ineffective, but it actually increases polarization, and with a polarized work force excellence will not be achievable in our work-places.

Co-determination committees

Already an encouraging sign in South African companies, for example, is the formation, at grass roots level – in parallel with works councils in Europe – of democratically elected committees. As long as these committees/councils do not become management-inspired and controlled, they can serve as excellent vehicles for the building and transfer of skills. If we seriously wish to develop the creative abilities of a broader spectrum of employees, we will see these developments as the beginnings of the bridge-building between capital and labor.

Moreover, we need to allow co-determination to be fostered outside the purely substantive areas of negotiation and dispute resolution. It must also be focused on the business problems with which we have to contend on a day-to-day basis, and on the manner in which we can attend to these problems in order to enhance our wealth-creating capacity.

The union and collective bargaining

By implication collective bargaining affects the balance of power between capital and labor, and the relative independence of each. This way of doing things serves substantive negotiations well, but is not very effective when it comes to chartering the future of the enterprise. To forge interdependence, companies should have regular meetings with the union on matters of information, consultation, and problem-solving. The reason for this is that, historically, no statutory requirement appears in most countries with regard to either capital or labor bargaining in good faith. As the law does not declare bargaining in bad faith an unfair labor practice, companies have to set mechanisms in place which build up good faith through understanding and interdependence. This could go a long way to start building up an effective industrial democracy.

Joint decision-making bodies

Although the majority of companies do not have any of these in place, it is envisaged that bodies of co-determination, with parity of representation, could become a thing of the future. To the extent that new-paradigm management becomes a function of the interdependent relationship between capital and labor, a broader base for industrial democracy will be established. This future controlling body could only exist once the maturity of both our labor force and current management had been raised to a level at which labor leadership is sophisticated and strong and where our current management has acquired leadership abilities rather than managerial expertise. It is imperative that if any semblance of success is to be realized within a new First, Second or Third World framework of industrial democracy, our pursuit will have to be one of trust-building. Mass education of our work force via our in-house video news desks will be needed and education will play a vital role.

Service cooperation

Under this system of participation, companies could look toward the economic empowerment of particular segments of their business such as maintenance cooperatives in which such groups would be paid a contracted lump sum for distribution to their members. In turn, these members will democratically elect their manager and decision-making body, and as a total group render a specific service to the business.

Structures to be Considered (a Background)

As much as change has to be acceptable to Second and Third World managers, participative management needs to be acceptable to the unions as and when they exert influence. This is not always the case, because of the fear of the loss of their credibility and power base. In order to understand this phenomenon we need to explore certain political and constitutional realities.

The current debate in countries such as South Africa (until recently) and the former Soviet Union has become bogged down in discussing the kinds of institutions which will bring about change rather than identifying the type of shared values on which a future society should be based. Logically, we can accept that common vision and value systems play a greater role in determining the institutions of government than the other way round.

If participative bodies are set up merely to share problems, then such bodies will be stillborn. They will always be viewed with suspicion and as a management ploy to exploit labor. A way has to be found in which to take account of the principle of the consent of the managed through genuine democratic institutions and structures within the organization.

Both socialists (old-paradigm unions) and conservatives (old-paradigm management) have always endeavored to devise codes to serve and protect their own interests and solve all problems by means of regulations. Driven by egalitarianism – the doctrine of the equality of mankind – the socialist tendency is to deprive individuals of those chances which alone can offer them the opportunity of choice over the direction of their efforts, that is, their human growth and opportunities. The egalitarian approach similarly deprives individuals of the one inducement which free persons can have to observe moral codes; namely, the relative esteem in which they are held by their fellow humans to the extent that they uphold moral standards. The pride and dignity of an individual, in relation to his performance in society, is therefore not seen as having social value, which in turn minimizes his or her own self-esteem as an individual. Coercion must therefore be used, in the name of law and order (systems and regulations), in order to make individuals conform to these egalitarian norms. Freedom of the individual is thus a lesser debate in such a society than is the freedom from a common enemy (poverty, apartheid, capitalism, socialism, or whatever).

On the other hand, the conservatives mistrust spontaneous forces amongst people and the human interaction required to forge freedom between them (let alone the consent of the managed). Neither therefore objects to coercion or arbitrary power, as long as that power is used (or abused) for what they regard as the right purpose. That is their vested interest.

Both of them show little concern for how the powers of a government should be limited, but focus their energies on who wields the power. Both regard power as their entitlement to force the values they hold on to other people. Neither of them actually believes in real democracy.

This poses a major problem for the humanist who can visualize the immense wealth-creation potential which could be liberated, if only the human elements within the organization were allowed the freedom to be enterprising. As old-paradigm managers react through fear they cling to the law for their protection when faced with obstacles. They even ask the government for more labor laws to protect their interest. The unions respond to this by asking for the limitation of these excessive powers, because previously they might have had the power in their hands. In the middle, you as the creator of wealth sit with two sides fighting it out through strikes, deadlock stoppages, and covert sabotage because both have forgotten the human issues of their differences, and both are now trying to resolve conflict through systems and regulations of law. The losers are all the people that work for you and your own productive wealth-creating process.

This all transpires because you never uncovered the common values held by all your people in order to establish a new and cohesive vision for a new post-Brezhnev, post-Honecker, or post-Pinochet society. All this arises because there is no common philosophy in place against which both parties can be judged.

The challenge which faces you then is to create an environment within your organization which is human and free. Through much consultation and deliberation certain freedoms have to emerge within your organization:

- the freedom to choose whether to grow and prosper, as an individual, as an organization, or as a business
- the freedom to influence the form of governance of the organization by democratic means
- the freedom to be enterprising, never fearing that initiative and creativity will separate you from the herd
- the freedom to associate and dissociate
- the freedom to be human, not treated as a pair of hands forever bound to slavery and coercion
- the freedom to cast a vote of confidence in a set of values which you helped devise, democratically by popular vote

Unions, through structures, cannot give these freedoms. Management, through structures, cannot expect loyalty from their people without these freedoms, because, in turn, their structures limit such freedoms.

The current protection of labor's rights and capital's rights through labor law still places the emphasis on the differences of each, regulating the interaction through structures. There is no underpinning, no common-ground value system. Could you imagine what would happen if you merely brought a man and a woman together, designed the most unbelievable ante-nuptial contract for the regulation of their behavior and protection of their rights, and then told them to move into the same house? You would be naive to think that they would live happily ever after, because at the first violation of a right they would resort to the legal document. Surely a potential married couple first court each other and share their views on life, and their feelings toward each other. Surely they first trade values,

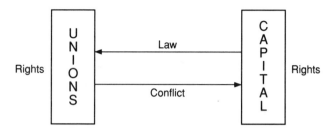

Figure 11.1 Rights protected by law

and establish common ground for the basis of their marriage, and only then do they resort to a legal document in case things go wrong, not a document to make things go wrong in an adversarial manner.

A Possible Future

Currently we have laws protecting rights and structures controlling relationships as shown in figure 11.1. If people continuously see their rights as defensible or indefensible, then who is to trust the judge in court, when the dice are politically loaded, and the integral relationship is conflict-oriented?

Labor and capital find commonality of purpose where there are rules set by labor law, but only where things go wrong, involving a system of governance in which a vote of no confidence can be cast by any person against any other person in the organization for a violation of the common purpose. It does not minimize the right to strike, nor does it minimize the right to make a profit. It is simply an open system in which a multitude of democratic mechanisms are put into place by mutual consent to give direction to the business unit which serves the economic interest of both parties. This is shown in figure 11.2.

You may minimize conflict but inevitably the management old-paradigm prerogative (whatever that is) would always rule the day simply because of the boss–worker autocratic relationship. The people will not have real influence, because no underpinning value system is in place against which mutual violation could be questioned, both from union's and management's side.

Surely a future labor dispensation could look as shown in figure

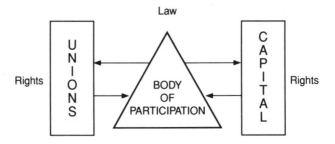

Figure 11.2   Rights protected by a Body of Participation

11.3. The law should be designed not to regulate the relationship between capital and labor but the relationship between all people in the organism and the organism itself – its philosophy, its rules and regulations as designed by all the people working in that economic entity.

We must start to move away from the debate of capitalism versus socialism in a linear manner, and rather add the very real dilemma of one world of managers facing another world of workers, attempting to find a pragmatic approach resulting in greater wealth-generation and more just distribution. We have to combine the strategic elements of the business with the culture of our people at the work-place. The rationalism of One World has to be integrated with the

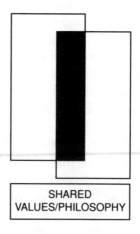

Figure 11.3   Dispensation by shared values/philosophy

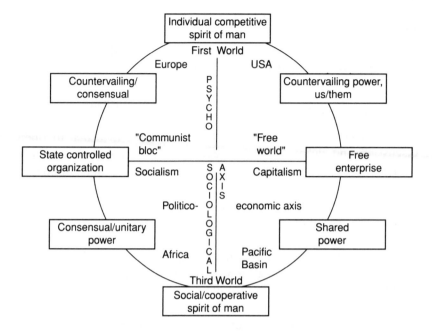

Figure 11.4 Combination of strategy and culture

spirit of another (see figure 11.4). We can now review how this was achieved in a building supplier retailer, in South Africa.

Philosophy of interdependence

The first stage in evolving a democratic structure in South Africa's "Cashbuild" – a currently highly profitable building materials retailer based throughout South Africa and employing some 1,000 people – was the formulation of the *Philosophy*. In essence, it was a controversial document, to say the least, as it did away with everything called social injustice, discrimination, privilege, prerogative, and class. All employees had to accept the common citizenry of Cashbuild and the rules of the game against which their interrelationship as members was judged.

In principle there was no objection to it save for the methodology of its implementation and the question of who would be the judge of right or wrong behavior. This emerged out of consultation with some 600 people in the organization as to about what they saw was right and wrong concerning the governance of the firm's employees. Management feared the tyranny of the majority if right or wrong were to be determined by vote. Shop stewards feared the same thing, as well as saying that if the people decided against each other they had to suffer the consequences of living next door to one another in the same township. At that time typical communalism would not work and trust first had to be built. To counter these fears, a vote of no confidence was raised and adhered to, both in order to open discussion and debate amongst aggrieved citizens and also to help people break down old stereotypes and build a new understanding.

Structured information-sharing and communication

The second stage was to develop a Shop Steward Committee of four (VENTURE-COMM – a new way of communicating) at each Cashbuild premises, who in turn elected a coordinator from amongst themselves. The coordinators met with management to review company performance and to discuss matters of common concern. Over a period of time this interim stage served to build mutual trust, maturity, and understanding. Not at any stage did we envisage undermining the rights of the union, nor could the union undermine Cashbuild's proprietary rights. It did, however, serve to build a platform for management as a joint function of capital and labor.

Possible structures for the future

The structures proposed in figure 11.5 are experimental ones, in no way to be taken as conclusive and final. Their eventual outcome will be determined only by the maturity level of both managements and unions, and by the degree of trust which will have to be built up over the years. Ultimately, moreover, innumerable consultations will have to take place prior to the negotiation of the final outcome.

The legislative body

This will be the highest forum within a company, established by both capital and labor.

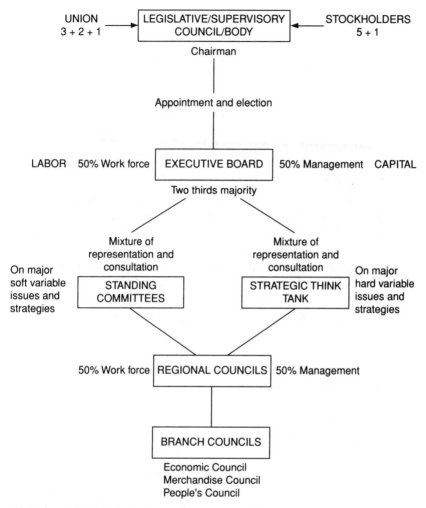

Workings of Councils:
- Majoritarianism on soft variables
- Suspensive vote on undecided issues for referral upwards
- Vote of no confidence against transgressors of the shared values

Figure 11.5   A proposed framework for democratic management

Representation

1 Stockholders elect five members to represent them from their ranks (directors, general managers, other salaried employees at a high level).
2 Employees elect three delegates from blue-collar workers, one from non-unionized workers and one delegate from white-collar workers, or whatever form is a proportionate representative of all workers.
3 Stockholders then elect one outsider, for example a legal adviser, to bring their complement to six and, similarly, through ballots at plants, employees select one outside union representative to bring their complement up to six members.
4 From among the 12 people present, a chairman is elected through a two-thirds majority, and similarly a deputy chairman. The chairman has the casting vote, which obviously means that at a point of equality of votes, if he comes from capital, he would favor capital, and if he comes from labor he would favor labor.

In the event of a dispute an avenue has to be found for arbitration without involving state structures, whether in a South African, Chilean, Polish, or Russian context.

The function of the legislative body

At this level the outside union member has to bring solidarity with the union to bear. He or she can discuss all unpopular issues, as they arise at the macro-level, so that this governing body can come to grips with the issues at hand.

1 The body will discuss everything pertaining to the business, and set clear objectives with regard to financial, marketing, personnel, and labor aspects – a total review of the affairs of the company. In short, it will guarantee the expansion and survival of the company as an economic unit and meet once every year for two to three days.
2 The body will set policy with regard to the functional areas mentioned above, as well as addressing social-adherence issues

such as job creation, retrenchment, equitable distribution of wealth, etc.

3 The body jointly appoints the executive body as one-third unionized members, one-third nonunion (including higher executives), one-third management (directors, etc.). All members appointed to the executive body must be elected by a two-thirds majority.

You can now observe that members of the executive body, in turn, will have to be leaders rather than functional managers, and that an immense amount of training will have to take place in order to develop an awareness of the differences between the positional power of the managers and the personal power required by a leader.

The executive body

The role of this body will be to see to the implementation of policy following set guidelines from the legislative body. It becomes the highest level of management.

Representation

1 **Capital**: one-third directors and one-third white-collar workers, representing buying, operations, personnel, finance/administration, production, marketing, etc.
2 **Labor**: one-third representing working conditions, staff matters, philosophy, quality of work life, and safety matters.

The function of the executive body

Jointly they discuss action plans and evolve ways and means of improving business performance and productivity. They seek procedural methods for the adherence to the new philosophy and its improvements. They analyze monthly results and information and ensure adherence to budget and economic performance. All hard variables will need only 50 percent of votes to resolve a problem and pass a motion. All soft variables need a two-thirds majority for a motion to be passed.

This means that capital, in the interim, retains functional power and can only be out-voted in so far as the conduct of business (albeit a hard variable) affects employees' lives or working conditions.

The executive body also becomes the core body with regard to negotiations. They can decide whom to call in, prepare agendas, and set parameters for negotiations on aspects such as:

- health and safety
- shops and offices legislation
- working conditions
- manpower planning and succession planning
- training required
- hiring and firing procedures/disciplinary procedures
- transfers
- organizational and work design
- wages, pensions, housing, etc.

If a dispute arises here, it is envisaged that such disputes could go up to the legislative body for arbitration, should the occasion require.

Regional councils

Representation

Managers of the region include one elected union member from each store or plant; one elected nonunion member from each store or plant; the regional manager or area manager as facilitator.

The function of regional councils

They resolve suspensive votes coming from branch council. They share and discuss hard variables but the regional council has no influence over conduct of business. Only on soft variables can they exercise a democratic vote – again with a two-thirds majority. If dissatisfaction occurs with regard to unresolved hard-variable issues, a suspensive vote by any individual can be passed up to the executive body for resolution. Regional councils also review performance within the region and discuss joint strategies for accomplishing company targets.

Branch/small business-unit councils

The branch council consists of three sub-councils each elected by the employees.

Representation

1 **Economic sub-council**: a manager and four elected people deal with matters affecting small business-unit performance such as shrinkages/losses; bad debts; statistical administration follow-up and control; and production targets and throughput.
2 **Marketing/merchandizing sub-council**: a manager and four elected people deal with marketing/sales review; lines/range actioning; stock levels; stock availability; sales service and training; and customer monitoring.
3 **People council**: a manager and four elected people deal with appraisals; employee matters; absenteeism; sick leave; days off, etc.; housing; and safety.

These councils serve to alleviate skill shortages within Cashbuild's small business units, and implement the transfer of skills through active involvement and discussion, thus bridging cross-cultural mis-understanding, misinterpretation, and lack of coordinated effort.

The manager's role in each of the councils will be to guide, coach, facilitate, and problem-solve. The councils will set their targets and the manager's role will be to follow up to ensure implementation/correction. They will statistically control all aspects of the business and from these analyses set guidelines for actions, objectives, and common-goal achievement to be communicated to all staff.

The function of branch/small business-unit council

They hold regular meetings to review tasks to be achieved and delegated; set objectives for month/week, etc.; monitor progress through involvement; statistically control all branch affairs; and on matters affecting people's lives, they exercise democratic voting.

When democratic voting takes place (on matters to do with people) any person can cast a suspensive vote if he or she so decides and this suspensive vote is to be passed upward to the regional council for resolution. The guiding rules of the game will be the document to base decisions on when casting a suspensive vote. Furthermore, a vote of no confidence can be cast against anyone who transgresses the philosophy, code of conduct, or negotiated rules of the game (call them what you want).

Disciplinary structures

The suspensive vote

On hard variables all information, problem-solving and discussion occurs in the economic sub-council. The manager is encouraged to listen to problems as put forward and to analyze the debate.

Let us assume that his problem was expense cutting, with regard to the excessive size of the luncheons served. This is a hard variable (????) affecting people's welfare (soft variable). At this point the council cannot influence the conduct of business and if the manager reduces the costs by giving French fries instead of steaks his decision is final. However, the employees might not be happy! The problem is then referred to the soft-variable council, the people's council, where a debate is opened. The manager now has to convince the council of the absolute necessity of cutting cost, hear all the arguments against this measure, and then put it up for a secret-ballot vote. A 60 percent majority sways the decision. If from the other side, hard facts are given as to why the cost-cutting measure would not serve the best interests of the company and its people, and they manage to persuade the manager, a majority decision would be reached and accepted.

The manager, however, feels strongly about his decision and he now would have the right to cast a suspensive vote. Likewise, at any of the People's Council debates, any other member has the right (against the 60 percent majority) to cast a suspensive vote to put an issue on hold for resolution by the regional council. The suspensive vote is therefore a mechanism to cope with the initial feeling of having a grievance against a particular decision. It can only be used in the people's council.

Similar debating procedures then occur at the regional council level. The case is heard and here a two-thirds majority will be the final decision.

The vote of no confidence

Should any employee's behavior be in conflict with the code of conduct or philosophy, any other employee has the right to cast a vote of no confidence against the offending employee. This will foster a climate for open debate, dealing with potential conflict long before there is a need to start completing grievance forms and time-consuming disciplinary hearings. It is less confrontational, less rigid, and fosters a spirit of trust and mutuality through an open system.

Normally if such a vote is cast against a manager it would be because of the way he is governing the people, and if cast against another individual it would be because that individual has broken one of the citizenry's rules.

Fears to overcome

Fear of erosion of power bases

True democracy enhances the strength of one's constituency and hence one's power base. If, however, as manager or shop steward, you do not believe that people are willing followers and stand behind you, you will always fear your legitimate right to lead. Hence, participative management becomes a threat.

Fear of the erosion of collective bargain process

Participation influences the collective bargaining process through information being shared and not withheld. Greater insight into the affairs of the company builds greater maturity and affords greater knowledge-power for a more democratic collectivity. This in turn serves to build up a better process for collective bargaining.

Fear of losing management prerogative

If management is authoritarian no legitimate basis, from a leadership point of view, exists for achieving objectives through people. Only once authority is earned, with people willingly following, will the need for managerial prerogative be negated.

Fear by the union of being integrated into the capitalist system

How else do we train and advance people except through involvement and active learning, by "swimming inside the swimming pool?" How else are we going to create wealth unless all people do their bit through unshackling the mechanisms which impede human growth? Anything beyond this human understanding is rhetoric.

Conclusion

As much as this entire structure is alleged to be totally democratic, when it comes to discipline within the context of a typical Third World socio-political climate, definite dividing lines have still to be retained between power as a prerogative and power as an earned right. Hopefully, these strong dividing lines will not be necessary once maturity and knowledge has been built up but, be that as it may, the system can survive given the constraint.

A new-paradigm manager needs to look at this industrial democratic model as a matter of necessity. If we sincerely want to be masters of our destiny then we must design that destiny through creative negotiation and not fall by the wayside, or possibly be sucked into the maelstrom. We simply have to grasp the opportunities as they present themselves, and in our case the opportunity is now!

At the same time, it is important to recognize that a fully fledged industrial democracy will only be approximate in some companies, in some places, at some times. What is essential is that our institutions are continually developing. The institutional base of the new-paradigm manager, then, is the learning organization.

PART IV

As an Organization – From Change to Learning

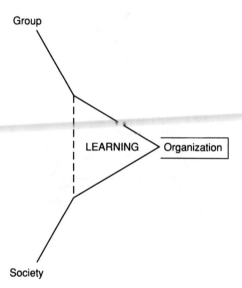

Group

LEARNING Organization

Society

From change to learning

The Developing Organization
Bernard Lievegoed

Change, Growth, and Development

The learning organization is a manifestation of continuing development. In the following chapters the concept of development plays a large part, particularly the development of forms of organization, along with management systems and styles of managing. It is therefore necessary to define this concept more clearly. To do so we have to distinguish between three concepts: change, growth, and development.

Change

The concept that we are living in a changing world not only appears regularly in this book but is expressed almost daily in newspapers and journals. As a generalization, however, it is fairly meaningless. It is given content only if we define and describe where and what changes are taking place. Then it becomes evident that the concept of change can have almost any content and that the same phenomenon is described differently by different people. The term "change" simply tells us that nothing is static and that everything is moving in the stream of time. Thus it becomes necessary to investigate whether change takes place haphazardly and by chance, or whether there are fields where one can find a system in the change.

If the latter is true, this could be a manifestation of natural laws. For instance, in physics we know the law of entropy: unequally distributed energy tends toward equal distribution and levelling out. This tendency toward the levelling out of differences appears also outside physics in "higher" biological and social systems. In biology we study a force of differentiation and a force of equalization. The former typifies life, and the latter typifies dying. David Riesman, the American sociologist, has described these two tendencies in the social field: "inner-directed" people create tensions through their personal behavior, and "other-directed" people seek an increased social entropy through conformism.

These indications will suffice at this point. The behaviorists have produced a wealth of literature based on the many aspects of emphasis on the individual or conformity to the community (e.g., "fight and flight").

Growth

We shall reserve the term **growth** to describe the kind of change that brings about a quantitative increase in size or weight within one and the same system. Thus growth depicts a quantitative increase within the same basic structure. In other words, growth describes a change not of the model as such but only of one of the variables (quantity). This kind of "genuine" growth takes place only in the inorganic world. A crystal grows in size and weight but its basic structure remains the same.

Once we enter the sphere of life we find that growth at critical points leads to a change in the whole structure of the system.

Development

We shall use the term **development** to describe this last form of change only. When an organism (or system) grows quantitatively, it reaches a point at which its increased size can no longer be held together by its original structure. Further growth will then lead either to a disintegration of the organism (biological death) and a return to the physical laws of entropy, or to a restructuring of the organism so that this new structure can continue to control the increased mass. This restructuring always leads to increased differentiation and a more complex structure. Kenneth Boulding, the American economist, defines development as "structural growth." This already expresses a first law of development.

Development is a discontinuous process. Development "grows" from structural crisis to structural crisis, passing through the following phases:

1 Growth of the whole system or parts of it (quantitative increase).
2 Differentiation and organ formation (subsystem formation), whereby functions initially carried out by the system as a whole are now concentrated in subsystems and thus made more effective.
3 Hierarchization: differentiated organs are governed by others and this is also termed "hierarchical integration."
4 Integration: this involves the formation of a new system of greater complexity and containing specialized subsystems.

The biologist Schneirla describes the process of development as growth (increase in tissue), differentiation (changes in structure as the organism grows older), and development (progressive changes during the course of a lifetime). Another European biologist Weisz points to the antagonism between growth and differentiation. After a period of rapid growth and tissue increase comes a period when growth slows down and an intensive inner differentiation of tissues into new tissues and organs takes place. Then comes a further period of growth, and so on.

The biological concept of development includes the principle of finality, which is inherent from the beginning and achieves its goal through a series of stages of development (blueprinted development). Heinz Werner points out that biological development follows the same basic rules as those described in the orthogenetic law of perception and learning. First comes perception, an overall generalized taking-in of the physiognomy of an object. Then follows a process of analyzing the specific nature of the parts (differentiation). Finally, in a process of synthesis, the parts are integrated again into the whole.

Seen biologically, development is a number of steps in levels of organization, with hierarchization, and with direction toward a specific objective. A remarkable trait of the concept of hierarchization is that the control of the lower levels by the higher ones does not take place by means of commands but through selective permission to function specifically. In other words, the higher levels in the hierarchy govern the lower subsystems by sometimes selectively restraining and sometimes selectively permitting their activity.

The question now arises as to whether it is permissible to apply the biological concept of development to the growth and development of social organisms. In our opinion it is permissible, provided that the following differences are not forgotten.

The biological organism develops from the smallest complete unit (the single cell) until it achieves its predetermined goal, the adult form of its species, which in the form of information has been present from the start (an unfolding process). A social entity can develop toward a predetermined goal only if this goal is consciously set by the people who are the bearers of initiative and power. These force the rest of the group toward the performed objective.

It is also possible to imagine an "adult" form of social organization in which all the members strive out of their own insight and conviction toward a jointly agreed objective. This does not mean that there is no hierarchization of subsystems. A conventional hierarchy functions from the top downward, but a new form of hierarchization can be developed at the level of social systems: this is a hierarchy that functions from below upward. It comes about when a higher level of insight, organizational talent, and expert knowledge is freely recognized by lower levels, which therefore voluntarily subordinate themselves in certain fields because they know their own place in the organizational model. It is then no longer a question of power, but rather a question of influence within a hierarchical order of subsystems.

An "adult" form of social organization is an entity that can bring to fruition the new and intrinsic qualities of this "social" level because its foundations are built upon adult human beings. Such "adults" have already brought to fruition the intrinsic quality of the social level; namely, the development of the self as an individual. "Immature" forms are those that are based on lower levels of system, as in the plant kingdom with its predetermined blueprinted information, or in the animal kingdom with its rigid insect colonies. In immature forms of organization the hierarchy is headed by those who most clearly perceive the target, are most strongly committed, and therefore master the necessary instruments for its attainment. In extreme cases the other members of the group are regarded, likewise, as little more than instruments directed toward the achievement of the target.

A natural biological organism can be regarded as a model for a social organization provided that one very great difference is not forgotten: the members of a social organization are independent human beings and not cells in a biological structure. For independent human beings who work together in a social organization, a jointly accepted objective must exist to which they are prepared to subject themselves out of their own conviction.

Wherever people rise above their merely biological level they will strive to form social organizations as described here. It is what we call modern mature forms of organization that are at stake in the present social and political conflict within human organizations. The path toward these mature organizations is the path of organizational development.

A second difference lies in the kind of objective. In a biological organism the target of development is the adult form of the species. In a social organization the adult form is a means of achieving an aim which lies outside the system. A social organization is an organization with an objective. The objective permeates the organization as it passes through the several phases of structural development. At the beginning, all functions are implicit and not yet differentiated; later, specialized subsystems such as departments are created through differentiation; and finally, through integration, everybody is oriented toward the common goal, while each individual fulfills his specialized task knowing that the others are fulfilling theirs, and that the objective can be achieved only if there is a concerted effort.

We can therefore describe the development of business entities as a process of progressive change in structure taking place throughout the life-history of the organization.

As a reaction to 19th-century views of evolution, the concept of development was for a long time regarded as suspect in social science. The objections to those theories of evolution were mainly that they were too generalized and could not be verified empirically, and that often in practice they did not appear to be correct. In recent years, however, problems of development have once again been receiving attention. This became possible when a start was made on the elaboration of a systems theory which replaced vague terms such as "totality" and "image" with defined systems and models. Unfortunately, these attempts have not yet led to a uniform usage of terminology. The terms most commonly used are therefore defined below:

- **Growth**: quantitative increase without any essential change in quality

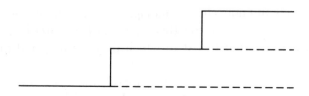

Figure 12.1

- **Maturation**: ripening or unfolding – existing predispositions are caused to mature (blueprinted development)
- **Change**: change in the value of related factors – this term is therefore always used in connection with structures and systems
- **Development**: this term is used for non-fixed change processes (that is to say, processes brought about by people) which are accompanied by qualitative transformation – the old pattern usually remains in existence in a more or less changed form in the background, as an undercurrent, or in a subordinated or repressed form, or as a historical relic (these could also be called "historical anachronisms")

So at the biological level we speak of growth and maturation, and at the human level of change and development.

In summing up, we can say the following:

- development is a discontinuous process, is irreversible, and takes place in time
- the time process follows the sequence of a general initial model, differentiation, integration in a model of greater complexity
- it is a process which takes place step by step, whereby earlier steps or levels may remain as subsystems in a dormant state
- thus development leads to the formation of a layered structure (see figure 12.1)

According to the concept of social development described here, a social organization is always "on the way" from a given past to its own future. The given past consists of a series of decisions which have been made and have resulted in entities with concepts, values, and motives which must be accepted as given. In the future lies the sector of freedom, which means a new choice of objectives and principles.

The development of a social organization always takes place within a wider field. Every social organization is a subsystem of a larger system. Internal development is always influenced from outside by concepts, values, and motives which are parameters affecting the system. Therefore every social organization must be regarded in the light of its cultural environment. Social change as a process thus has an internal and an external side. Not only is a social organization influenced by its cultural environment, but it in turn exerts an influence on this environment. An example will make this clear: the manner in which a firm conducts its personnel policy will have an influence on the extent to which aggressive or nonaggressive tensions emerge in a part of the community outside the firm.

In summary, development can be described from various points of view.

In looking at the direction of development we can speak of "evolution" and "involution." Biological and social **evolution** leads from simple to more complex structures in which differentiated substructures (or organs) emerge. This process is irreversible. **Involution** leads to increasing entropy, the dissolution of structures, indeed to chaos. In the social field, involution in development (the decline of a civilization or of a firm) can run parallel with the evolution of a new structure (e.g., the rise of a new civilization).

In looking at the process of development we can ask: "How does differentiation from simple to complex structures take place, and what laws can be discerned?" This aspect will be dealt with in detail in this chapter, because it constitutes the basis for planned development.

Development can also be described as a situation in which structures of varying degrees of complexity find themselves living together. In this case we can speak of structures which are developed to a greater or a lesser degree, and we can also mention international development aid. The degree of development varies in different countries and in different cultures. The same applies to the different departments with their varying functions within a firm. A highly differentiated production department can run side by side with a fairly primitive sales department, and so on. The existence side by side of social structures of different degrees of development leads to tensions (for instance, the racial or ethnic problems in the United States, in the former Yugoslavia, and in South Africa).

Finally, we can look upon development as an activity: planned change, guided innovation, and organizational development. It is obvious that, for an activity to be carried out, the direction as well as an activity calls for:

- goal setting (the direction of the development)
- policy-making (the strategy of the development process)
- planning (the concretization of practicable steps)

Policy-making is here the most important because a clear policy in connection with development as an activity can provide an action model. However, policies work only when they are converted into action, when they are accepted by the people concerned. The policies of separate social units can come into conflict with one another; this is a conflict of policy systems.

This chapter has focused on the development of organizations within the economic sphere, namely enterprises, whereby enterprises are seen as organizations directed toward an objective and encompassing an economic, a technical, and a social subsystem. A number of typical stages in the development of enterprises will be described, as it were, as the organization progressively learns.

Phases of Development

The pioneer phase

In its pure form, a pioneer enterprise is an enterprise that is still being run by its founder. It comes into being as the result of a creative act by a human being. This person is an entrepreneur; his or her personality structure is such that his or her perception and imagination are directed toward actual needs in economic life. He has a "realistic imagination."

At some point in your life then, as a pioneer, you notice a consumer need and, instead of saying "someone ought to do something about this," you decide to set about it yourself, providing a creative answer to the need at a price the consumer was willing to pay. With a few helpers and probably very little capital you set to work and found a small manufacturing firm, or a small transportation business, or some other service. Twenty years later you find, having learnt and developed, that through diligence and thrift you are now at the head of a flourishing little business with about a hundred employees.

Characteristics of pioneer enterprises

What does the organization of your firm look like at this moment? The pioneer is primarily interested in economic and technical performance (i.e., answering a need at a price the consumer is willing to pay). Your thoughts are occupied with the product you make and the market you create. You have a concept of a real objective and your organization is therefore the simplest form of an organization geared to an objective.

Leadership is autocratic

A pioneer often runs an enterprise with an autocratic style of leadership which is based on the prestige he enjoys in the eyes of "his" men. As we approach the next millennium, autocratic leadership of this kind is not very popular, but in the case in point it is socially acceptable and indeed accepted because the pioneer's autocratic behavior is balanced by the fact that he has the respect and trust of his employees at all levels.

If there is trouble, the "Guvnor" will always find a way out of it, and success in doing so proves that "he's done it again." As a pioneer you have a special charisma, you work "under a good star." Your absolute authority is also connected with the following factors:

- you know all your employees and their family circumstances personally – you engaged them yourself and they are your people
- you know all the jobs, having performed most of them yourself at one time or another – if you find someone making a mess of things, off comes your jacket for an impromptu demonstration
- you are successful in business, and in this situation success gives you prestige

Communication is direct

The pioneer communicates straightforwardly and directly with all employees. You give direct orders to your workers. Since everybody knows everybody, no difficulties worth mentioning arise out of this kind of behavior. Nobody knows better than the boss, and the method works efficiently. These direct contacts are also useful because they make many secondary communications possible and the order is given a personal touch. Long discussions become unnecessary when an incident referred to is remembered by all. (For example, *Pioneer*: "Those bikes are to have pedals like the one we sent to Middletown last year. You know, that black-haired chap you had a bit of a row with." *Employee*: "Oh, you mean those pedals! I noticed there were a few left in the store the other day.")

As a pioneer you speak the language of your employees. In many cases your roots are in the same milieu as theirs, and at least in the early years you have worked in very close contact with them. Close psychological proximity between yourself and your employees makes communication flexible and effective. There is as yet no need to formalize communication and set up information channels. There are no job descriptions to regulate each person's duties and rights. Neither are there such things as procedures, task descriptions, code numbers, stock transfer notes, specified regulations, and the like.

The style of organization is person-oriented

During the course of your career as a pioneer, you tended to pass on the tasks that did not appeal to you personally. Your employees have done just the same. Similarly, each person has sought to keep for himself the jobs that interest him and that he is good at. Thus gradually a kind of flexible division of tasks comes about, whereby each person creates for themselves a job which fits them like a glove. In consequence, work motivation is particularly high in a healthy pioneer enterprise. The pioneer strengthens this tendency systematically by employing people who appeal to him personally or whom he considers promising rather than functionaries who are to carry out specific tasks. When people are taken on they are told: "Have a go at this or that, and if you are any good you'll go a long way with me."

Unconsciously, therefore, as a pioneer you collect around you a group of co-pioneers. This can also have negative effects if the enterprise grows too large. In one case a pioneer enterprise had grown until it had six geographically separate production plants and one large head office. There was no official division of tasks within the company and everybody had at least five superiors who frequently gave contradictory orders. When it was gently suggested by a management consultant that perhaps the demarcation of tasks below top management should be examined, the 72-year-old pioneer director replied resolutely: "Certainly not, I like seeing the strongest come out on top!"

This pioneering style leads to a sort of patchwork pattern with little bits of purchasing and selling going on here and there, carefully hoarded little "individual" stores, and small pockets of administration all over the place. If you try to make a chart of the organization as it stands, the result is a jumble of lines. By any healthy organizational standards an enterprise like this ought to be seriously sick. And yet it functions excellently and shows good economic results.

The working style is improvisational

In a pioneer enterprise all problems are solved by improvisation. This ability to improvise is its real strength; it creates a high degree of flexibility. Because the employees of the company are skilled and can be called upon to do more than one kind of task, production can be rapidly adapted to demand, and the special requests of customers can be met.

The work force: "one big family"

In pioneer enterprises at the end of the last century, labor was the closing item on the budget. The labor market was open, and when work was slack workers were dismissed, while if work was plentiful more were hired. Those times are past. The 20th-century pioneer is economical with his workers. Those who feel at home in the firm make progress, those who do not usually disappear quietly and look for work elsewhere.

The labor factor is not an object of conscious policy, although the patriarchal efforts of the pioneer often touch even the very personal affairs of his people. In many cases the wife of a male pioneer is a kind of welfare worker for her husband's men and their families. "We're all one big happy family" is a favorite phrase of many a pioneer (until the first strike gives him a moral shock from which he usually never quite recovers).

The pioneer's market: known customers

As a pioneer you do not know what it is to operate in an anonymous market. You work in a limited geographical area and know all your customers. Your most important concern is keeping these customers through personal contact.

As a pioneer you work from one order to the next, so that you produce only what is already sold. You do not restrict yourself to certain set products, and keeping a stock of what you produce seems superfluous to you. You have a good, often intuitive, knowledge of your customers, and it is such relationships with them that is important. Your great strength is your ability to keep your customers. You make whatever they order, and you will often delay other work to oblige a long-established customer. The production method of the pioneer is really like an enlarged version of what goes on in a craftsman's workshop, with all the same advantages and disadvantages. As a result of improvisation, the pioneer does not know how much certain jobs and services cost. You are concerned with the total profit, which, however, you cannot determine until you have finished an order.

The long-established growing pioneer company

As a true pioneer you stand "head and shoulders" above your employees. This situation is unconsciously furthered by the pioneer who cannot tolerate any other true leaders either beside or beneath you. If you do choose a director, usually from among employees, to work beside you, the person nevertheless remains your subordinate.

If any of your children join you in the firm they fare no better. Many pioneers realize this and are sensible enough to have their children trained elsewhere. But even after many years they are unable to build up their own authority as long as "the old boy or girl" is still actively concerned with the running of the firm. The pioneer wants to lead without allowing any management to develop under him. Thus when he finally drops out, the company invariably faces a crisis.

The financing of a pioneer company is usually weak. There was too little capital at its inception and since then thrift and internal financing have provisionally supplied immediate necessities.

So far we have described the strong, successful, healthy pioneer enterprise with its great advantages of flexibility, readiness for service, and strong internal motivation. In a healthy pioneer company everybody is concerned with the company's objectives. They are simple and clear: success or failure (complaints from customers) can be witnessed by all. A pioneer organization is healthy as long as:

- the pioneer himself knows all the people
- the pioneer himself knows all the customers
- the production processes or services rendered remain relatively simple
- the accumulation of experience is an asset because technology and the market show stability

From the picture we have given we can conclude the following. As a pioneer, you regard your organization as a closed dynamic system of which your customers and your employees are a part. You are primarily interested in your economic and technical achievements. You think in terms of the product you make and the market you have conquered. For the pioneer, profit is personal income as well as the measure of success as an entrepreneur. Within the social subsystem you operate intuitively in accordance with the model of a craftsman's workshop. Differentiation into economic, technical, and also social subsystems is confined to a minimum. Improvising as you go along, as a pioneer you find your way within a world known to you personally. You reject any interference in this world. Your self-esteem is linked to your success. If the balance-sheet is positive "God has been good to you;" if it is negative "God has humiliated you."

The closed nature of a pioneer enterprise is at once its strength ant its weakness. So long as influences from outside do not disturb the system, a pioneer enterprise can grow and even be taken over by the next generation without much difficulty. But if the "external" world starts to move, if technology develops so that quite new products become available to satisfy needs, if market conditions start to change and competitors break into the pioneer's field with brand-new sales techniques, if the market grows so that personal contacts with customers are no longer possible, if extensive shifts take place in the social structure so that a patriarchal style of leadership is no longer acceptable, then the pioneer phase has reached its limits. If the company continues to be run in accordance with the model of the pioneer phase, despite external circumstances, it can be said that this phase of development becomes "over-ripe."

The first thing that happens when a pioneer company becomes over-ripe is that the employees begin to entertain doubts about "the boss." At the same time, his or her prestige begins to decrease and the autocratic manner becomes intolerable. Then a few mistakes begin to creep in. For instance, a crisis in the market is met in the same way as 40 years ago "when we also had bad times." The pioneer who has hitherto rejected any attempt at interference by the government now suddenly asks for protection for his "honest endeavors."

Once the influence of these external factors becomes so great that it can no longer be seen as an isolated incident but as something affecting the very structure, the pioneer enterprise has reached the threshold of a new development. The symptoms of such a crisis situation can be:

- decreasing profits
- leadership conflicts
- increasing customer complaints
- decreasing maneuverability
- communication blocks
- decreasing motivation

Summary

Just as the unicellular organism can accomplish all the functions that are essential for its life, so a pioneer company in its embryonic form can fulfil all the necessary entrepreneurial functions. The strength of a pioneer enterprise lies in its potentiality and in its strong identity, both of which are concentrated in the person of the pioneer or a successor carrying on in the same style.

The objectives of the company are visible down to the lowest level.

Each person knows what he contributes to the achievement of the objectives and how successful he is in doing so. The policy is not defined or discussed, and yet everybody knows what it is because it is the style in which the boss likes things to be done. Long-term planning is nonexistent. People improvise as they go along, fulfilling the wishes of the customers unless they are interrupted by one of the pioneer's new ideas. The organization is "shallow": there is usually only one level of management, or at most two, between the company director and the shop floor. The demarcation of tasks comes about historically on the basis of personal preference and ability and it therefore changes if there is a change of personnel.

Innovation comes from the top or in the technical field from motivated workers who usually put their own ideas into practice immediately. Control is exercised on the one hand through the direct contact with the customer and on the other by the annual results. The total performance of a pioneer enterprise is directly related to the total ability of all those working for it. If a particular person with a special skill drops out, then the firm can no longer fulfil certain tasks. The know-how is at shop-floor level and the level directly leading it.

The pioneer style described here can be found in the history of nearly all medium-sized companies. Today it is still present in garages, small construction firms, small transportation firms, and building contractors, and it is also a permanent feature of many trading organizations as well as of the agricultural sector and the hotel trade.

A healthy pioneer enterprise has a particularly efficient way of working: it has small overheads and great flexibility. The employees of a pioneer company are still people who have a wide range of skills and are very inventive. Their motivation in serving the customer is high, and they are not averse to lending a helping hand outside working hours as well.

The limitations of the pioneer model are obvious; the number of employees, the nearness of the objective, the vitality of the pioneer himself, the complexity of technical and market requirements – all these determine where this model can operate successfully and in a healthy way.

Many pioneer companies exist today only because the large concerns are not flexible enough to include the production of special series of parts or some semi-finished products or even some finished products in their production programs, and prefer to save money by passing this work on to smaller companies. Some examples of the articles and services supplied by these small firms are computer software, printed labels, screws, nuts and bolts, metal parts, wooden boxes, ship repairs, and scrap-processing.

If a pioneer enterprise becomes too dependent on one or a few large firms in this way, its range of products or services becomes too small. And if the large firms concerned stipulate a high standard of quality, higher investment in capital goods becomes inevitable and the advantages of low overheads and greater flexibility disappear. Then if a period of economic stagnation or decline should occur, forcing the large firms to limit production, the small suppliers will suddenly lack work and quite possibly face bankruptcy.

Further growth and significance of pioneer and family enterprises

In practice, in some cases the further growth of pioneer enterprises is coped with in the following ways.

The conglomerate

The original enterprise is split up into a number of smaller units, each of which is run in the pioneer style. The central unit becomes a kind of financing body. Young employees with a pioneering mentality are engaged or taken from the parent enterprise; they are given an initial capital sum and told to build a new subsidiary company or a special branch. All these "pioneers" are personally responsible only to the pioneer in the central unit. The whole operation could be described as an investment with risk. This conglomerate form, of which there are a number of examples, makes it possible to implement very successful and often aggressive market policies. The pioneer style can be maintained on a much larger scale and with a greater degree of diversification.

The family business

Although a family business need not be identical with the pioneer model, it invariably started as a pioneer company and bears some characteristics of this model for a long time, especially in the style of leadership.

We speak of a family business:

- when the management has been in the hands of a particular family for more than one generation
- when the spouses and children of a former director are members of the board of directors
- when the style of the company is identified with the style of the family concerned
- when the activities of members of the family concerned can help or damage the firm even if they are not employed by it
- when the family finances are firm even when losses occur
- when the careers of employees are a matter of discussion in the family council
- when a person's position in the firm determines his standing in his relationship with the family

Since the family business is still the most frequent form of medium-sized enterprise, and since the medium-sized enterprise is still the backbone of our whole industrial society, we must examine the advantages and disadvantages of this form of organization a little more closely.

The weak points of the family business (which should be avoided) are as follows:

- conflicts within the family and between different family interests, which have an effect on the business
- lack of knowledge about real production costs, continued production of "image" products on which the firm was originally founded, and prestige actions of competing members of the family
- immobility of market position – new markets are not covered quickly enough, and there is insufficient development of new products
- nepotism – some members of the family have to have a position in the firm even if they are incompetent
- rejection of external financing on the capital markets and concealment of the actual financial situation

The strong points of the family business are as follows:

- the family is prepared to advance capital, even in difficult times, and also temporarily to forgo dividends – as a rule the family is prepared not only to share the profits but also to make sacrifices
- the respected family name opens the door to good business relations
- the staff of the firm is loyal and is dedicated to making every effort for the firm
- the body of shareholders is united and is interested in the continuity of the firm
- there is an acceptance of social responsibility (the reason for the firm's good name)
- continuity and integrity of management

In some families, extensive enterprises are managed with success. Strong principles are often the foundation:

- family members are allowed to participate actively in the running of the firm only if they can achieve at least a comparable position in the outside world (it is cheaper to send "nephew Harry" to the Riviera with quite a large annual compensation than to let him earn even a small salary causing confusion in the firm and undermining the authority of the family)
- family members and sons-in-law judged to be suitable are carefully trained elsewhere and prepared for their future tasks
- good specialists are given important positions and take a valid part in decision-making

Family enterprises that recognize these principles can function in a healthy way.

The Phase of Differentiation

The historical answer to the problems of the over-ripe pioneer enterprise came in the form of scientific management. This form of management is conventionally looked upon as "classical management." In the terms of this book we may describe it, like the pioneering approach, as belonging to the "old paradigm."

In the second half of the 19th century, as a result of rapid changes in the technical and economic spheres, firms and enterprises – particularly in America – were confronted for the first time with industrial production on a large scale. These new conditions, which became manifest in the appearance of large-scale enterprises, called for reorientation and reorganization of management. For the first time the organizational problem was systematically examined in the search for new and effective methods.

Two people laid the foundations for a new philosophy of management: Frederick Winslow Taylor in America, and Henri Fayol in France. Both were already engineers of some calibre when they were quite young, and they complemented each other. In the years following the First World War their two methods of organization, which had already proved themselves in practice, were combined to form what we now call "scientific management." No doubt the term "scientific" was deemed necessary as a means of distinguishing the method from the "unscientific" personal style of organization during the pioneer era.

Taylor (1856–1915) came from a wealthy home. At the age of 18 an eye ailment forced him to abandon his medical studies at Harvard University and he decided to undergo an apprenticeship as a pattern-maker in a pump factory and later to work as a laborer in a machine factory. And there, as a young intellectual on the shop-floor, he experienced all the inefficiency of what was later called in Germany the *Meisterwirtschaft*.

The directors reigned supreme and were interested purely in the commercial side of the enterprise. The engineers were regarded as simple technicians for whom the office milieu was inappropriate. The master-craftsmen were the ones with the real know-how, based on well-tried skills specialized over decades of experience.

In this situation Taylor began to think about two things: on the one hand, the lot of the workers who had low wages and long working hours coupled with a high accident risk; and, on the other hand, the possibility of rationalizing production so that it could be increased. If the latter could be achieved, the workers would be able to earn higher wages with less effort and in more dignified conditions, and the entrepreneurs could make higher profits which would in turn pay for technical improvements.

This attitude had tragic consequences for Taylor himself. A number of organizational principles elaborated in his scientific management were taken up, but his social ideas were rejected as those of a clever but impractical idealist. Against his doctor's advice, Taylor spent his evenings studying to become an engineer. After passing his exams he soon patented a number of important inventions and quickly became financially independent. Thus at the age of 37 he was able to become the first independent management consultant, devoting all his time to publicizing his ideas. When in 1912 the American Federation of Labor finally pronounced him workers' "enemy number one," his life's work collapsed and he died in hospital three years later, lonely and embittered.

Taylor had a brilliant personality, was exceptionally gifted technically, and was also socially inspired. And yet a study of his life reveals a trait of character which also found its way into his theories. Today one would say Taylor was an obsessional neurotic, and this showed itself even in his youth in numerous, almost compulsive, actions. A similar compulsive kind of thinking appears in his system: whatever can be distinguished must be separated. All his principles were absolute. The system was more important than the people, for whom nevertheless he wanted to do so much. Taylor thought that he could grasp a social organization in a deterministic system in which all variables were known and could be stipulated.

The best way to rediscover Taylor's greatness is to read the report of his hearing before Congress. His answers are those of a brave and clear-thinking man in a highly awkward situation. Patiently he explains his system, answering all the unpleasant questions and leaving us in no doubt as to who is really leading the discussion.

His system was one-sidedly worked out by his successors who saw in it nothing but a striving for efficiency. In this form it came to Europe after the First World War, where far-sighted entrepreneurs founded such institutions as the Dutch Institute for Efficiency (1925).

Fayol (1841–1925) was another highly gifted personality. At the age of 19 he became the youngest mining engineer in France. At first it seemed that he would devote himself to science as a geologist, and his book on geology was a standard work in this field for a long time. But then he was asked to take over the running of an ill-functioning, almost bankrupt, mining company.

With the same systematic thinking he plunged straight into his new task, and was able to transform the whole organization in a short time. Thereafter he was called to ever-higher positions. During the First World War he held a high position in connection with the economic organization of the war effort in France. He attained a ripe old age and was a celebrated man until he died.

Fayol built up his administrative organization according to a number of definitions, elements, and principles. The following 14 principles have become the best known:

1 division of labor
2 authority and responsibility
3 discipline
4 unity of command
5 unity of direction (objectives)
6 subordination of personal interests to company interests
7 good remuneration of personnel
8 centralization
9 hierarchical structure
10 order
11 justice
12 stability in the position of personnel
13 initiative
14 *esprit de corps*

Having studied the first 12 principles in this list – centralization, discipline, order, subordination, unity of command, and so on – one wonders where there is any room left for initiative. Indeed, Fayol's principles of organization could have been formulated by the Sun King himself!

With these two personalities, Taylor and Fayol, we have two biographies, two characters, and two entirely different attempts to save the over-ripe pioneer enterprise.

Taylor begins from below, with a rational organization of the workshop, with improvements of resources and machines, and with a systematic division of labor and specialization of performance. Not until decades after his death did his principles penetrate to other spheres beyond production; and they never reached top management.

Fayol, as a good Frenchman, starts from the top with a centralized organization and works downward. His principles hardly reached the shop-floor. Rational management for him was called "administration" and his question was: "How can I control the whole company from the top by means of a logically constructed hierarchical order of authority and responsibility?" He made the first large organization charts of the well-known "Christmas-tree" type (i.e., with the star at the top, and below at every level small parcels with the names of interrelated functions and tasks).

Before his death, Fayol was himself able to end the argument between the Taylorites and the Fayolites by declaring that the two systems were not contradictory but complementary. Since then, through the merging and further refinement of the two systems, scientific management has continued to grow.

The efficiency of production methods was developed on the basis of engineering science as a whole (Taylor's successors), and the corresponding efficiency of economic administration grew out of a theory of internal control and management developed by economists (Fayol's successors). We shall discuss the principles of the resulting organization theory, which are essential for an understanding of company structure in the second phase.

Seen historically, scientific management has led to a form of enterprise. That is why, as a classification, the second stage of development of a system or organization geared to an objective has been called the phase of **differentiation**.

Scientific management is based on a logical ordering of functions, tasks, things, and processes. It assumes that the productivity of an organization increases the more the people concerned succeed in behaving according to the formal organizational plan. The norms for human behavior in the work situation comply first and foremost with the demands made by the technical process.

Some characteristics of the phase of differentiation

Taylor and Fayol and their successors were not primarily concerned with providing a scientific explanation of what occurs in the actual running of an enterprise. They gave practical organizational procedures, the application of which was intended to guarantee maximum efficiency. The main organizational principles of the phase of differentiation are mechanization, standardization, specialization, and coordination.

The principle of mechanization

This principle implies that technical resources must be used wherever possible. Human labor must be replaced by machine labor as far as possible. Mechanization is not concerned exclusively with machines, but covers the whole production process and also the information processes.

The principle of standardization

This second principle is concerned with interchangeability and uniformity. Standardization means that everything, every process, every working method can be whittled down to an exactly described standard. From a number of alternatives one possibility is chosen and is declared to represent the norm for reasons of expediency.

The mechanization of production processes would not be profitable if standardization had not made serial and mass production possible. The principle of standardization, however, affects human beings as well as things. In addition to interchangeable standard parts and standard quality norms, we find standard function descriptions, uniform performance requirements, standardized assessment techniques, standard instructions, interchangeable functionaries and so on.

It is impossible to stipulate production norms without carefully analyzing the cause and effect of relevant phenomena. When this is done, the complicated interplay that goes on in an enterprise becomes controllable and predictable and can be planned. As development continues in the second phase, however, this controllability threatens to become an end in itself. As norms and standards become more and more refined, the controllability of the production process increases, although this is usually at the expense of the necessary flexibility. For the departments directly or indirectly involved in the production process, the actual objective becomes the meeting of planning requirements. The real objective of the firm, namely to satisfy a need of the market, disappears more and more into the background.

While methods and techniques for controlling and developing the internal organization become increasingly scientific, the sales department continues to function anachronistically in the pioneer style. It still works from one order to the next, relying on personal contact with customers. On the one hand the elaboration of norms and standards has led to a thorough knowledge of production costs and production output, but on the other hand much less is known about sales costs and the benefits obtainable from possible alternative sales techniques. This development leads to an aggressive sales mentality: the firm's products are "forced" on to the market.

The principle of specialization

This third principle means that the restriction of effort to a small field leads to improved performance in quality and quantity. Mechanization and standardization lead as a matter of course to specialization. Mechanization requires an ever-increasing perfection of equipment as well as concentrated knowledge and experience with regard to every part and every technical aspect. Standards can be met only if all the causes and effects that could influence the object to be standardized are minutely controlled in every detail. This can best be achieved through specialization.

Three modes of specializing appear in the phase of differentiation:

(1) **Functional specialization**: similar activities are concentrated in a single department under one specialized department head, who in turn engages further specialists. Purchasing, selling, production, administration, and any research, become separate departments. According to need, further departments are divided off. Thus, for instance, departments for production planning, maintenance and storage are divided off from the production department.

(2) **Specialization of management levels** leads to a vertical management structure. The top is concerned only with policy-making: constitutional management. In the middle these policies are translated into organizational measures such as organizational management; and at the bottom of the hierarchy immediate direction and control are exercised over the shop-floor level: i.e., supervisory management. The relationship between superiors and their subordinates is one of direction and control.

Management is interpreted on the one hand as the right to give orders, and on the other hand as the duty to see that these orders have been correctly carried out. This form of management is formal and autocratic. It is formal because the exercise of authority (as seen in Max Weber's model of an ideal bureaucracy) is to a great extent based on a person's powers resulting from his position in the hierarchy; and it is autocratic because the traditional style of management behavior of the pioneer entrepreneur is usually copied.

(3) **Specialization by phasing the work process**: in this mode, the principle that everything that can be distinguished must be separated is applied, so that the three essentially interrelated phases of human work, planning, execution and control, are recognized as being distinguishable and are duly separated. Departments are organized for the sole purpose of planning and preparing (general planning offices, production planning, drawing offices, and so on). Other departments appear with exclusively controlling functions (e.g., quality control, cost control, auditing). What remains in between is "pure" operating labor.

With the help of work analyses and time-and-motion studies the entire work process is broken down into basic elements with corresponding standard times. On the basis of the requirements of the production process with regard to layout, the supply and dispatch of materials and parts, and the speed of the production flow, tasks for human beings emerge which consist of basic elements rationally joined together. These tasks are attuned to one another according to technical norms and have to be performed by a prescribed method (the one-best-way principle). The resulting unskilled work is void of content and calls almost exclusively for manual dexterity. Human labor is reduced to an automatic activity.

The phasing of the work process in this way is not restricted to the factory. For white-collar workers, research workers, and even in the domain of the expert, increasing specialization leads to much routine work.

The principle of coordination

This fourth principle is introduced to counterbalance the centrifugal force of differentiation, which becomes increasingly prevalent in the second phase. The numerous and varied activities which come into being have to be held together. Coordination comes about directly and indirectly in the following ways:

Unity of command: in order to avoid the issuing of contradictory instructions, each person has only one superior. In principle, horizontal communication between two employees should take place via their superior.

Span of control: since the relationship of a superior to his or her subordinates is one of direction and control, he must have a detailed knowledge of all his subordinates' activities in order to have his department well under control. This is possible only if the number of his subordinates is not too large.

Staff-line differentiation: as the number of specialists increases, it becomes more difficult to maintain the principle of unity of command. Staff-line differentiation is a solution to this problem. Specialists are placed in staff departments outside the line of command. They act in an exclusively advisory capacity while the line of command keeps its full authority.

Performance remuneration: the assumption is that good pay is the only thing that motivates people. A person acts rationally and tries to reap the maximum benefit from the bargain, in this way safeguarding his own interests (the concept of economic man). In an enterprise, this negotiation situation means the execution of work for a return in the form of good financial remuneration. By roundabout means, self-interest is used to direct the activities of the employees toward the interests of the firm. Put briefly, organization is, therefore, directing resources and people toward an objective.

Communication techniques: a complicated network of information distribution is set up. This must ensure that management remains informed about the activities of its personnel and that they in turn are informed about the plans decided on by management. Internal post systems and mailing lists are methods applied.

Introductory courses and training programs: systematic transmission of knowledge and skills ensures that people will do their work in the way prescribed by the formal plan. It is typical of this kind of coordination that it takes place outside the work situation to which it pertains. The higher level coordinates the lower level.

With regard to the task of top management, the above development shows that its attention in the phase of differentiation is directed

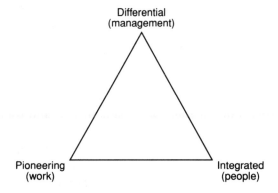

Figure 12.2

mainly inward. In the pioneer phase, the external marketing function was the most important. The internal set-up had to give the least possible trouble and had, as it were, to translate the smallest hint into action. In the following phase it becomes more and more necessary to give attention to the internal organization. Administering and controlling the internal structure of the company becomes the most important task of management.

In the triangular relationship of management, work, and people, the pioneer directs his attention primarily to the people and motivates them to do the work. In the phase of differentiation, management concentrates in the first instance on an analysis of the work processes, which it then passes on to the people divided up into portions (see figure 12.2).

Through the technical and organizational structuring of the company, scientific management has achieved an enormous increase in productivity. The method of analysis and differentiation has made it possible to investigate in detail, and learn to control, every activity in the firm. Mechanization and standardization have led to new methods of production aimed at the mass markets, which have considerably increased the living standard of sizeable groups of the population in the western hemisphere.

In the pioneer phase it was a matter of piece production. Each product was manufactured by itself as a whole. This form of production is still found in capital-goods industries, such as ships, diesel engines, electrical installations, telecommunications systems, and so on. Items are produced individually or in small lots. The work is completed in consecutive homogeneous segments, and the division of work is already present to a considerably greater degree than in craft production. Where piece production is still undertaken, the acquiring of order, that is, the external marketing function, is in the foreground. The cost price is relatively high. In the phase of differentiation, old-style mass production, new-style mass production, and process production appear side by side and sometimes also successively.

Old-style mass production usually involves standardized interchangeable components and standard manufacturing methods, and the end-product is also fixed. There is only one variety (remember Henry Ford's remark that "people can have whatever color they like, so long as it's black"). Old-style mass production means that the end-product and the production process are rigid. The customer has to learn to be satisfied with the available range. Individual customer relations are less important than an effective sales organization and the penetrating and covering of a wide market. Long production runs make the cost price relatively low.

New-style mass production combines the advantages of low cost prices with those of a relatively flexible production process and a very varied end-product (e.g., automobile production). The problems here lie in high investment, inventory costs, working to capacity, running the organization, and marketing. Although the introduction of operational research and network-planning technically creates the conditions for entering a third phase of development, the organization and management style of the phase of differentiation prevent a company from doing so.

Process production makes the end-product strictly dependent on the technical installations. Production calls for high capital investment and the production-line installation can really only do the task for which it was designed. A new product requires an entirely new or considerably altered installation. Basically, production is secondary; the main concern is selling, finding, and cultivating markets which are prepared to accept the end-product in one or only a few of its variations in large numbers at low prices.

Thanks to these new forms of production, Taylor's social ideas, namely that scientific management should bring about low cost prices, good wages, less need for physical effort, and a high degree of social security, have been more than realized. Thanks to scientific management, an entrepreneur can now cope with a wider "area": a larger enterprise, a more varied assortment of products, a larger market; in short, a greater complexity.

Clearly, the organization itself now claims a large part of management's attention, which is focused upon the profitability and productivity of the production process. In a certain sense, contact with the market is lost as a result. Management is faced with marketing problems for the large series it has produced, while at the same time competition increases. Decreasing profit margins strengthen the need to give attention to internal efficiency and rationalization. Selling tends to become aggressive, and production pressures arise.

This also explains why the organized aspect of a company's internal structure, its formal organization, becomes so important. The rational ordering of tasks, things, and processes becomes the organizational principle of the phase of differentiation. The integration of human activities is based on a formal hierarchy of authority and subordination.

The phase of differentiation is in many ways the antithesis of the pioneer phase. It is rational instead of intuitive, mechanistic instead of organic, impersonal instead of personal, and based on organizational instead of situational principles.

The limits of the second phase

The differentiation that takes place in the second phase is an essential condition for a company if it is to function on a long-term basis on a larger scale and with greater complexity. Specific "organs" have to be developed. Differentiation leads, of necessity, to a diversity of parts which have to be bound together and oriented toward the company's objective.

In the second phase this is done through formalizing relationships and interconnections. The informal and personal pioneer style, which continues for some time in the second phase, for instance in the style of management, ensures that the negative sides of the formalizing process do not become apparent immediately. In a certain sense the informal organization makes it possible for the formal organization to exist.

In some cases management realizes this and in its policy-making gives particular emphasis to personal relationships within the organization. This kind of policy often grows out of a nostalgia for the earlier pioneering days. However, it is impossible for anachronistic elements of this kind to compensate sufficiently in the long run for the bureaucratic tendencies of the organization. On the whole, people cannot be expected to solve the problems of the second phase by "knowing each other personally." The relationship of company structure and company behavior is then dysfunctional.

Although at first scientific management brings clarity and order into the over-ripe pioneer situation, as growth continues, crisis phenomena begin to appear again, indicating a need for restructuring and orientation toward the next phase of development. Some symptoms are as follows.

Rigidity

The flexibility of the organization is drastically reduced through formalization and bureaucratization. This can become fatal if the dynamics of social and market conditions increase. The possibility of a rapidly adjustable policy is reduced.

Coordination problems

Through specialization and sub-specialization the departments draw further and further apart; they lose their understanding of each other's tasks and can no longer communicate because they no longer speak the same language. Small functional kingdoms with their own objectives and their own standards arise, and this makes coordination even more difficult. Personal assistants begin to act as "liaison officers;" coordination committees are set up, but are little more than stopgaps. Finally, in an effort to solve the coordination problem, stronger managers are called for, which is a step back to the days of the pioneer. In addition, fewer and fewer top managers are produced by the system. The "promotion ladders" up the various functional "pillars" are so long that, by the time they have reached the right age, managers have become unsuitable for general management tasks as a result of their ingrained one-sidedness.

Vertical communication problems

Communication is distributed not only between departments, but also vertically. It has already been pointed out that management in the second phase is autocratic and formal (lower levels are derived from higher levels; tasks are created through the downward delegation of authority). This style of direction and control, together with the organizational measures of unity of command and span of control, leads to an ever-increasing number of levels in the hierarchy. At the top, less and less is known about what is going on at the foot of the pyramid, and vice versa. The need for official distribution of information increases, and signalling data systems are established. In consequence, the number of indirect workers increases disproportionately, administration grows, and overhead costs rise. Because lower down in the organization people lose sight of the totality, they find it very difficult to bear responsibility for decisions of which the consequences lie outside their vision, and therefore problems are unloaded upward. Accumulation of responsibilities and overloading at the top emerge.

Staff-line problems

The staff-line structure, which is built on the difference between advice and command, is found to be untenable in the long run. The expertise of the specialist staff means that their advice takes on the characteristics of command, while within their departments superior staff members acquire line authority. In addition, the line manager will often find himself giving advice to his colleagues. So the difference between staff and line becomes blurred because there seems to be no way out of this cul-de-sac. These problems will continue as long as the difference is formally maintained.

Motivation

One of the most serious problems is the decrease in motivation and individual productivity. The reasons for this are manifold: people feel that the work is devoid of intelligent content and therefore experience a kind of qualitative under-employment; they feel reduced to a number, a mere extension of the system; they no longer perceive the overall work. To identify with the objectives of the company becomes well-nigh impossible. The place of the motivating objective has been taken by a closely prescribed task which leaves little room for personal identification. Tasks are fixed and adjusted to technical requirements and change insufficiently with the growing ability of the worker. He is forced to use an ever-decreasing proportion of his capacities the more his task is sharply defined on a long-term basis. He is taxed only with regard to speed and manual skill.

Management by drives

The more complicated the structure becomes in the second phase, the more top management attempts to solve its problems by initiating special drives such as efficiency drives, cost-cutting drives, productivity drives, etc. Without fundamental structural changes, these drives become less and less effective. The law of diminishing returns is in operation here: the result of management drives, expressed in the difference between expenditure and returns, becomes increasingly disproportionate until finally it becomes negative.

We have described the second phase as a causal deterministic one in the form of a "pyramid" command organization, oriented mainly toward the expansion of the technical system as regards both production technology and organization techniques. As a result, top management devotes a large proportion of its time and attention to running the internal organization.

To begin with, the economic system did not grow in proportion to the development of the production process. The managers chosen by the shareholders behaved in the style of the owner–entrepreneur and found it very difficult to accustom themselves to the new specialists who were expected to "manage through organization." In production organizations the technical mentality of the engineer was dominant, and in commercial and survival-oriented organizations the old merchant mentality remained in the foreground.

The specialists became advisers, left in a siding and having to sell their advice to the line organization which had developed as the line of command in the late stages of the pioneer phase. In the whole logically constructed model, with its network of minutely coordinated tasks and competencies, there was no room for co-pioneering and individual initiative.

Because of the depth of the organization (almost always more than five levels of management between top and foreman), the objectives of the company as a whole were no longer visible and recognizable below the third level. Instead, the subsystems now had their own objectives; e.g., purchasing, production, administration, and selling.

At shop or office-manager level, people's horizons did not extend beyond their own work-place or office. In the model of the second phase a wider horizon was unnecessary. The relationship with people was instrumental; they were regarded as tools serving the achievement of objectives. Organization meant directing resources and people toward an objective. For this to be achieved, human beings had to be reduced to organizational variables behaving in a predictable and rational way and reacting to financial stimuli. The peculiarity of this kind of financial motivation was that work satisfaction was achieved not through the actual work but through being able to spend one's wages away from one's place of work. There was no genuine satisfaction to be gained from the work in office or factory, since it was devoid of real content and meaning.

Whereas in the pioneer phase the emphasis was on objectives and direct control of these objectives, we now find that planning and organization come to the fore, though entirely within the technical system of the company.

The company's external relations also undergo an important change in the second phase. In the pioneer phase, external relations meant promoting customer ties and producing what had already been ordered. The customer was part of the system; he or she was a known factor who always wanted things done in a certain way. In the second phase the customer is no longer a known factor. The rationalization of the production process, brought about by an analysis of production techniques, has led to an enormous increase in productivity. Machines have to be used to a certain capacity and the production flow must not be interrupted. Mass-produced articles flow out of the factory and have to be sold to an anonymous market. This anonymous market is no longer included in the system of the company.

Instead of satisfying needs, the moment comes when it is essential to push products on to the market. The customer becomes an antagonist. Formerly, the customer was given what he asked for.

Now selling becomes aggressive and the customer is expected to adapt his wishes to what is offered. In keeping with the second-phase attitude, this problem is also approached in a causal, analytical way, and a new specialization of sales promotion arises. Advertising and persuasion techniques place the consumer under pressure. He is seen just as much as an instrument as is the internal work force: he must not think or judge or choose for himself; he must simply reach for the branded product at the command of his influenced subconscious.

The internal work force, oppressed by the impersonal organization model, increases the counter-pressure by organizing its own power against the employer. The workers still cherish the old image of the entrepreneur pocketing all the profits as his personal property; and the consumer, bombarded with an avalanche of advertising and temptation, is today also beginning to found consumer organizations as a counter-force. Tension builds up on both fronts with the result that the "image" of the employer becomes worse and worse, although he is himself no more than the recipient of an annual salary who works for objectives controlled by others.

The development from the first to the second phase can be summarized as in figure 12.3. Workers and consumers stand at the end of an impersonal process of rational analysis and construction. Both are under the same kind of pressure. The strange thing is that it is the same people who feel oppressed by the same model both in and outside the work situation. Henry Ford was the first to see this connection, when in the 1920s he decided to pay his workers a wage high enough to enable them to buy his cars.

The second phase was a historical answer to the over-ripe pioneer phase. The pioneer–entrepreneur consciously gives preeminence to economic achievement and wants as little trouble as possible from his organization. In the second phase, managing and running the organization become preeminent. The economic achievement gradually comes under pressure from the swelling stream of production or the demand for continuity of services.

In the second phase the economic system works against an ever-growing resistance coming from within and from outside in the form of decreasing motivation on the part of the worker and increasing mistrust on the part of the consumer: a kind of social law of diminishing returns.

In order to escape from the dilemma of the over-ripe second phase

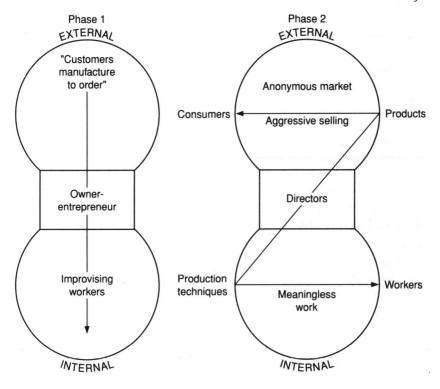

Figure 12.3

in which most "old-paradigm" companies find themselves today, the time seems to have arrived for a complete revision of the model. The "new-paradigm" model would be a third phase in the development of the enterprise.

The Phase of Integration

When we consider the phase of integration, the important thing to bear in mind is the development of the social subsystem and its integration with the already developed economic and technical subsystems. This leads us to an entirely new concept of organization, which seeks to make it possible for every employee within the organization to be able and willing to act intelligently in the interests of the whole. This aim can be achieved only a step at a time.

Requirements of the third phase

The third phase will have to give answers to the following problems of the second phase.

Communications

With regard to internal communications, the line of command is too long. The company objective becomes vague and is replaced by sub-objectives. Reporting upward breaks down at every level; hardly any information is available at the top about what is really going on a few levels lower down. Horizontal interdepartmental communication is hampered by a specific deafness to the language and basic mentality of others. With regard to external communications, live contact with the customer or consumer is lost. The manufactured product or standardized packaged services, rather than the solution of problems for others, are in the foreground. Contact with the authorities and the trade unions has become antagonistic. A model of the third phase will have to reveal new possibilities for internal and external relations.

Process management

The process of accumulating value between input and output runs falteringly through a number of departments. In each one a series of activities is concluded, and then the throughput is taken up again elsewhere and dealt with once more. The control of a process in time is satisfactory only where there is a static situation; as soon as varying or unrepeated activities are required, the throughput takes too long. A model of the third phase will have to create the possibility of surveying, steering, and controlling all the different process flows as one great flexible, adaptable network. It is for this reason that "business re-engineering" has become so popular today.

Rigidity and qualitative under-employment of personnel

By the end of the second phase, integrated co-pioneership has been lost. Nevertheless, people still like to be master of their own house (subsystem) and to fight their own little battles. Changes are met with deep-seated resistance and are covertly or overtly sabotaged (the reorganization of a large administrative department was once nick-named by the staff "Operation fasten your seat-belt"). There is qualitative under-employment at almost every level; this means that people have far greater potential than they are permitted to use in their prescribed work. The resulting latent dissatisfaction is expressed in aggression or apathy. People have learnt to use their creativity outside their work, while they do their work for the most part "with more brawn than brain."

A model of the third phase will have to ensure that co-entrepreneuring, integrated with the total objective of the company, is extended right down to the level of the foreman and the worker. This means that:

- Alertness to change, and intelligent participation in and thinking ahead about innovation, must become an inherent attitude in the whole of the social system. The organization itself will become a supporting function changing according to need.
- The superior-oriented vertical-line system will have to be replaced by horizontal orientation toward those who come before and those who come next in the sequence of activities. This means that each person will be oriented toward the output of the processes and that there will be joint interest in maintaining an optimal throughput within the boundaries of policy and network planning.
- Management development and task enrichment must be able to raise the personnel resources of the company to ever-higher levels.
- Continual innovation becomes normal; its consequence is continual education; its source, today, is often constant improvement and total quality management.
- Finally, after the economic and technical subsystems have evolved, the social subsystem – through the empowerment of people – must also be brought to maturity and integrated into a

totality consisting of all three subsystems. Only then will the enterprise have reached full maturity.

Having set out the requirements of a new, more highly differentiated model, we must show how the transition from the second to the third phase can be achieved.

If we start with the entrepreneurial initiative of the pioneer as our thesis, then scientific management is in a certain sense the antithesis, and a third step will have to be the new-paradigm synthesis: a synthesis of the positive elements of the first and second phases with the addition of a new element that makes this synthesis possible – the mature social subsystem. For lack of a more suitable name, we term the third phase the **phase of integration**.

An Overall Picture of the Third Phase

The phase of integration is based on a conception of the human being which rests on the conviction that every person is able to (and wants) to develop, and that real work satisfaction is connected with the question of whether any personal fulfillment can be achieved in the work situation.

Such a situation is approached when the organization allows individuals as well as groups to act intelligently in accordance with the objectives of the totality. For this the objectives must be known, and the resulting individual sub-objectives must be visible. Furthermore, there must be a policy known to everybody which depicts the style and the standards according to which the objectives are realized in the company concerned ("This is the way we do things here"). Finally, a continual training program is required, to ensure that people can carry their new responsibilities.

With regard to the execution of tasks, efforts should be made to leave some of the planning (micro-planning) to groups and individuals (no one-best-way regulations, but objectives with a margin for initiative and self-control).

All this becomes possible if there is a change of attitude in management. As mechanization increases and islands of automation begin to form toward the end of the second phase, it becomes increasingly difficult for those at the top to cut Gordian knots by power of command. Complex problems are already increasingly solved by joint consultation among experts. These consultation structures, which were originally rather rigid both in their composition and in the time pattern of their meetings, have, of necessity, begun to take on a more flexible character in the form of task forces and problem-oriented consultation groups. The permanent committees have thus been relieved to a considerable extent.

Through all this the social system begins to unfold. But in order to achieve the integration of the economic, technical, and social subsystems, a form of organization is necessary which is significantly different from those of the previous phases.

The pioneer phase had a shallow, broad form of organization; the phase of differentiation had a deep, pyramid form, with the controlling board of directors at the top (Christmas-tree organization). And now, for reasons that will be dealt with in detail, the phase of integration demands a form of organization which we introduce here as the learning organization.

12

Building a Learning Organization
Ronnie Lessem

Introducing the Learning Organization

The 19th century was the age of pioneering, economic man. Economic achievement, endorsed by both Church and State, became the hallmark of the industrializing societies. The 20th century, however, has seen the rise of "differentiated" organizational man. Institutional power, endorsed by both "free" and socialist enterprise, has supplanted personal power. The 21st century is likely to herald the successor to economic and organizational man – the "integrated", whole person. Thus, the 19th century was the age of the pioneering entrepreneur; in the 20th century the scientifically rational executive has taken command: business administration has taken over from business entrepreneurship, the bureaucratic organization from the pioneering enterprise, the 21st century, as we see, will be the era of the integrated learning organization. In this chapter we shall introduce you to such a developed enterprise, in both theory and practice.

Within such an organization a healthy array of individual managers, institutions, and cultures holds interdependent sway. In the vertical dimension, each engages in an on-going evolutionary process of learning and development (upward), and a continuing transformative process of innovation and creativity (downward). In the horizontal dimension, each participates in an interactive process of learning with and through others.

The Limits to Learning

The learning project

As long ago as the late 1970s, the Italian industrialist and management philosopher Aurelio Peccei set up a learning project to deal with the whole question of societal learning.

> Tangles of mutually reinforcing old and new problems, too complex to be apprehended by the current analytical methods and too tough to be attacked by traditional policies and strategies, are clustering together, heedless of boundaries. There is a desperate need to break these vicious circles. An entirely new enterprise is thus required. Focusing on people, this new enterprise must be aimed at developing the latent innermost capability of learning so that the march of events can eventually be brought under control. (Botkin *et al.*, 1979: 17)

Maintenance learning

The American Jim Botkin, who headed Peccei's learning project, and two colleagues, from eastern Europe and north Africa respectively, distinguished between two forms of learning. The first, **maintenance learning**, involves the acquisition of fixed outlooks, methods, and rules for dealing with known and recurring situations. This is the realm of the analytical manager, suitably at home when internal and external environments remain the same. Maintenance learning, therefore, is indispensable for the stability of the individual, the organization, and our societies.

Innovative learning

For long-term survival, however – particularly in times of turbulence, change, and discontinuity – another type of learning is more essential, one that is more compatible with development. It is a type of learning that can bring (both individually and collectively) change, renewal, or total transformation.

Botkin's innovative learning is divided into two types:

- **Anticipative learning**, which corresponds to our vertical variety, involves the consideration of trends and the making of plans, so as to shield institutions from the trauma of learning by shock. Through anticipative learning, the future, for the individual and the organization, may enter our lives as a friend and not as an assailant.

- **Participative learning**, which corresponds to our horizontal variety, involves cooperation, dialogue, and empathy. It requires not only keeping communications open but also constantly testing your own operating rules and values against those of others. Without participation, anticipation is futile; and participation without anticipation can be misguided.

On the one hand, then, managers within learning organizations have to be able to enrich their context, keeping up with the rapid appearance of new situations. On the other hand, they must communicate the variety of contexts through continuing dialogue with other individuals, institutions, and cultures. The one is pointless without the other. Whereas anticipation stimulates "vertical" learning in time, participation allows "horizontal" learning across space.

The Learning Organization is Born

Comino – Dexion

A learning organization of both vertical and horizontal varieties came into existence some 60 years ago, when a Greek–Australian resident in Great Britain started up the Krisson Printing Company in a basement in central London. Out of those humble origins Demetrius Comino developed his company Dexion, creating, in time, an industry for storage and materials-handling equipment that has spread world-wide.

More importantly for our theme, however, Comino created an organization geared toward innovative learning. We shall take Dexion International as our example of the learning community or organization, making due reference to Comino's pioneering thoughts and actions:

In Dexion we believe that a company is a living organism; in order to be really healthy, it must grow and develop. We therefore regard growth as fundamental. The most important single requirement therefore laid on us is the requirement of learning, or, to put it differently, it's how it is that we can become effective systems for our own transformation, as individuals and as organizations. Such self-transformation (learning) must become a continuing process, a way of life[1].

Participative learning

In 1927 Comino, a qualified mechanical engineer, left his employer to set up a venture of his own. He had no idea what business he wanted to go into, but he did have some very definite intimations of the kind of organizational learning he wanted to create. He described this later in a letter to one of his employees during the war:

Our equipment now consists of half a dozen lathes, a couple of milling machines, a drill and diverse other small devices. Most precious of all is the experience gained, literally at the cost of sweat and blood. We don't know what kind of economic and social system we will finally find ourselves in, but it will certainly be a gain to work out our salvation as a group rather than as isolated individuals. Whatever kind of place it is, we should be able to make some sort of centre in it for ourselves (I almost said corner, but centre is the word.) It is a radiating centre we want, not a retreat[2].

Comino went into printing because he had some Greek business friends who needed materials printed. From the outset he employed school-leavers from the East End of London for both economic and social reasons. At an early stage there was established a complementarity of managerial effort between Comino the visionary and agent of change, and Fred Riley the action man, who helped Comino turn his dreams into reality. In time Norman Bailey, the only one among the initial recruits who had been to a grammar school, became the analytical manager, and George Thomson, another East End lad (who rose from floor-sweeper to production manager), emerged as the animator. The sales force, duly encouraged to win friends and influence people, was unashamedly American in approach, though British by entrepreneurial heritage.

Anticipative learning

It turned out, in fact, that the printing business was an ideal learning environment for young people. It provided a training not only in production methods but also in literacy. The business was very varied, and everyone got involved in the selling and promotion of merchandise.

However, Comino came to realize, soon enough, that he would not be able to devote his life to printing. He required wider product and market horizons. By 1937 he had begun experimenting with a metal construction material. In his printing works there was a space problem. As business expanded he continually had to dismantle and rebuild his storage equipment. Throughout the war he searched for a versatile system of storage construction, with the minimum of components, simple to erect and cheap to buy. His failure to find one led him to invent "slotted angle," a "grown man's version of Meccano."

Slotted angle was only the beginning. Whereas Dexion (the Greek *krisson* means "better" and *dexion* means "right") started out as a one-component solution to a storage problem, Comino's close contact with industry led to customers exploiting the product's versatility. Dexion, particularly in the hands of an inveterate problem-solver and agent of change such as Comino, became a packet of possibilities.

Product and Market Development

We can no longer rely on the next generation learning the new things and taking the next steps forward. We have to re-educate ourselves two or three times during our lifetime. We have reached a stage where we have to keep learning and re-learning if we are not to become obsolete. It is not merely that things are changing in the sense that we now build racks with speedlock instead of slotted angle. What is important is the increase in complexity and interrelatedness.

Products used to be "things;" lengths of slotted angle, speedlock components, and so on. But now products have become a system, a service. What advanced companies do is solve customers' problems. The customer can no longer say "I want a rack." He says "I want the solution to a problem." We and our customers must learn to think in terms of wholes, not parts. A product is no longer a thing, a piece of ironmongery. It is what we do in our part of the industrial system to take account of what is happening in some other part (Comino, 1970). Today the Dexion Group has a series of divisions that range, in their product-market scope, from the original slotted angle to electronically integrated handling systems.

Innovative Learning

Learning: the departure

Individual or organizational learning of the vertical kind involves a departure and a return (see figure 13.1): the departure begins with adventure and ends with creativity; the return begins with vision and ends with action. Both involve successively different combinations of behavior, thought, and feeling. We shall illustrate these learning processes through references to Comino, as the individual learner, and to Krisson and Dexion as models of the learning organization.

The adventurous role: the physical transaction

Comino responded to the call to adventure, as a first, physical step, when he left his job in a large company because he wanted to set up on his own. Not only did he venture into the unknown, without a burning idea to drive him on, but he started his business just before the Great Depression.

You can do it!

Hunting around for something to do, Comino, a first-class graduate in mechanical engineering, set up his printing business in the heart of London through a series of accidents. Because of his Greek roots he had some Greek friends who happened to be in the cigarette business. They needed their paper and packaging to be printed. So he started with two or three machines in a basement in Oxford

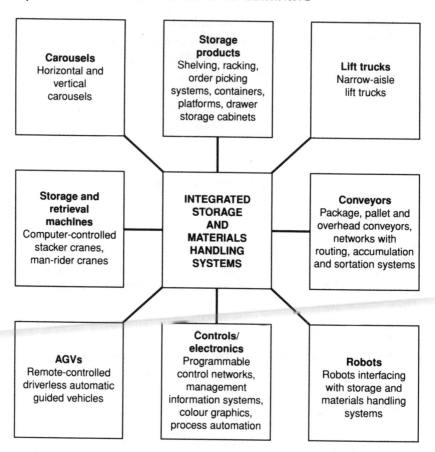

Figure 13.1   Dexion's molecular structure

Circus. Because of his location there he ended up doing jobbing printing for the rag trade[3].

Comino started from nothing, with virtually nothing, in a depressed economic climate. That combination of circumstances instilled in him the idea that you have to fight for yourself, but if you put in all the hours in the day and use your brains you can do it. At the time he had no business picture. He simply wanted to be independent.

It so happened that the printing trade offered marvellous training opportunities for people, including Comino himself: design, copy-writing, visual aspects of printing, the engineering and chemistry of the printing process. Above all, because the job was so physically as well as mentally demanding, it was useful continually to remind everyone "You can do it!" Moreover, in this distinctive environment, at once spatially restricted but technically instructive, seeds were being sown for the ultimate conception of slotted angle.

The communal role: the social transaction

Learning involves a continual interchange between challenge and support. Those who are brave enough to respond to the call to adventure, more often than not (if they are open to it) find in it their source of social support. In time such support builds up into the family feeling that plays so important a part in any learning organization. For Comino's initial source of support was Fred Riley, and that earthy, warm-hearted influence was subsequently to be nourished by the influx of youngsters from the East End, where poor communities were strongly bonded together.

Riley was one of the first few boys Comino took on as apprentices from the slums of London. While he had enormous innate ability, he had no formal education. Comino gave him (and innumerable others) confidence in himself; in his turn, Riley helped Comino to build up a learning organization. The master had the vision of the learning community but it was the disciple who knew how to turn it into a reality. The resulting family feeling is best exemplified by the response of Krisson conscripts during the war years (see panel 13.1).

Panel 13.1
The Krisson Gang

Dear Gang and all responsible for the parcel I have just received. Quite frankly I do not know how to put my appreciation of what I have just received into words. Apart from monetary value, which I realize is quite considerable, the admirable choice and variety of gifts really makes me think I must have chosen a firm and a gang of workmates in a million . . . a firm which, to my mind, has no equal in the world. This must sound a lot of balderdash to you blokes but to me it's just an inkling of how I feel. Anyway if I ever get a chance to repay the firm for the kindness and consideration it has always shown to me, believe me, I'll take it. Thanks for everything gang[4].

The community feeling has continued to manifest itself not only in a "Dexion pride," which still exists some 60 years later, but also in the "classless Dexion society," which stands out in class-ridden Britain. That classless community has provided the context for a family of products and processes that unite "metal-bashers" turning out a "grown man's version of Meccano" on the one hand and professional marketing in international arenas on the other. But such a communal spirit has to be continually renewed if it is to maintain its supportive part in the learning organization. For everything and everyone is relentlessly subject to change.

The intellectual role: learning must be greater than the rate of change

For Comino – a "new-paradigm" leader – one of the most important functions of the manager was to stimulate the problem-solving and learning behavior of others. At Krisson the youngsters were turned into printers, doing staggering things by the standards of the trade. As a result the company found itself in the vanguard of developments in letterpress printing.

Besides on-the-job training there were regular evening classes on problem-solving on the one hand, and on political and economic developments around the world on the other. As Norman Bailey recalled: "I was a country boy who'd been to grammar school before I joined Krisson at the age of 17. Comino saw something in me. I went to his home twice a week. We talked till midnight. He pushed Shaw, Wells and Russell at me. He was my university education."[5]

Once again this focus on learning and questioning, rather than teaching and answering, was borne out during wartime (see panel 13.2).

Panel 13.2
A Boat Sailing Through the Storm

Thank you for the K.P.L. Bulletin – a typical Krisson masterpiece and something to be proud of. How it brought back personalities and showed in a wonderful way how K.P.L. will be making every effort and sacrifice to keep the boat sailing through the storm.

If I kept count of all the useful things I learnt at Krisson that have assisted me here I am sure I should be amazed. It is only occasionally when I ask myself "How did I arrive at that?" that I find Krisson's experience is the answer. Take this for example. I was accused of using too much new round belting. I complained that the quality was not as before. I am proving it by running two sets of 16 side by side doing the same work and noting all the breaks, tightenings, etc. I ask you – where did I learn that?[6]

Some 30 years later, Demetrius Comino was calling for change and learning to become a way of life among managers:

We must train people how to learn for themselves. Learning must become part of the normal work of every manager. Education must be for change and not for a static world. No solution, no process, no knowledge can be permanent or static in the face of change. What can be basic is a set of Basic Unifying Problem-Solving Concepts. In particular Dexion must be a learning organization with a basis of such concepts[7].

The commercial role: the emotionally laden transaction

Krisson, and then Dexion, particularly in their early days, were companies brimming with ideas. Both companies moved with their times, adapting to a changing environment. But whatever ideas were developed intellectually had to be put to the test in the market-place. That required emotional resilience as well as intellectual ingenuity. It also necessitated a collective ability, within the learning organization, to "win friends and influence people."

Krisson, under Comino's influence, unashamedly drew on the Americans for insight into salesmanship. John H. Patterson of National Cash Registers and Dale Carnegie, of public-speaking fame, became gurus to the fledgling companies. In the 1950s Dexion people were often asked whether their firm was American. "Our sales literature was direct and simple. It will do this for you. No fluff. We had a direct approach to selling."[7]

Because neither Comino himself nor his Krisson apprentices had any entrepreneurial or sales background themselves, they felt a need to learn from the most outstanding salesmen and sales-oriented culture. They also realized that they needed to undergo a transformation in emotional as well as intellectual attitudes. While product and people development was therefore "invented here," approaches to market development were learned and adapted from American practice. The adaptation proved so successful that Dexion established a reputation as the company for budding salesmen to join because of its professionally based sales training (see panel 13.3).

Panel 13.3
Winning Friends and Influencing People

I recently attended a Dale Carnegie class. It was a thoroughly enjoyable evening and our class of 50 were all attending for the first time. Hearty laughter and sometimes sympathy was the order of the day when the almost petrified speakers got up to say their piece for two minutes. The girls of the class made charming pictures as they stood on the platform in front of a grinning, predominantly male audience and tried to free their tongue from its glue-like attachment to the roof of their mouth. Their poor faces registered all colours and they sat down at the end with a sigh of relief.

They were all nationalities and all classes, that is porters and executives. After all had made their speeches the instructor told them their faults and would not let them go until they had corrected them[8].

As a learning organization Krisson realized that no matter how good its product or service, how friendly its people, or how brilliant its ideas for improvements, markets had to be exploited and customers had to be won. To succeed in that respect the company had to outgrow its culturally ingrained limitations, through a combination of training and development. These had to be built into the fabric of the organization.

The organizational role: the coordinating transaction

As the learning organization succeeds in projecting its fledgling products or services into the market-place, it comes to realize that a further developmental step is required if it is to establish its identity as separate from the owner's. By the later 1930s Comino had already given Krisson an organizational identity of its own, but it was not a substantial enough organization for someone who wanted, increasingly, to change the world. For Comino had no unique product to call his own. So, during the Second World War, he proceeded to devise one, to be produced by a separate division of the existing organization.

Comino had always been strongly influenced by Henry Ford. The challenge of identifying a broadly based need that could be satisfied through mass production greatly appealed to him. He wanted to be able to multiply the impact of his organization's socially, technologically, and commercially instigated learning on the world stage.

Through the product concept that Comino was exploring he therefore sought to marry up the need – and willingness to pay – of millions of potential industrial consumers, with an intellectual idea realized in a particular physical form. The marriage between demand and supply is what he was after, an integration of technological capability and commercial need. Moreover, he wanted to implant the social form that his people had so carefully nurtured and developed into a technological innovation. He devoted much more thought to new technology and the social form than to any formal organizational or financial arrangements.

The enabling role: the evolutionary transaction

Comino spent several years pondering on a simple, but versatile solution to his own storage problem. He was also well aware that his problem was similar to one faced by thousands of organizations that had to handle and store materials in confined spaces. While still a small printer, he ransacked the trade journals, spent endless hours at the patent office, and went to the Hanover Fair to develop his ideas. Eventually, after some ten years of research and development, and many a false start, he came up with slotted angle. And by the end of the war he had worked out not only the product but also the production process, at least in general terms.

Slotted angle was essentially an enabling technology, just as semiconductors are today: as speedier, more versatile chips are produced every year so the new computers, facilitated by ever more varied computer software, are "enabled" to perform new functions and satisfy an ever-changing range of customer needs. Similarly, the

Dexion product turned out to be a universal building material, the versatility of which was demonstrated in the 1950s at the time of a series of earthquakes in Greece (see panel 13.4).

Panel 13.4
A Universal Building Material

The people of the Greek islands are still clearing up the wreckage of the recent earthquakes and rebuilding their homes. A firm in London is helping in the relief work by sending materials for a number of prefabricated houses as a gift to the island. Today a specimen bungalow of this type was handed over to the Greek ambassador.

The firm that made the gift weren't builders before. This is the first house that they have ever put up. What they do is to supply industry with angled lengths of steel with slots in it. These slotted angle lengths make almost anything – storage racks, machinery platforms, gantries, towers, bins and boxes[9].

Thirty years later the basic slotted angle still sells, but today it is accompanied by an integrated range of allied products, many of which have resulted from subsequent research and development activity.

The creativity role: inventing the product

The inherent originality of Comino's invention lay in its combination of simplicity and versatility. Indeed, because of the product's range and scope, Dexion essentially created an industry for materials – storage and (later) handling equipment – where virtually none had existed before.

In the 1940s the extent to which Comino would be able to follow in Henry Ford's footsteps by turning his dream of large-scale production into a reality was open to question. Like Ford, Comino was interested in producing an economical product for "everyman." Unlike his predecessor, though, his ambition to create a learning organization transcended even his aspiration to beat a path, by means of his new product, to every part of the globe. Ford was quintessentially a car man, an engineer, and a manufacturer; Comino was essentially a renaissance man, a humanist, and a builder:

Resource building was our objective when we started Krisson Printing in 1927. It still is, and I believe it is largely the basis of our success.

I would go further and say that any individual, any company, any nation that deliberately and continuously has as one of its major objectives the building of its resources will inevitably rise above the others and become a leader[10].

Innovation: the return

Learning, or development, for the individual and for the institution, cumulatively involves:

- physical adventurousness and a bias toward action
- social engagement and a family feeling
- mental ingenuity and a learning capability
- emotional resilience and sales orientation
- coordinating ability and integrated controls
- individual openmindedness and enabling institutions
- personal creativity and innovative systems

Innovation, or transformation, for the individual and the organization, turns the potential created into actual performance. The upward movement from physical reality to creative imagination is now reversed into a downward movement from vision to action. The starting point is the vision.

Innovative Management: Actualizing a Vision

Now that the individual and organizational vision, as the culmination of the learning process, has been developed, it has to be communicated. The innovative manager has the task of articulating his or her personal sense of mission, so as to indicate how, in actuality, the vision will serve to solve a universal problem. Moreover, by illustrating how such a vision can transform the world, the innovative manager taps the imagination of all those involved. Finally, and quite obviously, this is not a once-and-for-all process but – like each aspect of organizational learning – needs to be reinforced and renewed continually.

Comino's vision was of a self-governing learning community, spread around a world that had become increasingly "slotted angle conscious." He saw the company as a constructive element of proven value, offering not a take-it-or-leave-it product, but something that people could fashion for their own ends, something fundamentally simple and progressive.

The vision was at the forefront of the company's activities in the 1960s, once Comino had created the new industry. Dexion's products were being used around the globe to build houses for earthquake victims, to construct grandstands for independence celebrations, and to equip explorers for expeditions to the poles – quite aside from its more everyday uses. Toward the end of the 1960s, Comino the innovative manager began to take a back-seat role in the business, devoting his attentions now to the development of people rather than products or markets. The power of the vision henceforth was (potentially if not actually) reduced.

Developmental Management: Recognizing Potential

Recognizing the potential in people and things, in products and markets, is the next important stage in the innovative process. For, whereas the visionary creates potential, the enabler recognizes the emerging technological, social, and commercial opportunities. Developmental management, then, involves a recognition of the underlying needs within and among people and communities, products and market-places. Such recognition leads to organic development of the company and its people.

In the early stages of its development, Dexion was able to recogize the "packets of possibility" in its product-market inter-face. As a result, the enabling technology contained within the original "grown man's Meccano applications" was brought to fruition. Norman Bailey, as managing director in the 1960s, was able to translate this enabling philosophy into sales management. "We're not here to tell the sales force what to do, but to enable them to do what they need to do. Our job is to make it possible. They're the front line."[11]

However, during the 1960s, a series of diversifications took place that involved a transformation of the business rather than a further evolution of it. The innovative and entrepreneurial impulses supplanted the developmental ones. Above all there were shortfalls in executive capacity.

Analytical Management: Structuring Activity

The analytical manager is engaged in:

- defining policies and procedures
- establishing strategies and structures
- articulating the production-market concept
- allocating roles and responsibilities
- delineating boundaries between departments and divisions
- channelling the flow of resources through formalized planning and control mechanisms

Such analytically based activities should represent a channelling of the potential created by the innovator, duly recognized and enriched by the developer.

The executive role played at Dexion by Norman Bailey in the 1960s and 1970s was a somewhat isolated one, preceding as it did the takeover of the company by a new management regime. Bailey recalled that, even in the Krisson days, quarterly reports were issued to parents about all aspects of the apprentices' work. In the 1950s Bailey issued a quarterly report to the sales force; it gave a statistical picture of sales performance, including budgeted versus actual sales, and a commentary on variance.

This kind of analytical role was anathema to Comino from the outset. His meticulous problem-solving processes were applied to production and marketing rather than finance and organization. Moreover, the role of the accountant was never strongly established in the company. Comino himself, aware of the problem if unwilling to confront it head on, maintained in 1965:

> Though we are a successful firm, our success and further progress is hampered by one serious failing. We are not good at routine work, at carrying out procedures according to the rules, promptly and rigorously. The result is that a percentage of our profits are needlessly frittered away. (Comino, 1965: 2)

The reluctance to engage in what we might call maintenance learning was to cost the company dear at the time of economic recession in the early 1980s, when cost-cutting became the order of the day. Yet Comino was able to claim, in terms of personal theory if not of Dexion practice, a fundamental belief in the efficacy of systems (see panel 13.5).

Panel 13.5
The Well-oiled Machine

Rules are unintelligent, they make no distinctions, they restrict our freedom and use of intelligence and initiative. Yet if there were no rules the world in general and our business in particular would be chaotic and unworkable. Rules restrict our freedom on details, but they give us freedom on major matters. . . .

It is true that rules tend to make an organization run like a machine, but machines free us from the details and permit us to use our intelligence on more important things. Because we have an engine in a car that looks after the procedures and details of injecting petrol into the cylinders and igniting the mixture at the right moment, we are free to steer a car. But engines stick to the rules and that is why they operate so smoothly.

It would play havoc with their running if the ignition had initiative and tried alternatives or if the fuel tried to take short cuts. Everything must run to rule and on time; precisely. Rules and procedures are deliberately designed to cut out alternatives in order to make the routine and repeated operations in an organization run like a machine. Just as in a machine it is fatal if people operate one erratically, ignore it or take short cuts. (Comino, 1965: 3)

In practice Comino hated going through the motions – the routine – of running formal meetings. According to Bailey, "I must have run a thousand meetings having the chap with the ultimate authority sitting there, alongside me. Demetrius could not be bothered with following an agenda. That was superficial stuff. He was only interested when it came to some human or industrial policy."[11]

Enterprising Management: Doing Deals

Comino reflected that those of us who drive cars often feel how silly it is to sit waiting for traffic lights to change when there is an obvious opportunity to slip across. This inclination to take a risk, to commit ourselves, and to be enterprising is what brings an organization to life. An original invention, serving an underlying need, located within a structured organization, nevertheless remains still-born. It has yet to be sold.

Panel 13.6
You Can Do It!

In 1949 we granted an American steel company a manufacturing licence to make slotted angle. After two years the company had hardly sold any. There was no market for the product, they claimed. So Comino went over himself. "Take me round some factories," he said to the Americans. As he went around he demonstrated how this and that could be made at half the price using Dexion angle. All the applications could be made at half the price using Dexion angle. All the applications one could imagine lay under their noses. Demetrius subsequently sent over a team of six salesmen from the UK and demonstrated how the Americans could do it. Cheeky. "You don't see what's in the product," he said, "and I do."

I started out as a southern region salesman twelve years ago. After a fortnight I'd had enough; that was until I went out on a call with Arnold Dyer. I became transformed. He brought the job alive. We went to see this plant engineer, bringing with us this sample of five foot high speedlock. We plonked it in the reception area. The guy said we were wasting his time. He'd already placed an order with a competitor. Arnold assured him that it was never too late, and persuaded him to take us on a site visit. Through his persuasive powers Arnold turned the guy completely around. It was magical. A challenge. A contest between two opposing forces. With Arnold selling was a way of life. It stayed with me forever[12].

What are the activities of enterprising management?

The answer might be:

- securing a competitive advantage
- championing a product's cause in the market-place
- taking a calculated financial risk
- selling yourself to others

These are all part of it. In a corporate context this managerial ability is spread throughout the organization to the extent that people's self-centered motives are tapped in the common cause.

One of the American books favored at Dexion in the 1950s was Frank Bettger's *How I Turned Myself from a Failure into a Success*. Bettger's approach was in sympathy with the "You can do it!" philosophy (see panel 13.6), which was inculcated into the original "scout troop" at the Krisson printing works. From the outset Dexion was looking for self-starters in the sales force – people with a will to win. Comino was totally dedicated to the idea of payment for results. From the very start daily records of sales were kept. At the same time people felt themselves to be missionaries for the product. "I took a cut in salary to join this company in 1972. Dexion enjoyed the reputation for having the best sales set-up in the country. You were expected to give 100%" (Bettger, 1941[13]).

Focusing on Dexion's most important managerial concepts, Comino stressed:

1 the dominant position of marketing in top management, orienting the organization toward its customers
2 maximum delegation, enabling the organization to move quickly
3 a willingness to trust youth with responsibility early
4 the creation of stimulation in the work environment
5 the establishment of frank relationships between bosses and subordinates
6 the need for involvement of all personnel[14]

One of the younger salesmen in Scotland, Ray Higgins, represents the continuity of this approach today:

My boss Jim started out selling packs of angle. He's never lost the feel. One of the things I love about selling is that you're getting inside the client's problem. We're geared around ideas. We have what I do believe is the best product. But our competitors don't produce a bad one. Anybody can produce a piece of metal. It's the relationships with our clients that count. People in Scotland are consistently successful with Dexion. They know the Dexion people. A lot of the older clients say "I used to build this out of Dexion Angle."[15]

The Management of Change: Adapting to the Environment

The establishment of any business is not a once-and-for-all operation. Continuing adaptation to change is essential, especially in the fast-moving environment in which business is conducted today. As a result, continuing programs of experimentation and adaptation form a critical part of any organizational development. Such uninhibited experimentation is more often the prerogative of youth than of age.

Yet experiment, problem-solving, and the generation and selection of alternatives remained as important for Demetrius Comino in his sixties as it had been in his youth. If anything he caused damage to his company in the 1970s by continuing to challenge, to diversify, and to probe when Dexion should have been consolidating, focusing, and directing its powerfully constituted energies.

PACRA

Progress arises in science, as in evolution, from the increasing weeding out of error. Thus truth, in scientific terms, is not approached as one would seek a goal, by heading straight toward a distant beacon, visible or visualized. The individual scientist may proceed that way, but as for science as a whole, what it regards as truth is but the strip of possibilities left over after all demonstrable errors have been trimmed away. And this will remain a fairly broad band of uncertainty, including the indeterminate, the unknown, and the indeterminable.

In the process of natural selection or evolution, and in the development of science, two clear and distinct processes stand out: throw up, find, collect a wide range or variety of possibilities, and eliminate rigorously all those that do not fit a set of criteria. This is the basis of PACRA – Purpose, Analysis, Criteria, Resources, Alternatives, and of course eliminate and select.

The original slotted angle emerged out of the PACRA process that Comino has described. The learning community established at the Krisson works was replicated, to some extent, by the research, training, and development that emerged at Dexion. But it has never assumed the same dominating force. In fact, in the business context in the 1970s, the generation of alternatives overbalanced the rigorous elimination of ill-suited diversifications. In the 1980s, however, a balanced learning community existed in Dexion's Scottish plant:

> We take a philosophical view in Dexion Scotland. The attitude here is that mistakes are to be learnt from. It's a question of getting the basic rules right, and then expressing ourselves as individual sales people. If I'd merely come and gone, I'd have seen Dexion as a metal basher. Instead I see ourselves as people who work together to sell solutions to problems. I tend to sell from the perspective of a consultant. Why do you need shelving? What do you want to achieve?[15]

Such processes of action and reflection, trial and error, idea generation and problem-solving have also been built into the high-tech end of Dexion's operations. The handling and electronics divisions of the company are in the business of solving complex problems. At the engineering end of the main storage division the 25-year-old production controller James Cadman, with youthful enthusiasm, is grasping the experimental nettle:

> If there wasn't excitement, I wouldn't be here. In manufacturing we see changes everywhere. The Japanese will soon be selling techniques, not cars. To bring down cost we have to look towards new manufacturing techniques. I've started putting up notices all over the place. SCM. It stands for "Short Cycle Management". We've got people thinking. I'm in the factory solving problems[16].

People Management: Establishing a Learning Community

The "scout group" of young apprentices that Comino brought into Krisson became not only a family but also a learning community. Everyone felt they belonged, there was a sense of community and shared values, productivity was achieved through people, and the whole work force felt close to the customer. Above all, though, it was a learning community in that everyone learned and developed together, as managers, as businessmen, and as human beings.

The challenge that the company has since faced is that of maintaining and developing a learning community, suitably reformed, within the larger-scale Dexion. Such a community would need to emerge out of the broadly based vision of the Dexion Group in the context of Europe in the 1990s, and subsequent to an American takeover.

The takeover followed a period of severe recession, exacerbated by a prolonged steel strike and a three-day working week. It may also be seen as a result of the relatively weak managerial and financial control exercised through Dexion's early life. A change of management regime and waves of redundancies made sharp inroads into "family life." At the same time Comino's move into the background weakened the force of the "learning" side of the Dexion community, for his learning principles and practices had never been formally codified within the company. Nevertheless, the family influence, so strong in the formative years, and the original shared values, continued to exert an influence in the late 1980s, even if they were less all-pervasive. In James Cadman's words:

> When I first joined it was a friendly environment. It came out in the initial interviews. They were looking for someone who could fit into Dexion. Someone who is enterprising, good at communication, and not limited to a profession. My initial view of the organisation was subsequently confirmed. There's an incredible atmosphere. A lot of loyalty. Although things don't always go well the company bonds together[16].

The bonding and the learning have become set somewhat apart over the years. The plight of the company in the late 1970s led the new management to believe that safety through profit was a higher priority than learning through trial and error. As a recent Chairman of the Group, Steve Hinchliffe, indicated:

> Dexion had always been seen as a growth company. Sales and personal relations in the seventies were good. Problem-solving was of a practical rather than of a financial nature. It was also communal in outlook. Everyone and his aunt had to be in on a minor problem. Sometimes no decision was made at all. I tried to get the appropriate individuals responsible[17].

An appropriate blend of responsibility and responsiveness, of communality and of learning, seems to have been arrived at, once again, by the storage center at Dexion Scotland and its sales region.

You can't throw a team together and say "communicate." We like each other. If somebody feels comfortable with their job they have no need to keep somebody else in their place. Youthful enthusiasm here is combined with experience. The vitality of youth is intermeshed with the wisdom of age. We're doing great things. We're becoming leaders in the new technology. We've a new story to tell. We made the slotted angle years ago. Now we're in the electronics business. We've moved on with our customers. We can give them the whole package. We paint a picture of Dexion as a group[18].

The family image, then, in terms of people and products, continues to dominate at Dexion.

Action Management: Making Things Happen

The image of the Dexion product has both a cerebral and a practical element – the problem-solving and the "metal-bashing." For, at the end of the day, any organisation has physically to produce something. For all his intellectual sophistication, the physical product was dear to Demetrius Comino's heart. Furthermore, physical productivity is part and parcel of the company's heritage, as Bill Bates, the production manager, explains:

We built our families on the back of Comino. George Thomson, who started out as a sweeper on the factory floor and ended up as our managing director, would come in with Comino's ideas, and between them they'd make it work. During the Skopje earthquake we worked 24 hours a day to get the product out. During the three-day week in 1971 it happened again[19].

When the company achieved production levels of one-million feet of slotted angle per week there were great celebrations. The physical image of the powerful "metal-bashers" or steel men is also central to the company ethos. Brian Stringer, a youthful but senior buyer in the storage division, joined Dexion not only because of its reputation for training and developing its people but also because "it is a big player in steel, and I love steel."

Finally, as the umpteenth Dexionite extols the Dexion bedrock that forms the firm foundation of his personal and corporate working life, it is plain that vision and action, invisible dream and visible reality, remain connected. To turn such an original vision into continually repeatable action is to complete the productive circle of learning departure and innovative return. The cycle of anticipative learning and precipitative creativity revolves as part of the continuing spiral of business life. And, as in a round of golf, if you fluff a shot or get stuck in a bunker you have to make up the loss later in the game, so in business life any false step or a period of standing still means that later you will need to revisit old ground in order to maintain your progress.

Conclusion

You have now been exposed to a particular learning organization, in Great Britain, viewed also from a particular learning perspective. In order to make it work for you, you may wish to work your way through panel 13.7, an organizational learning exercise, in relation to your own institution. You may explore the implications of organizational learning further through chapter 14, in which we introduce the concept of "total quality learning."

Panel 13.7
Organization Learning

React – the call to adventure

How does your unit keep itself physically and sensually – in terms of touch, smell, taste, sight, and sound – collectively alert?

Respond – making societal connections

How do you attract to your communities what will enhance your organizational learning?

Adapt – learning from organizational experience

How does your organization maintain its exploratory stance and institutional experimentation?

_____

_____

Expose the organization to risk

How does your institution continually expose itself to commercially, technologically, and culturally or socially risk-laden situations?

_____

_____

Conceptualize the organizational activity, systematically

How do you continually conceptualize your unit's activities, both in part and as a whole?

_____

_____

Develop insight – penetrating to the organization's source

How do you develop your powers of insight?

_____

_____

Imagine – enhancing your organizational originality

How do you draw out your people's and your organization's origins, and consequent originality?

_____

_____

In the final analysis, though, organizational learning is only a means to an end; that is, continuing organizational transformation.

Notes

1 D. Comino, "The learning organization," unpublished paper, p. 4.
2 Letter from D. Comino to staff, reproduced in the company journal *Dexion Angle*, June 1964.
3 N. Bailey, interview with the author, 1989. Norman Bailey was formerly the managing director of Dexion.
4 S. Clift, letter in *KPL Bulletin* no. 2, 1940.
5 Bailey, interview, 1989.
6 H. Treasdon, letter in *KPL Bulletin*, 1940.
7 D. Comino, in *Dexion Angle*, July 1966.
8 J. Deller, letter in *KPL Bulletin* no. 2, 1966.
9 News bulletin read by Godfrey Talbot, "BBC Radio Newsreel," February 1957.
10 D. Comino, in *Dexion Angle*, June 1963.
11 Bailey, interview, 1989.
12 T. Reynolds, interview with the author, 1989. Tony Reynolds is the sales director of Dexion Storage Division.
13 Bettger's book is discussed in *KPL Bulletin* no. 3, 1943.
14 Bailey, interview, 1989.
15 R. Higgins, interview with the author, 1989. Ray Higgins is the sales manager of Dexion Scotland.
16 J. Cadman, interview with the author, 1989.
17 S. Hinchliffe, interview with the author, 1989.
18 R. Higgins, interview with the author, 1989.
19 B. Bates, interview with the author, 1989. Bill Bates is production manager of Dexion Storage Division.

References

Bettger, F. 1941: *How I Turned Myself from a Failure into a Success.*
Botkin, J. *et al.* 1979: *The Limits to Learning.* Oxford: Pergamon Press.
Comino, D. 1965: The need for rules. *Dexion Angle*, June.
—— 1970: Change and what it implies. *Dexion Angle*, September.
—— 1971: Why is scientific method so successful? *Dexion Angle*, November, 5.

13

Total Quality Learning

Ronnie Lessem

"Total Quality Management" has taken the business world, in recent years, by storm. However, all too often, such "TQM" merely represents a recontextualizing of old wine in new bottles. For the new-paradigm manager then, "total quality learning" may be a more appropriate concept.

Total Learning – Quality Management

Our underlying premise, in this context, is that quality lies in conformance to human nature, that learning is a natural extension of being human, and that management is an externalization of learning. In so far as "arete" (Greek for excellence) incorporates a duty to yourself, learning is the means to acquire it; in so far as it also encompasses a duty to others, management is a means of applying it. Quality, in that context, forms the bridge between self – the internal – and the external world. Management becomes an extension of human "being," represented in inner-directed learning (arete) and outer-directed quality (excellence), as is indicated in table 14.1.

The problem is that the neat, linear representation, as indicated in the table, is a gross misrepresentation of reality. Strategy, for example, may be quintessentially an exercise of the imagination, but actually it is often a more conceptual, or mental, exercise. Marketing may have an essentially wilful thrust to it, but it is also highly conceptual in its character. In effect, learning and management, like quality, are essentially holographic in nature.

Table 14.1 Management and learning

Human attribute	Learning field	Learning style	Manager's self	Managerial skill	Management knowledge
Imaginative	Holographic	Inspire	Innovative	Create	Corporate strategy
Intuitive	Molecular	Harmonize	Developmental	Facilitate	Organization development
Conceptual	Functional	Deliberate	Analytical	Organize	Finance and accounting
Wilful	Proactive	Energize	Enterprising	Influence	Sales and marketing
Mental	Adaptive	Experiment	Agent of change	Learn	Information management
Social	Responsive	Respond	Animated	Socialize	Personnel management
Physical	Reactive	React	Action-oriented	Direct	Operations management

The Holographic Organization

The holographic paradigm

A hologram is a special type of optical storage system that can best be explained by an example. If you take a holographic photo of, say, a personal computer, and cut out one section of it – the keyboard, for example – you will obtain a picture not of the keyboard but of the whole computer. In other words, each individual part of the picture contains the whole picture in condensed form. The part is in the whole, and the whole is in each part.

The technique of holography was first invented in the mid-1950s, by the Hungarian Nobel Prize winner, Denis Gabor. Some 30 years later, the English nobel physicist David Bohm (see Wilber 1982) concluded (p. 59) that: "In the explicate or manifest realm of time and space, things and events are indeed separate and discrete. But beneath the surface, as it were, in the implicate or frequency realm, all things and events are spacelessly, timelessly, intrinsically, one and undivided." In other words, the physical universe itself seemed to him – just as the organizational universe does to me – to be a gigantic hologram.

The implications of all of this for total learning and for quality management are huge. In the first instance, it becomes apparent that all the elements of learning and of management, identified in table 14.1, are explicitly separate but implicitly integrated. In the "explicate" order, for example, the deliberative style of learning is separate from the reactive one, and such a reactive style is separate from operations management. However, in the "implicate" order they each unfold out of the same unified source.

Within a holographic organizational universe, then, the whole, albeit in condensed form, is contained within each part. The appreciation and manifestation of such a whole, within whatever part, is the essence of quality. Moreover, the more intense the awareness of the whole, within each part, the more total the quality: simplicity means onefoldness; it comes from some simple germ but it might unfold to encompass the complexity of the universe.

The Unfolding Organization

In essence, then, management and organization are not classically ordered in a linear manner. Simple divisions between marketing and finance, or between "energized" and "harmonic" learning, are merely explicate, surface manifestations of a deeper, implicate reality. In such a holographic view of reality, the most profound, inseparable reality is the absolute and infinite state of interconnectedness: within this ultimate source all individuals (or organizations) are contained in potential form. Above that individuals are aware of themselves, but also of their connectedness. On the immediate surface individuals (or, again, organizations) consider themselves to be totally separate. Let us begin on the surface, organizationally speaking, and descend progressively toward the absolute source, relating aspects of learning (chapter 13) to levels of organization.

The reactive organization

The reactive organization, at its most basic, reacts to individual people and events, in a tangible, immediate, and short-term way. Therefore, it exhibits a reactive style of managing and learning, and a myopic operational outlook, individually associated with the exuberance of childhood.

The typical street trader – offering you whatever he happens to have in stock, just to physically capture your attention – is a reactive case in point. His senses are alert, but his thoughts and feelings are comparatively inert. "Managing by wandering about," incorporating Tom Peter's famous "bias for action," is an inherent part of this reactive approach to management and organization. Similarly, "short-termitis" comes from reactive individuals and organizations reacting to surface changes and to tangible phenomena.

The responsive organization

The responsive organization, at the next level down, is immediate and short term in outlook, but responds to individuals' feelings rather than to their actions. For example, if a customer stops buying a particular product the reactive organization would immediately offer it, or any available alternative, at a lower price. The responsive one, on the other hand, will first gain a feeling for what the customer likes and dislikes about the product, and then respond accordingly.

A typical such organization is the family grocery store, also positioning itself "close to the customer." Personal service is its hallmark, and people – whether employees or customers – are treated like personal friends, rather than as either functionalized staff or depersonalized consumers.

Thus the emphasis here is, again in Tom Peter's terms, on "productivity through people" rather than upon optimal human relations, or on any other such abstract notion of social responsiveness. Current approaches to "customer care" and even to TQM often assume such responsive overtones, in the course of taking managers "back to basics." People-managers and responsive learners gravitate toward this homely form of organization, as does the group-oriented young person.

The adaptive organization

The adaptive or "interactive" organization is able to form and reform itself, in continual response to specific environment changes.

As a temporary, rather than permanent organization, it is frequently project- rather than function-based, and thrives on "ad hocracy" as opposed to bureaucracy. Managers of change and experimental learners are therefore best suited to this sort of network-based organization.

Typically small in scale, and high-tech in nature, such enterprises "thrive on chaos." Populated by footloose and fancy-free knowledge workers, adaptive organizations have permeable boundaries, and therefore are easily able to interact with the outside world. Networks, as opposed to hierarchies, are the order of the day; moreover, change – as opposed to continuity – is considered desirable.

Capable of learning at a rate that is faster than the rate of change, such organizations have no need to engage in particularly long-term thinking. They are also unlikely to be able to grow very large, because of their attachment to the temporary and exploratory identity of youth, and due to the fickle character of their networks.

The proactive organization

As you can now see, the simplified polarity between the "reactive" and "proactive" manager or organization represents a vast oversimplification. There are distinctive shades – both responsive and adaptive – in between, and further shades of difference to follow.

The proactive organization is, in fact, the one that most strongly exhibits "autonomy and enterprise." Like its constituent managers, such an organization is demonstrably going places and, for the first time, is not primarily short-term in its orientation. Entrepreneurial managers and energized learners, who thrive in such proactive enterprises, seek out prospectively lucrative and far-reaching commercial opportunities, in the course of dynamically engaging with the external environment.

Such "intraprises" are freewheeling, decentralized profit centers, in which self-selecting "intrapreneurs" are given free rein to pursue their practical imaginations, just like young adults gaining their new-found independence, although bound together in their "club" by shared communal values.

The functional organization

While Charles Handy (1982) regards what we have termed the
adaptive organization as "task-centered," and the proactive enterprise as "power-centered," the functionally based institution is
"role-centered." Typically identified as a bureaucracy, such a role
culture is built upon enduring functional pillars, and is characteristic
of large-scale organizations which are built to last. Analytical
managers and methodical learners thrive in this kind of organization,
which is ordered hierarchically in pyramidical form.

Corporate, regional, and nationally based plans, both short- and
long-term in nature, are – by intention if not in reality – characteristic of these stable and predictable organizations. Relationships are
necessarily compartmentalized and depersonalized. As a result
institutions and their formal representatives, rather than individuals
in informal groups, are their focal point.

This form of functional organization has, up to now, been the
predominant and prevailing form of large-scale organization, both
public and private, capitalist and communist. Not surprisingly, such
an "accountable enterprise" has been championed by the Austro-
American Peter Drucker rather than by the Anglo-American Tom
Peters.

The molecular organization

Whereas the reactive organization is an agglomeration of disconnected people, the responsive organization is a family unit, and the
adaptive organization is a network of professionals, the proactive
organization is an independent enterprise, albeit often built around
an enterprising individual. In other words, such a proactive enterprise, legally represented as a limited company, is the first of the
organizational forms to acquire an "ego" identity, independent of
the people associated with it.

Moreover, the functional organization transcends this independent identity. Those working within it are dependent on outside
stake-holders for their ultimate existence. At the same time –
whether as an IBM, a Singapore Airlines, or as an Ecole Polytechnic
de Lyons – it retains a self-centeredness. In other words, there is a

clear dividing line between itself and the outside world. People remain employed by the institution, shareholders (in a business context) hold shares in the organization, and it is ultimately legally constituted as a corporate whole. What we have called the molecular organization is therefore the first institutional form to lose its independent identity completely, and to be subsumed under not a dependent, but an *inter*dependent one.

A genuine joint venture (see chapter 9) is typical of such a molecular organization. In fact, as dealings with institutional suppliers and customers become progressively more long-term and complex, an enduring molecular form of relationship supplants the merely horizontal or vertical ones. This form of inter-organization comes naturally to the developmental manager and to the harmonic learner. Individuals in mid-life, in seeking to recognize and subsequently harmonize the different parts of themselves, are potentially receptive to such molecular form. In effect, it results in a trans-personal, trans-organizational and transnational orientation which supplants the individual, corporate, and national ego. In that context, the humility and "ego lessness" of the east is better suited to such molecular organization – witness "Japanese Inc." – than the egotism of the west.

The holographic organization

We finally reach down to the ultimate organizational form which underpins this whole book; for whereas the molecular organization involves intense interconnectedness, the holographic form transcends even such interdependent form. As Marilyn Ferguson (see Wilber, 1982), the American organizational psychologist and futurist has pointed out, in the course of linking ancient wisdom with contemporary brain research:

> In the heaven of Indra there is said to be a network of pearls so arranged that if you look at one you will see all the others reflected in it. In the same way, each object in the world is not merely itself but involves every other object, and in fact is every other object.

In other words, Pirsig (1990) finds his Godhead in the circuits of a digital computer, and the organization becomes a gigantic hologram.

For Pirsig the "classical" is concerned with the separate parts: the

A particle   A wave

Figure 14.1   Particle–wave duality

"romantic" brings together the interconnected whole. In this holographic field of the creative manager (as well as the inspired learner,
and the wholly mature individual) learning and managing, operations
and finances, knowledge and skill, manager and organization, product and market, institution and environment become, on the one
hand, discrete and separate phenomena and, on the other, holographic reflections of each other. In fact, this complementarity
between part (classical) and whole (romantic), like that between
particle and wave, is the characteristic of total learning and quality
management, just as it is of quantum physics.

The Principle of Complementarity

The quantum physicists, as distinguished from the Newtonian
classicists, have demonstrated that at the atomic level matter has a
dual aspect; it appears as particles and as waves. Light, for example,
is emitted and absorbed in the form of "quanta" or photons, but
when these particles of light travel through space they appear as
vibrating electromagnetic fields which show all the characteristic
behavior of waves (see figure 14.1). Similarly, in this chapter, we
have alternated between "particle" and "wave" orientations, both of
which are required for total learning and for quality management.

Particles of learning and of innovation, of development and of
transformation, are the seven discrete "horizontal" elements, or
states, of the spectrum. Waves of learning and innovation, of
development and of transformation, are represented by the "vertical" and essentially interconnected flows. These involve both the
inner journey, between physical reality and creative imagination, as
well as the outer journey, between vision and action.

Alternatively, these complementary forces – "classical" particles
and "romantic" waves – also make up the two sides of quality.
Moreover, in David Bohm's terms, they represent the respectively
explicate and implicate orders (see figure 14.2).

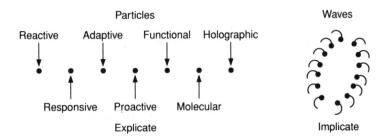

Figure 14.2   The explicate and implicate orders

Conclusion

The prolific and popular writer on biology and ecology, Lyall Watson (1980), has used an analogy to describe the principle of holography, which will ultimately help us to integrate quality and learning. If, he says, you drop a pebble into a pond, it will produce a series of regular waves that travel outward in concentric circles. Drop two identical pebbles into the pond at different points and you will get two sets of similar waves that move toward each other. Where the waves meet they will interfere.

If the crest of one coincides with the trough of another, they will cancel each other out and produce an isolated patch of calm water – the same thing as Robert Pirsig's "peace of mind," which arises when the craftsman, or new-paradigm manager, is so at one with his or her work that true quality results.

In fact, there may be many different combinations of interacting waves, particularly if you increase the number of pebbles dropped from two to seven, equal to the full spectrum. The final result is a complex pattern of ripples, known as the "interference pattern."

Light waves, then, behave in exactly the same way as the ripples in the water. When two laser beams touch they produce an interference pattern that can be recorded on a photographic plate. The record, if reflected off an object, will be a hologram. In equivalent terms, it takes communication between any two waves on the learning spectrum – for example, reactive and responsive ones – to produce an interference pattern. Such a pattern, if accommodated by a wholly receptive learning organization (the highly sensitive photographic plate), and subsequently reflected off an object (a product or service), will provide a holographic picture of quality.

When quality and learning become holographically integrated no part can stand in isolation of the whole. The reactive organization becomes a reflection of the unified whole in the same way as the commodity sold by the manager–trader is perceived as an explicate entity of an implicate unity. Duty to yourself, as an individual, is integrated with duty to others, within the organization, as an interference pattern. To the extent that the division between managing and learning, or between producer and consumer, is an explicate order divorced from an implicate one, a part disconnected from the whole – then true quality cannot exist.

As we learn and develop, then, as a managerial and organizational species, we need to transform our institutions – from reactive and molecular, or even adaptive, proactive, or functional ones – into molecular and ultimately holographic entities. Once we mature in this way the whole notion of quality will change its functional identity – Crosby's (1978) "fitness for purpose" or "conformance to standard" – to a holographic identity, Pirsig's "Godhead." In the process, and as Jagdish Parikh (1992) has indicated, we will develop from "innocent" and professional operators into true "master managers." As such, we differentiate and integrate the parts – reactive, responsive, adaptive, proactive, functional, and molecular – within a holographic whole. And whereas the inward manifestation is a process of learning, the outward realization is a product of quality.

References

Crosby, W. 1978: *Quality without Tears*. London: Pan.
Handy, C. 1982: *The Gods of Management*. London: Pan.
Pinchot, G. 1985: *Intrapreneuring*. New York: Harper and Row.
Parikh, J. 1992: *Managing Your Self*. Oxford: Blackwell.
Pirsig, R. 1990: *Zen and the Art of Motorcycle Maintenance*. London: Black Swan.
Hampden-Turner, C. 1990: *Charting the Corporate Mind*. Oxford: Blackwell.
Watson, L. 1980: *Lifetide: the Biology of Consciousness*. New York: Simon & Schuster.
Wilber, K. (ed.) 1982: *The Holographic Paradigm*. Colorado: Shambhala. See articles by D. Bohm, I. Bentov, and M. Ferguson.

14

Requisite Organization
Elliott Jaques and Stephen D. Clement

Hierarchical Layering

The progressive unfolding, or indeed layering, of organizations has been a preoccupation of the prominent Canadian management thinker, Elliott Jaques, for decades. In seeking after his so-called "requisite organization," he has developed his own concept of organizational learning. Three works, published between 1976 and 1991, chart this development.

Central to managerial organizations, for Jaques, is the meaning and structure of the hierarchical layering, since that is what these organizations are fundamentally about. This method of layering is a true human discovery, like fire or the wheel, which originated in China some 3,000 years ago. It was a major event in the transition from the family/tribal society to the more dispersed type which we take for granted.

How many layers should any organization have? Layering should be such as to encompass successive categories of task complexity within each stratum of organization. Seven categories of task complexity are used in managerial hierarchies. Equivalent firm boundaries of real managerial layers have been found by Jaques to exist at time spans of one day, three months, one year, two years, five years, 10 years, and 20 years. The prime act of managerial leadership in any organization, therefore, is to establish an effective and efficient work organization where the work gets done by competent individuals, at just the right organizational strata to deal with the inherent complexity of the work itself.

Levels of work

Work is defined by Jaques as that plane of human activity in which the individual exercises discretion, makes decisions and acts in seeking to transform the external world in accord with a predetermined goal. Bureaucratic systems are social systems which call upon individuals to work in a setting in which the goals of the activity are set by the employing institution through its managers in the form of assigned tasks, rather than by the individual.

Bureaucracies, moreover, are hierarchical systems. They contain a range of different levels, reflected in different levels of work. Jaques's definition of level of work is given in the form of a measuring instrument based upon the maximum of time spans during which people are required to exercise discretion. He suggests, as a first proposition, that there is a universally distributed depth structure of levels of bureaucratic organization, of natural lines of stratification. The second proposition is that the existence of the stratified depth structure of bureaucratic hierarchies is the reflection in social organization of the existence of discontinuity and stratification in the nature of human capacity. The capacity is referred to as work capacity, which is further analyzed in terms of a person's level of abstraction. A multimodal distribution of capacity is postulated.

The third proposition is that the rate of growth of your work capacity follows predictable paths. Maturational shifts in the quality of your capacity occur as you move across the boundary from one level of abstraction to another. The discovery that measured time span, or measured distance of goals into the future, corresponds to subjective feelings of levels of work, is like the discovery that the measured length of a column of mercury in a thermometer corresponds to subjective feelings of warmth. This leads Jaques on to the keystone of his argument, relating to cognitive processes.

Making information available for work

The concept of cognitive processing, for Jaques, lies at the heart of any possibility of understanding the nature of competence at work. Cognitive processes are the mental processes by means of which you are able to organize information to make it available for doing work. This processing enables you to deal with information complexity. When your cognitive processing is up to the complexity, you are comfortable. Cognitive power is the potential strength of cognitive processes in a person, and is therefore the maximum level of task complexity that he or she can handle at any given point in his or her development. Just as we find that the greater a person's cognitive power, the larger is the mass of information that can be coped with, so we find that the greater the person's cognitive power, the longer is that person's time horizon.

Levels of mental processing

Cognitive processes are the mental processes by means of which you are able to organize information to make it available for doing work. Not only do cognitive processes come in greater or lesser degrees of complexity, they proceed in discontinuous jumps. Each of these steps is characterized by a change in the nature of the cognitive process, just as some substances change in state from crystalline to vapor when they are heated. For Jaques, there are four types of cognitive processes:

1 (First-level) **assertive processing** organizes information and pulls it together in a form that is directly relevant to the immediate situation.
2 (Second-level) **cumulative processing** reasons by accumulating possibly significant pieces of information and organizing them in relation to each other so as to be able to combine them into a decision.
3 (Third-level) **serial processing** reasons by putting information together in some logical sequence – a progressive story, an algorithm or a decision tree.
4 (Fourth-level) **parallel processing** reasons by organizing information into a number of separate trial processes, and then deals with the information in each of these processes in parallel, showing how they impact upon each other.

A fundamental point is that as we mature, we progress through developmental stages, moving from one type of cognitive processing to the next more complex type. But there is more to management, for Jaques, than cognition. Such layers of mental processing, in the person, are therefore interspersed with layers of complexity in the task environment.

Cognitive processes: the worlds in which people manage

In the same way as there are layers of ever-greater complexity within our managerial heads, so there are such layers of progressively increasing complexity in the world in which we manage. Such increasingly complex groups of data in the external world we must assimilate and use to inform our cognitive processing in our internal world to solve problems. There are, according to Jaques, four orders of complexity of information:

1 First-order concrete things, that is, specific things that can be pointed to. The variables are clear and unambiguous ("use this tool;" "employ him, not her"), they are not tangled together, and they are relatively unchanging.

2 Second-order verbal abstraction, through which we are able to discuss our work and to issue instructions to others in a manner that makes it possible to run factories, to design new products, to discuss orders with customers, to record data and produce financial accounts, to maintain information systems and generally carry out the activities necessary to manage a business unit. Concrete variables have to be grouped into useful categories in order to see the wood and not get lost in the trees.

3 Third-order conceptual abstraction, whereby, for example, balance-sheet values serve to bring together a wide range of accounting categories, which can in turn be translated into a large array of items of revenue and expenditure, assets and liabilities. The factors, such as financial policies and political circumstances, are very ambiguous, continually changing and inextricably entangled together.

4 Fourth-order universal abstraction, whereby concepts are grouped together into the universal ideas that are required for handling the problems of whole societies.

Cognitive processes in the instrumentation business

These also follow the four orders already mentioned.

1 Concrete things are encountered regularly in selling products to technical buyers. Questions such as "How big is it?" and "How hot does it get?" require immediate answers.
2 Verbal abstraction is home ground to the designer or scientist. Concepts such as bandwidth, frequency and risetime can only be discussed and measured if there is an appreciation of the theory underlying each.
3 Conceptual abstraction becomes part and parcel of work with the client organization. "Preferred-Vendor Policies" or "Ethical Purchasing Policies" are likely to change with world events. While the individual salesperson may seldom encounter such concepts, they are an essential part of marketing as a whole.
4 Universal abstraction in the sales-and-marketing context seldom impinge on the business, and are usually broken down and addressed as lower-order abstractions.

Categories of Potential

Layers within layers

As we mature, we move not only from less to more complex cognitive processes but also rise in the orders of information complexity that we can handle. We obtain a series of recursions of the four cognitive processes in each of the four worlds of information complexity. Different individuals will mature to different levels of complexity at different stages of their lives. Jaques refers to "category of potential capability" (CPC) as a particular cognitive process within a given order of information complexity. Whereas the first order of complexity, A, is clear-cut, the second and third orders, B and C, each have layers to them. Finally, category D, like A, is equally definitive but now at the highest order of complexity.

Second-order cognitive process (B)

Verbal abstractions, then, unlike the definitive nature of concrete things, can range from unsupported assertions – "I can't stand my boss" – to arguments supported by logic – "My boss is a difficult person because. . . ." More specifically, there are the following:

B1: Unsupported verbal assertions, through which people argue with unconnected strings of assertions – "Well, it's wrong, isn't it?", or "You don't know what you're talking about", or "I disagree with you."

B2: Arguments supported by data, whereby people support their views with accumulated information to justify them: "We're selling the wrong product; look at the declining sales figures over the past six months" or "He's the right man for the job, look at the high-powered positions he's held over the past ten years."

B3: Arguments supported by logic, whereby an argument is organized in sequence, in which one thing leads to another, or may have led on, one from another, in the past. "My experience has been that such an approach to promoting our cars is a bad idea. I've worked in Germany and I have found that the Germans there are not receptive to a brash line of advertising approach. And they have good reasons to react against it. Their whole educational background is oriented, especially when it comes to matters of technic, to quality rather than quantity."

B4: Parallel processing of several lines of argument, whereby two or more arguments are pursued and aspects from each related to one another. "When I think about it, neither promotion from within nor selection from without is exclusively right. Let me outline the pros and cons of each, and then make my intermediate case."

Third-order cognitive process (C)

We now move on from second-order to third-order categories of processing potential, identifying three layers of possibility.

C1: Conceptually formulated assertions, whereby statements of principle are grounded in practical examples – "Look, let me get back to the principle I was putting forward" – without being able to articulate it, support it with data or relate principles.

C2: Arguments supported by related concepts, whereby mutually reinforcing concepts are interrelated (say, of salesmanship and of consumer motivation). "Salesmanship, as a matter of arousing attention, interest, desire, and action (AIDA) – in that order – can be related to Maslow's hierarchy of personal motivation."

C3: Serial conceptual arguments, whereby the values pursued are linked to progressively higher-order issues, such as profitable sales being associated with the advancement of individual learning, or the betterment of social welfare. There is an overall difference, finally, between what Jaques terms "hollow" language, mere words or academic arguments, and "solid" language, based upon real, personal experience.

We now turn from the individual and managerial to the institutional and organizational, albeit still within a cognitively based analytical as well as hierarchical framework.

Role Complexity and Task Complexity

Layers of complexity

What Jaques postulates, as we have seen, is the existence of a universal bureaucratic depth structure, composed of organizational strata with boundaries at levels of work represented by time spans of three months to 20 years. These strata are real in the geological sense, with observable boundaries and discontinuity. They are not mere shadings and gradations. Requisite organization of bureaucracy must be designed accordingly. In other words, strata of organization need to be built up that are "requisite" for the complexity of the task at hand. The complexity of a task lies in the number, variety, rate of change, and degree of interweaving of the variables involved in it.

Jaques identifies seven such levels, or strata, of organization, drawn from a combination of categories of inner and outer complexity, of the first and second order. Whereas first-order complexity – that is, the concrete world – stands prior to organization, the fourth order – universal world – for Jaques, lies beyond it. The work of a single craftsman, on the one hand, and of an individual "guru," on the other, lies outside the realms of Jaques's organization.

Strata of organization

Second-order complexity

(1) **Stratum 1: Direct action** (B1): These are shop-floor – or office-level – activities, requiring a person to proceed along a prescribed linear path, getting continual feedback in order to do so, for example drilling holes with a hack hammer, or typing a letter.

(2) **Stratum 2: Diagnostic accumulation** (B2): These kinds of task are found at first-line managerial level; the individual must anticipate potential problems through accumulating significant data – designing a new jig for a machining process, working out the design as the job proceeds.

(3) **Stratum 3: Alternative serial plans** (B3): Increasingly complex situations require alternative plans to be constructed before starting out, one to be chosen and serially progressed to completion – heading a project team to create a new software program, having initially to select between alternatives with varying times, costs, specifications.

(4) **Stratum 4: Mutually interactive programs** (B4): These comprise a number of interacting programs which need to be planned and progressed in relation to each other. Tradeoffs must be made between tasks to make progress along the composite route – new venturing requires a combination of overlapping product development, market analysis, product engineering, and commercial assessment, with mutual adjustment along the way.

Third-order complexity

(1) **Stratum 5: business-strategy formulation** (C1): These are the kinds of tasks faced by presidents of strategic business units in large corporations. Practical on-the-spot judgements must be used to deal with a field of ambiguous conceptual variables, and to make decisions envisaging second- and third-order consequences – such

as setting half a dozen critical tasks to achieve a seven-year plan, continually picking up important areas of impact and likely consequences of change, keeping profitability at a reasonable level while maintaining customer goodwill, high employee morale and a growing asset base.

(2) **Stratum 6: developing a supportive business environment** (C2): At this level executives must build up a picture of likely critical events worldwide, using international networking to accumulate information about potentially significant developments that could affect the business and its units, forestalling adverse events and sustaining a friendly environment for corporate trade.

(3) **Stratum 7: envisioning the future** (C3): At this ultimate point Chief Executive Officers (CEOs) work out strategic alternatives for world-wide operation, using complex conceptual information concerned with culture, with values, and with the business of nations and international trade well into the 21st century

Because, in the final analysis, each category of task complexity has a corresponding category of cognitive complexity in human beings, complexity in work can be matched with complexity in people in the same organizational layer.

These propositions can be applied not only to the design of organizational structure for bureaucracies but also to coping with changes in these systems induced by the developing capacities of their employees. If the propositions are valid and reliable, Jaques argues, they will show that the relationship between bureaucracy and individuality is not an unresolvable conflict to be softened by uncomfortable compromise. Rather, it is a dilemma which can be dealt with by creative interaction between social institution and individual.

Levels of abstraction

The functionalist type of argument, Jaques maintains, that bureaucratic systems are economically efficient in themselves, and that these systems were established in order to get the necessary work done, is, at best, incomplete. Social systems cannot endure if they are not closely attuned to a person's nature. If, for example, all people were equal in work capacity, the bureaucratic hierarchy would be an impossible social system. Employees would have worked together in leaderless groups, but a bureaucratic hierarchy, Jaques asserts, never! Nor can the nature of tasks readily explain the phenomenon. For tasks are artificial things. They are products of human desire and aspiration, created by human imagination of the objects to be produced as the output of the task. According to Jaques, any evidence that there might be not only a hierarchy of tasks but also an inherent discontinuous stratification of tasks would therefore point to stratification of populations with respect to the mental functioning of its members. Each of the discrete levels described is a level of abstraction. These levels, or strata, of cognitive complexity are central to Jaques's notion of "requisite" management and leadership.

We now turn from this richly laden perspective on cognitively based learning and development to Jaques's more limited affective and behavioral orientation.

Managerial Leadership

Effective leadership

Effective leadership, for rationally minded Jaques, is indistinguishable from "requisite" management. It demands four straightforward and basic conditions.

1 A person must have the necessary competence to carry the particular role, including strongly valuing it.
2 That person must be free from any severely debilitating psychological characteristics that interfere with interpersonal relationships.
3 The organizational conditions must be requisite, that is, conforming to the properties of hierarchical organizations and human nature.
4 Each person must be encouraged to use their natural style, namely, to allow the full and free expression of their natural self.

Cognition and capacity

Central to Jaques's concept of "requisite" management, as we have seen, is the manager's powers of cognition. In that sense, Jaques is a direct disciple of Piaget. However, he is also concerned with values, knowledge and skills, wisdom and temperament. Ever inclined to use mathematical formulae, Jaques describes the relationship between capacity and a group of seminal learning concepts:

current actual capacity (CAC) $= fCP.V.K/S.Wi \; (-T)$, where CP is cognitive capacity (that is, mastery of complexity); V are values, interests, and priorities; K/S is the skilled use of relevant knowledge; Wi is wisdom about people and things; and $(-T)$ is the absence of serious personality/temperament defects.

Current potential capacity (CPC), moreover, is the maximum level at which a person could currently work, given optimum opportunities and conditions, provided that the work is of deep inherent value for the person, even though he or she has not had past opportunity to acquire the necessary skilled knowledge. A person's CPC is determined by his or her cognitive power alone. Such cognitive power determines the level at which he should be employed. Future potential capacity, finally, is the maximum level at which a person will be capable of working, say, at five, ten or fifteen years into the future.

Values, knowledge, wisdom, and temperament

Values and motivations

Jaques's experience is that everyone will put their best effort into doing what they value. People, he says, are spontaneously energetic with respect to things that interest them. The issue is not to encourage output by incentives but to provide conditions in which the work itself has its inherent value and allows the individual to release and direct his or her energy and imagination into the work.

The core of motivation, then, lies in valuing something. If we value something we will try to attain it. Values range from generic to specific. **Generic** values are usually referred to as our philosophical or ethical position. **Specific** values are the things we currently give priority to, or spend our energy pursuing. To be an effective managerial leader a person must really value the opportunity to work with subordinates and value being able to unleash their enthusiastic and effective collaboration. Get the values right, Jaques argues, and such factors as style and personality will fall in line.

Knowledge and skills

We learn from our experience, from teaching, and from practice. We store our learning in the forms of knowledge and skill in the use and application of that knowledge. By knowledge, we refer to objective facts, including procedures, which can be stated in words, formulae, models, or other symbols that one can learn. By skill, Jaques refers to the application of facts and procedures that have been learnt through practice to the point that they can be used without thinking.

The key issue, for Jaques, is not that leadership capacities, such as communication or listening skills, can be taught but that the necessary conditions for effective managerial work must be set. It is specifically necessary to have a requisite organizational structure, with layers sufficiently wide and few to call for managers who are one category in cognitive complexity above their immediate subordinates, and who are working at a level of task complexity that is also one category higher. It is also necessary to have established a range of requisite managerial practices for managers to carry out, which can be taught and which managers can, with practice, learn to use without having to think about them.

Thus education in managerial leadership, according to Jaques, should be approached not in terms of the inevitable vagaries of "leadership skills" but, instead, by learning standard practices that have been formulated for clear understanding and teaching. Our knowledge provides the verbal framework within which we organize and set contexts for our work. It enables us to set contexts for subordinates as the prime act in managerial leadership. Knowledge and its appropriate skilled use enable us to organize our field of work so that our nonverbal cognitive process can handle the complexity of the field more readily.

Wisdom and temperament

Action without sound theory, Jaques believes, can be counterproductive. Unsound theories distort our experience, narrow our vision and leave us none the wiser about the effects of our actions on others. Wisdom can be developed in people, especially by good mentoring by a more senior person. For rationally minded Jaques, though, in the final analysis, focus upon personality traits is misguided. Emotional make-up has little effect upon the person's in-role leadership work, unless these qualities are at unacceptable or abnormal extremes, and the person lacks the self-control to keep from disturbing his or her work relationships. In the English language, Jaques maintains, there are over 2,500 personality variables which are possessed to a greater or lesser extent by everyone. This large range of commonly occurring characteristics combines in infinitely varied patterns to give the great richness in personality make-up, all of which is likely to be better or worse. For Jaques, "Our argument is that the personality variable figures in managerial leadership in a negative rather than a positive way."

Many people would argue that it is precisely by understanding and attending to the special emotional needs and personality styles of each individual that a "leader" can best motivate a follower. But that can result in the "difficult" personalities getting special attention as compared with their more collaborative colleagues. This is not what managerial hierarchies should be about. Managerial hierarchies are not seller–buyer situations, nor families. It is simply not acceptable, Jaques argues, for individuals to behave in ways that are disruptive of working relationships. How, for Jaques, are people developed?

Fostering the development of individuals

Mentoring and coaching

The art of the development of individuals is:

1 To take note of the rate of growth of their potential and try to provide work opportunities consistent with it.
2 In addition, they should be given the opportunity to consider

their values, gain the necessary skilled knowledge, fortify their wisdom, and take the necessary steps to get rid of any seriously abnormal personality quirks they may have.

Mentoring, in relation to the first of these, is the process whereby a manager–once–removed (MoR) helps the individual to understand his or her potential and how it might be applied to achieve full career and organizational growth. There are three major approaches to the second. Coaching is the process through which a manager helps subordinates to understand the full range of their roles and then points out the subordinate's strengths and weaknesses.

Teaching and training

Teaching is the imparting of knowledge to individuals by lecturers, discussion, and practice. Training is a process of helping individuals to develop or enhance their skill in the use of knowledge through practice, either on the job or in a learning simulation. Skill enables individuals to use their knowledge in problem-solving activities without having to think, thus freeing up discretion and judgement.

Career progress and level of aspiration

Whereas an individual's aspiration toward equilibrium between work capacity and level of work is absolute, that between level of work and payment is relative. In the case of pay, Jaques argues, each person's aspirations appear to be geared to a sense of fairness of economic reward relative to others. In the case of work, however, each person's level of aspiration is geared to his or her deepest feelings of reality and freedom.

The construction of adequate grading and progression systems, therefore, is an essential mechanism for making individual freedom real. For if their levels of work in time-span terms are shorter than their time-span capacity, individuals will be deprived of the opportunity to test their capacity at full stretch, that is, to maintain their relationships with reality over as wide a spectrum as possible. Conversely, if their levels of work are longer than their current work capacity, their freedom will be destroyed in that their relationship to reality will be disorganized and their deepest anxieties aroused. Whereas, Jaques believes, all employees should be entitled to receive periodic assessments of the adequacy of their performance from their immediate managers, MoRs should be responsible. Such judgements need to be made at least from the next higher level of abstraction, Jaques says, if they are to be genuinely detached.

Growth of Bureaucratic Systems

Bureaucratic systems, for Jaques, are internally live and changing, as the occupants of the systems join, develop, change, and leave. There is a continual ebb and flow, with stable periods and critical change periods. At the same time, different parts of the system change at different rates, as do the individual members of these parts of the system.

It is precisely by identifying such differences in individuals that a society can accomplish two important social ends: firstly, it can arrange social procedures to make it possible for everyone to gain a level of work and career consistent with his or her work capacity; secondly, it can bring political power and legislative control to bear to ensure that bureaucracy is managed in a manner consistent with the political outlook of society. Thus, whether or not bureaucratic organization would lead to economic elitism would be a political decision.

Size of organization, Jaques maintains, tends commonly to be regarded as a function of size of market, the nature of the economy, the type of technology and other such external factors. They are necessary but not sufficient. For Jaques, ultimately, the distribution of sizes of bureaucracy will be determined by the distribution in level of work capacity of those available to manage the bureaucracies.

There is a kind of Archimedes' principle at work, whereby bureaucratic systems grow to the level-of-work capacity of their chief executives; conversely, chief executives stimulate bureaucratic systems to grow to the level consistent with their work capacity. In fact, in posing the existence of up to seven strata of organization, preconditioned by executive work capacity, Jaques is following in the structural footsteps of Jean Piaget.

Progressive abstraction

According to Jaques, as the strata of operation ascend, from the practicality of the operational world to the abstraction of general management, the total field is available now to the manager only in conceptual form, in histograms of performance, drawings of product families and other such conceptual models. He must have that sense of security in his abilities to let go to some extent of the concrete outside world, and to rely upon an interplay between data of immediate experience and data culled from mental constructs. The manager or administrator must learn how to work from an office, not in complete detachment but with sufficiently frequent contact with the various parts of his domain to keep lively examples in mind of the activity of the situation he is dealing with in abstract.

Conclusion

In so far as managers are able to deal with progressively higher degrees of abstraction, so they will be helping their institutions to evolve through their organizational strata. At the same time, to the extent that any organization is "requisitely organized" so it will enable its members not only to manage appropriate levels of complexity but also to learn and develop as they mature. Managerial learning, for Jaques, is reflected in an individual's ability to cope with progressively higher levels of complexity, as he or she matures. Moreover, organizational learning and development takes place when there is a good match between organizational strata and cognitive capacities. Such development is individually preordained and organizationally orchestrated.

Finally, in this section on organizational learning, we turn to Charles Hampden-Turner's approach to "Charting the corporate mind," by managing dilemmas.

References

De Madariaga, S. 1968: *Portrait of Europe*. Hollis & Carter.
Gardner, H. 1974: *Quest for Mind*. New York: John Wiley.

Jaques, E. 1976: *A General Theory of Bureaucracy*. London: Heinemann.
—— 1989: *Requisite Organization*. Arlington, Virginia: Cason Hall.
—— 1991: *Executive Leadership*. Oxford: Blackwell/Arlington, Virginia: Cason Hall.
Revans, R. 1980: *Action Learning*. London: Blond and Briggs.

15

Charting the Corporate Mind
Charles Hampden-Turner

Introduction

A living system

If we assume, as we did in chapter 13, that our learning organization is a living system, then there are dilemmas which arise from this:

- any biological or social system is differentiated in its function, yet these need to be integrated if the whole is to develop
- its members must have some local freedom and discretion, yet all remain subject to the captain's authority and command
- orders must go from the top down, yet these cannot maintain their quality unless information goes from the bottom up to educate decision-makers
- the captain empowers his subordinates to make certain judgements and decisions, yet expects their exercise of such responsibility to confirm his own power and influence in the ship
- all crew members may legitimately compete with each other to achieve the skills of seamanship but all must cooperate in furthering the effectiveness of the ship itself

We could multiply such tensions indefinitely.

Virtuous and Vicious Circles

Not all so-called cybernetic systems are benign and not all result in leaders or organizations learning. Systems can grow "virtuously" or they can regress "viciously" and it can mean life itself to recognize the

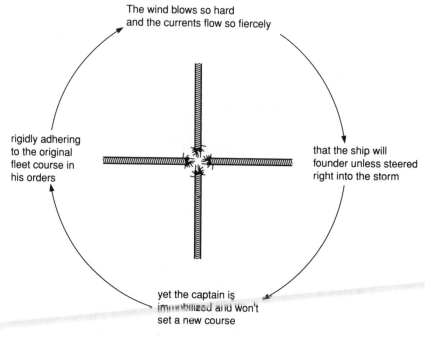

Figure 16.1

difference. In vicious circles the tensions between opposing "sides" of the circle (or horns of the dilemmas) become so severe that "the rope snaps." In other words, the mutually constraining influence of values in tension is lost and the system "runs away." Let us return to our nautical metaphor and consider the case of Captain Queeg on the bridge of the *USS Caine* at the height of the typhoon, described in Herman Wouk's *The Caine Mutiny*. Because the storm is clearly in charge of the situation we have begun with the unruly elements (figure 16.1).

Note what happens when the "tensions snap." The captain no longer responds to the typhoon, and the ship's course no longer responds to the danger of capsizing. Yet the arrows feeding around the circle continue their vortex of mutual intensification. The more the storm rages, the more the captain is immobilized, and the more the ship is inundated by the waves, the more rigidly the captain repeats "Fleet course is 110 degrees!" Each opposed element is escalating the force of its opposition. The storm and the ship's increasing danger is immobilizing and rigidifying the captain, while the latter's rigidity is increasing the peril of his ship and the dire effects of the storm, with a vicious circle resulting.

The anthropologist Gregory Bateson called this process **schismo-genesis**, "a growing split in the structure of ideas." In this example "the wind blowing" gets split apart from "how the captain should steer the ship," and the ship's "imminent foundering" gets split apart from "the jbest direction to steer." The splitting in this story occurred within the paranoid mind of the captain. The Navy dealt with this split by court-martialling the officers who relieved him but finding them innocent.

Note that only an organization that heals its split can learn as the US Navy learned in this story. Split systems "run away" until they self-destruct. This is what would have happened to the Caine had not Lieutenant Maryk relieved Captain Queeg and then headed the ship into the wind so as to give its screw some purchase in the water. This action reconnected the snapped nerves of the ship's social system and it survived.

Vicious circles are not usually the products of a psychotic break within a leader or the disintegration of his or her mind. It is more common for leaders to prevent their own disintegration by siding with one clique or faction against the others. In this way they "save" themselves, yet the organization is severed. Whether or not a leader has personally contributed to the "growing split in the structure of ideas," the dynamic has a momentum of its own, and the leader may be as one "tied between wild horses" and is pulled apart psychologically by the "snapping ropes" at the center of the vicious circle. Because dilemma is so painful, many managers prefer to rend the system rather than rend themselves; yet this will blind the managers to the polarity they have rejected and may fatally cripple the organization's capacity to learn.

Splitting, then, which precipitates a vicious circle, is an often inadvertent response to painful stress and anxiety from which the individual flees to find support within a clique. This can happen in all kinds of corporate conflict. Automobiles designed and made by even the most dedicated producers will not necessarily delight their intended customers. Workers will not necessarily see the purpose of the organization as identical with their own purposes. Rather than assume a unanimity which is not there, or an ideological antagonism which is everlasting, why not recognize a dilemma the pain of which must be endured so that it can be resolved? Resolve means to solve again and again. Just as the helmsman keeps noting errors and correcting them, so dilemmas do not go away but perpetually represent themselves in changing forms and varieties. Employees may develop (or regress) in their levels of skill. Shareholders may prefer the bid of a corporate raider. Customers may change their tastes to grow more sophisticated with the help of your product. The environment may suddenly deteriorate, the community clamor, the government interfere. The struggle to resolve the claims of different stakeholders in the organization never ends.

Yet the cybernetic "virtuous circle" presented here is above all else a form of organizational learning which can accelerate to help us win the learning race or can lag and lose us a prosperous and creative future. It is not just leaders or helmsmen who learn. The whole "ship" can organize its experience to perform more effectively. Some lessons can be automated, much as a stabilizer corrects for disturbance or a compass shows the course that must now be steered if the original destination is to be attained. But other types of learning are relational, as when the crew of a racing yacht learns to act as one.

Producers can learn to combine their aspirations with those of customers; workers, despite the fact that their goals are different from those of managers, can learn – with management's help – how to design congruence between differing priorities. We shall see how branches who seek autonomy can resolve this value with corporate headquarters seeking to exercise their authority and how learning and business objectives can combine. It is possible to plan yet remain spontaneous and flexible, and to enjoy the economies of both scale and scope. Where, then, does this leave your vital business imperative, that is, profit?

A Critique of Profit

None of us can doubt that the generating of profits is among those processes which are vital to the survival and expansion of a business. It does not help to stigmatize as greedy an ingredient so important to the learning race and so necessary to its acceleration. Unfortunately, the emphasis on profitability goes much further than this. From being a necessary condition for long-term survival, it is often extolled to the point of being a sufficient condition, nay the be-all and end-all of economic activity itself, the "pure essence" on which all other measures dance attendance and to which all other concerns can be distilled.

This attitude seems to have a curious fascination for those schooled in the Puritan ethic, with its yearning for some unambiguous sign of divine favor, something with which to confound bishops, princes, and feudal vestiges, whose authority rested upon a vague mystique and an alleged organic place in the great chain of being. Countable, methodical, and demonstrable success was the banner of the bourgeois revolution, the yardstick used to belabor political opponents, rooted in the soil of an earlier tradition. Today this attitude is strongest in Britain and the United States, two countries who pioneered the industrial revolution and whose middle classes had to fight rhetorically much harder against an uncomprehending and resistant government and against their land-holding classes. Later industrial revolutions in France, Germany, Scandinavia, and Japan used "catch-up" strategies in which government and business and the rural and industrial classes were less ideologically polarized.

The issue then is to what extent are profit and self-interest ideological slogans rather than tested means of learning to create wealth? Is the enthronement of the profit motive at the very pinnacle of bourgeois triumphalism the best way of generating wealth or the best way of defending that wealth once it has been amassed? A mere glance at Anglo-American politics in the last decade shows that "the profit motive" has been a political winner, and that unregulated competitiveness well describes the conduct of politicians. But are such values also conducive to generating wealth or have we fatally confused the politics of wealth retention with the arts of value creation? There are major objections to the "unicorn" of pure profit:

1 profit comes too late to steer by
2 motivationally, the desire for profit is too narrow to learn from
3 profit conflicts with values of equal importance yet higher priority
4 putting profitability first makes business strategies too predictable and too easy to defeat
5 profiting is a "text" which needs a "context" to support it
6 profitability is an organic not a mechanical attribute
7 profiting may not apply to all the units within a strategic alliance
8 when imitated by factions and persons within the corporation, profiting becomes suboptimal
9 it cannot deal with societal and environmental "addiction"

Finally, we shall examine the place of profitability in an overall synergy of created values and wealth.

Profitability comes too late to steer by

The evidence that a company is profitable can, in many cases, come too late for the organization to be steered by those numbers. This is not always so. A restaurant gives you feedback on what customers have ordered and what they enjoyed on the same day that the food was served to them, and within days or hours of the ingredients being purchased. But most businesses are more complex. Managers of Shell International have estimated that current profits were the consequences of investments made up to 30 years earlier, yet it was hard not to take credit for something initiated before you heard of the company.

If you use present profitability as feedback on the success of current operations, the implications could propel you from behind foremost into the future. You could have doomed yourself by a decision taken last month and not know it for another ten years or longer. Moreover, present profitability may be the consequence of several hundred decisions taken over the past decades. Knowing which of these decisions contributed more or less to current surpluses is a hopelessly complex calculation. Steering by profit is as difficult as steering a boat by the shape of its wake left three miles astern. It is ludicrously cumbersome and it would take a helicopter to look backwards in this way.

The map coordinates drawn up here may not have the precision and objectivity of profits, but they are at least contemporaneous. You steer between phenomena to port and starboard and, although their interpretation needs personal judgement, the financial performance will come later. Moreover, the fact of present profitability will not save you from the rocks or whirlpools in your path. Because profits are historical they are realized up to the very second that you are holed and start to sink.

General Motors, in the early 1970s, paid all its senior executives a profit-sharing bonus which they enjoyed right up to the sudden surge in the price of oil and the simultaneous assault of Japanese compacts and subcompacts. Because smaller cars made less profit per unit, GM executives were motivated not to emphasize or defend that end of the market and their destruction was nearly complete. They ran on to the rocks while counting their profits.

Motivationally, the desire for profit is too narrow to learn from

There are good reasons to suppose that a single-minded emphasis on profit and personal gain could reduce social learning. Anyone familiar with a nursery knows that clamorous self-concern does not need to be learned. What has to be taught and developed is how to resolve your own needs with those of others – at first parents and siblings, and then working colleagues, customers, workers, stakeholders, and, finally, the inhabitants of distant lands and different cultures.

The crucial capacity is to cross these ever-increasing distances between departments, between technologies, between classes, between suppliers and customers, and between continents. In the world race to achieve such competencies, personal obsessions with what we can gain or grab are very likely to impede our understanding. Indeed, what needs to be emphasized is not gaining, but contributing in order to gain. Profit, like happiness, popularity, and self-fulfillment, is best gained indirectly. If you are all out "to close a sale" you are likely to run into resistance. Customers realize that you are much less interested in them than in extracting their money.

You may smile and reply that "of course" you must convince customers that you are there to serve them. This is the essence of good sales technique. But our objection remains. Your real motive is one that cannot be authentically communicated without arousing suspicion and dislike. If, in fact, your customers' satisfactions and those of your employees are simply a means to an end to your own profitability, then sooner or later they grasp this and repay you in kind.

Nor should you expect even a fraction of the loyalty, commitment, and concern from those whom you regard as mere instruments of your purpose. Why should they confide in you, risk revealing genuine needs, or trust you with their most creative concepts? In short, you will learn less from them than you would if you reconciled their welfare with your own need in order to gain, and realized that the fulfilment of creative employees and the satisfaction of customers were strategic priorities for those seeking to profit thereby.

For some curious reason, many Anglo-Saxons have a love affair with the manipulative ethos. "How to Win Friends and Influence People" through a series of memorized techniques leaves most continental Europeans cold. America's only home-grown psychology is behaviorism, in which the experimenter, standing outside the subject in every sense of that word, shapes his or her behavior by schedules of unilateral reinforcement. Huge excitement was generated in the late 1950s by Vance Packard's *The Hidden Persuaders*, the account of a (failed) experiment at subliminal persuasion, in which advertisements were flashed upon the screen for microseconds. The intoxicating prospect of making them want it without them realizing that you have even tried to exert influence was enough to make the book a best-seller.

We find the same affection for lovable rogues in American popular culture, for example the Music Man, selling boys' bands without the benefit of music, uniforms, or instruments, The Wizard of Oz, a transformed medicine man, and W. C. Fields in *Never Give a Sucker an Even Break*. In *We're No Angels*, Humphrey Bogart sold empty jars labelled "sea air," "country air," and "all-purpose air." You unscrew the top and inhale deeply. The sheer hilarity goes on from there.

While it probably does a "low-tech" economy little harm if Barnum quickens the flow of crowds through his exhibition by a notice saying "To the Egress," it starts to matter a great deal when products grow in sophistication and become extensions of the human nervous system, as with computers, cameras, telephones, and fax machines. To have the makers and sellers of such products predominantly concerned with their own profits could be counterproductive in the extreme. In Arthur Miller's play *Death of a Salesman*, the myth of self-fulfilling confidence and the salesman's empty optimism were shown to be the ingredients of a tragedy, not comedy. Willy Loman is nearer to the truth than "Professor" Harold Hill.

But is there any evidence that the drive to profit is being taken too far? The European Management Forum periodically surveys several thousand managers in the world's developed economies to see how they rate themselves, their own country and other economies on such measures as "reputation for sales push." By taking various indices from their survey and selecting measures of quality that might reasonably be expected to be in tension with each other, we can estimate whether various values are being maximized or reconciled.

Now the "sales push" of Americans, the single loop of "getting them to want it" is likely to be in tension with the eventual quality of the delivered product. If Americans push too hard, harder than the quality of the product or service justifies, or push instead of improving the product, then this is likely to reduce the credibility of the communicator and the corporation being represented, so that "sales push" and "corporate credibility" become dilemmas instead of being reconciled.

The dilemmas shown in figure 16.2 illustrate just such a problem. We see in Dilemma 1 that in reputation for market push the United States scores 76 out of a possible 100 and is third in the world behind Japan and Korea. But in reputation for product quality, the product which the pushing was all about, the United States scores only 65 out of 100 and is 15th in the world, behind Sweden, Denmark, Finland, Italy, West Germany, The Netherlands, and others. Moreover, the world pattern is to have a product somewhat stronger than your push. Switzerland, Denmark, West Germany, and Japan are all above 85 in product quality.

Corporate credibility probably increases if you are better than even your own publicity suggests. Dilemma 2 shows that, once again, America is near the top in its sales orientation; only Japan exceeds it. But if we ask how much of what American corporations say is believed, then the reckoning is clear. She scores only 49 per cent. Over half is wasted as the public simply discounts for puffery and manipulation. So, far from following the Japanese maxim of "minimum effort and maximum impact," what we have here is maximum effort with minimum impact, the mountain belly of hype heaving to bring forth mice. The United States drops again to 15th place. Britain is worse on all measures, lacking the push, the credibility, and the quality.

These are, of course, broad national aggregates, and not true of Hotpoint, Apple, Hanover, Dow, ICI, and specific US or British corporations we may encounter. Dow especially may have learned more from the Japanese than most Japanese corporations have learned from each other. We must examine cultural weaknesses without falling for cultural stereotypes or generalizing the data to every company in that culture.

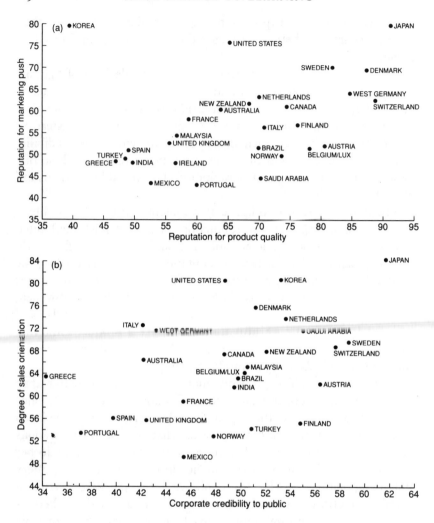

Figure 16.2   Two dilemmas
Source: European Management Forum (1985)

Profitability conflicts with values which are equally important yet of higher priority

The problem with giving profit some special status, or a supreme place in a hierarchy of values, is that it conflicts in the short term with other crucial values. If we hold profit inviolate, then we condemn all illicit intercourse between profit and those who belong in the same bed. Profit is a fruitful lover, not a sacred goddess, and like a human being, she lives in a state of alternate tension and reconciliation with other people.

Profit, in effect, comes into creative tension with the rapidity of corporate growth, with investing in human resources and with increasing one's share (or the overall size) of the market being served. If you want to grow very fast, doubling and redoubling the market for VCRs or fax machines, then what most western companies pay out in dividends would be better spent on reinvesting in the company for faster growth. Asian companies are better adapted to this strategy than most western ones because their shareholders want growth, not dividends. Leaders of western corporations face very real dilemmas in combining these values strategically.

These are very critical questions, as we have seen, and are not solved by simply giving to profitability some higher standing. Interestingly enough, Japanese culture gives its strongest emphasis to market share and does not celebrate profitability at all. What is publicized is what the corporation has done for customers, as opposed to what it has done for itself and its owners. Market share is not only a more contemporary indicator of success, but it arguably measures the mutuality of suppliers and customers more reliably and more consistently than does profitability. For, while present profitability is usually a sign that value has been delivered to customers in the past, it is no guarantee that this is continuing in the present. Market share measures what has been put into market relationships, while profit measures what has been taken out – with all the perils attendant on taking out too much.

You can be profitable in making carbon paper for some time after the Xerox machine has started to destroy your market, or making gas-guzzling cars after the oil price shock has struck, but not for long. The signs that you are in trouble are generally elsewhere, and the profit stream itself may give false comfort. Creating value means "taking the bull by both its horns" and resolving dilemmas. Consistent with that view we must stop believing in the sacred unicorn of profitability. The beast, however beautiful, is a myth.

None of this denies the market share can also be idolized, pursued one-dimensionally and end disastrously. What is crucial is how we think – linearly or systemically. If we see either profit or market share as measures of mutuality, we are thinking systemically; if we see these measures as straight lines of rigid rectitude, we are in trouble. There are important issues of priority here. The word is often loosely used in the sense of "more important." But priority means before or prior; putting one value before the other in a strategic sequence is to give it priority. However important profitability may be to the fate of the corporation, it is not usually as effective to put profits before growth, before investment in human resources, and before the enlargement of market share, as it is to put this afterwards. This is because taking profits out of an organization will usually slow its growth. The money paid to shareholders cannot be invested in upgrading the skills of employees, and higher margins may limit market share. The reverse sequence is generally more effective. Rapid growth will increase profitability in the longer run. Investing in human resources can make employees more productive, and an increased market share may cause competitors to withdraw and, in any event, can usually be turned to profitability later. It follows that profitability may be more attainable strategically if it is postponed, i.e., realized in the longer run rather than the shorter run.

However, this is very unlikely to happen if profitability is prized above all else, or is seen as the only conclusive evidence of corporate success. It is this attitude which produces the short-termism for which much of western industry is blamed and which financial markets are said to demand. It must be stressed that this is an attitude of mind more than a visible result. Long-term strategies, begun years earlier, come to fruition today and tomorrow. The long-term strategic player gets his jam today, once the virtuous circle is well developed. Indeed, the long term includes many short-term concerns. But the reverse is not true. Managing short term can mean the loss of longer-term objectives. As we might expect, then, the United States and Britain, the bastions of profit maximizing, are less able to take long-term views than most other nations (see table 16.1).

Putting profitability first makes business strategies too predictable and too easy to defeat

Japanese strategy may be likened to judo or karate: Will he strike first from the left or from the right? Which way will he swerve when I attack? Will it be more variety of products at the same cost,

Table 16.1   The extent to which firms take a long-term view

Japan	83.61	1
Sweden	75.64	2
West Germany	74.55	3
New Zealand	72.50	4
Finland	70.48	5
Switzerland	70.24	6
Singapore	66.90	7
Norway	66.67	8
Denmark	66.50	9
Netherlands	66.27	10
South Korea	65.00	11
France	64.26	12
Taiwan	62.35	13
Thailand and Canada	60.00	14
Malaysia	59.39	15
Belgium/Luxembourg	59.29	16
Australia	59.21	17
United States	57.53	18
Italy	56.96	19
Ireland	54.67	20
United Kingdom	54.59	21
India	54.43	22
Austria	52.73	23
Mexico	52.67	24
Turkey	50.59	25
Brazil	50.00	26
Hong Kong	47.50	27
Spain	44.50	28
Portugal	43.12	29
Greece	38.57	30

Source: European Management Forum, 1986.

the same variety at lower cost or, worse still, lower costs and more variety? Will he buy market share and shave profits, or raise margins, make profits and go to the market for more investment, and try then for market share? The important thing is to keep your opponents guessing, most especially about which values will be sought in which order to make the more potent synergy.

If you know what your opponent will do next it is not too difficult to defeat him or her. The overriding concern of many western corporations for short-term profits greatly limits their likely moves. If Asians attack the market at its broadest and take market share among the lower-priced popular lines, most western corporations will obligingly retrench around a few profitable up-market niches where they can hold their margins.

You can easily defeat a profit-maximizer by the simple expedient of taking the profit out of a particular product for several years and out-waiting the opposition. Unable to pay the dividends expected, and more conscious of any decline in the share price, the western corporation will withdraw.

This situation is particularly serious when Asians have several reasons for still making a product and we are looking only at the profitability of that particular unit. For example, a medical imaging technology may be the basis of a dozen more envisaged products. Its production and development may be teaching 2,000 employees valuable skills of development, production, and assembly. Its capacity to detect tumours may save an estimated 60,000 cancer patients a year and save on far more expensive treatments. The more reasons there are for making it as well as possible, the more its price can be forced down temporarily until the western supplier gives up.

Yet we in the west may be narrowing our attention as our competitors broaden their own. Those in retreat become preoccupied and anxious about the very profits they are losing by being narrow in the first place. When Asian inroads into western markets began to bite seriously in the late 1970s and early 1980s, western voters rushed to elect the advocates of profit and laissez-faire in Britain, the United States, Canada, Holland, and West Germany. The attack on our markets led to a creedal crisis, which led in turn to a reaffirmation of that creed. We were being punished for dalliance with the mixed economy, for not letting business be as profitable and self-interested as it wished. We must return to Victorian values!

But if the right wing is wrong, so is the left. Indeed, the tragedy of western wealth creation is that left and right on the political spectrum have split the solution between them and each extols a part, not in itself viable. Profit is neither good nor bad in itself. Rather, it is strategically ineffective unless woven into a larger configuration of reconciled values. It is not profits or people but both, not merit or participation but both, not competition or cooperation but both. The danger is that, under pressure, we shall fall back on profits, merit, and competition as eternal verities and tear ourselves asunder.

The effect of having one unicorn in our midst, one value the pure extension of which cannot be questioned, is that this idolization spreads to other values and dilemmas. Consider Michael Porter's famous bifurcation between the low-cost generic strategy and the strategy that seeks a premium product with an abnormally high return. The attempt to do both is specifically warned against. Muddle the otherwise clear issue and you will fall between two stools.

Porter is correct, of course, but only if you think short-term about how to make profits quickly. The shortage of time makes an either–or choice necessary. One absolute, the need to profit now, makes a second choice between absolutes necessary – *either* a low-cost generic strategy *or* a premium product. Unicorns beget more unicorns, while bulls beget bulls.

But suppose that we were willing to postpone profitability. This makes the dilemma resolvable. A company makes an original and excellent product, yet offers it at an extremely economical cost, slashing its own margins. This will effectively deter other entrants to this market, who will probably doubt their own capacities to achieve so much for so little evident reward. The result will be that, after several years of low or nonexistent profits but rising market share, the Asian competitor will find itself supreme. In contrast, after five years of profiting hugely from its patent, the western firm finds itself besieged by low-cost imitators. The better strategy is surely the first, although it requires the submerging of any emphasis on "the bottom line" for several years.

Many of you may react to this argument by emphasizing that profitability should be long-term not short-term. The bottom line should be extended in time! But this is rout disguised as a tactical retreat. We live here and now, in the short term. Either profits are to be maximized or this objective is going to be qualified by other considerations. If qualified it loses its status as fundamentalist dogma. If we must forgo profits now to recoup them later, to what criteria should our allegiance be transferred? What should we do now to make our strategic moves less stereotyped and less predictable?

Profiting is a text needing the support of a context

Profit-making figures against a ground which is in contrast with it, standing out from the background. Profiting, then, is a text within a context. It follows that any profit orientation needs a contrasting orientation to make it work effectively. Societies have sectors which are for profit and not for profit, but ideally the latter will support the former. For example, a good health service shores up employees in their work, allowing them to take greater risks because a major source of avoidable insecurity has been taken care of. A very high standard of public education makes private enterprise considerably more prosperous, since all children, regardless of economic circumstance, are given the opportunities they need. A private enterprise economy grows in public soil and the nutrients, irrigation, and care of that soil are priceless advantages, yet do not compete in the same manner as the plants themselves. As Lester Thurow has pointed out, competition for profit between US automobile companies was literally underwrought by the National Highways Defense Act. Private vehicles compete on public roads.

This much is obvious, but the dilemma between profiting and supporting is found within the corporation as well. Most especially is it true of the highest reaches of top management at Hotpoint, Apple, Hanover, Dow, AKZO, ICI, Shell, and others. These persons act as coaches, mentors, score-keepers, and cheer-leaders for the profit-making activities of their companies, but their own roles are largely nurturant and supportive, giving aid, advice, encouragement, and rewards to their front-line troops. They do not think first and foremost of how they can use their high status to win from the rest of the company. They cooperate so that others may better compete, think so that others may better act, and reflect so that others may better practise.

The danger with profit orientation is that no one will be willing to play these more supportive roles, or symbolize the learning which makes profiting possible. Support is especially important in recessions. It is estimated that Britain lost around a quarter of its manufacturing capacity in the 1979–83 recession. "These companies could not profit so they should die, right? They should release their resource for more profitable use by better managers." Perhaps. Certainly, the performance of the surviving manufacturers has been as impressive as we might expect from such culling of the weak. But today there may be simply too few producers, with the result that any increase in demand sucks in imports and pushes the trade gap further into deficit. More support for the profit-making sector in its earlier troubles might have been wise. Profiting gets its resilience from support by other values. It is too brittle to go it alone.

Profitability is an organic not a mechanical attribute

The case for profitability as a supreme arbiter is based on a mistaken metaphor. The corporation is conceived of as a machine in something akin to a demolition derby with competing machines. Losers are junked and their unusable parts cannibalized by other, more successful, competitors. In this way machines and drivers improve with losers feeding resources to winners. The assumption is that these "losing" bits and pieces can be reassembled quickly and easily into winning combinations by better managers. Despite some waste and destruction in the demolition process, there would be far more waste if the less able were not pushed off the track. Profitability is the sum of each contestant's strength, speed, and skill.

If we conceive of companies as social organisms which have grown over 10 or 20 years, then destruction takes on aspects of trauma and death. Their parts may be less valuable than the living creatures from which they were stripped. Years of growth and learning may be irreversibly lost by one bad decision. Unprofitability may have been temporary, a growing pain, but disintegration is for ever. When the recession ends, the plant will not recover, and it may take decades or more to grow its replacement. In the organic or holographic metaphor, profitability is but one important sign of healthy growth, but is its temporary absence sufficient to condemn the company? Not if we wish to expand rapidly after the recessions are over; not if the complex learning of networks is to be preserved; not if we want resilient corporations.

Profiting may not be applicable to all units within a strategic alliance

A seventh objection to profit maximization is that it may not be applicable to all products and services in a particular collaborating network. What about an investment bank which makes little or no profit yet lends money to a key national industry which, enhanced by its low cost of capital, becomes a world-class competitor, eliminating several rivals? The bank did not maximize profits, yet the organization, taken as a whole strategic alliance, won valuable markets.

The same issue applies to products that "give birth," such as first-, second-, third-, fourth-, and fifth-generation computers or microchips. The question is less whether one particular generation is profitable, taken as a single range of products, but what their making contributes to the next generation and the next. The experience learned through volume development and production becomes the basis of moving to the next level. It might be worth forgoing profits on stages one, two, or three if the consequence was to out-run and out-learn competitors so that all subsequent stages belonged to that company.

This issue comes down to the question of who is competing with whom. Is each bank, each supplier, and each subcontractor out for itself, or can more effective combinations of these be regarded as a strategic entity, a supra-company? Now that airlines are joining with other airlines and with hotel chains, car rentals, and travel agents, which is the entity that must profit and by how much?

Likewise, if the Japanese government leases its robots at a loss, that could still make every factory that employs these robots and turns them in for the latest models more competitive than they would otherwise have been. The problem with the profitability criterion is that we are never sure to what units it should be applied, nor how wide is the strategic alliance which, taken as a whole, needs to be profitable in how long a time-span. English-speaking countries are not generally sympathetic to the idea that one unit might be content to sacrifice its local income for the benefit of the larger whole, yet alliances formed with such sacrifices may be unbeatable as a combination, with profits returning to those who only appeared to give them away through the success of the whole alliance.

When imitated by factions or persons within the corporation profit orientation becomes suboptimal

Our eighth objection to profit maximization as a strategy, and the self-interest which is its rationale, is that an organization's employees are likely to model their own behavior on that idealized by their firm. If the corporation is all out for itself, why should not each employee, each department, each function, each faction and each union place its own perceived interests above those of other groups, including customers, shareholders, and the community? In such a value system people will work together only when they can directly gain by doing so, but will scurry down the rigging at the first sign that the ship may not be seaworthy or if a more attractive craft comes alongside.

Why should a corporation invest in its human resources and in the future learning of its employees if each individual promptly takes that training to the highest bidder? British and American corporations make lower "invisible" investments in their people because they fear to pay twice, once to raise the competence of employees and again to prevent their selling that advantage to a rival corporation. Self-interest, which is qualified neither by gratitude nor loyalty to the firm, is clearly suboptimal. Yet firms themselves extol the value that undoes them.

For accelerated corporate learning of the kind that can win the learning race has to be much more than the knowledge carried around within single heads. Knowledge is becoming so complex that only stable human networks can encompass it. The more subtle and difficult the communication, the closer human relationships need to be, and the more damaging to the larger system does narrow self-interest become. Turnover rates of 25 per cent per annum or higher are catastrophic. No one will wait for their profits because they will be long gone from the corporation and care only about gains which can be made during a brief occupancy. Profit maximization as an ethic atomizes the organization into adversarial pieces. It has become our Achilles' heel and we may never learn, because to want profit too much is to overlook its necessary preconditions.

Profit motives cannot deal with societal and environmental "addictions"

In practice, the free market is severely limited in key areas. We do not encourage trade in addictive nonmedical drugs, or in babies, or in certain kinds of porn. Just as the human body can crave more and more of a drug that is actually poisoning it, so a society can crave lethal weapons, cadavers, or human organs which, if freely traded, would inflict social damage.

As we shall see in the next chapter, the environment can become addicted to chemicals, especially pesticides. It can take more and more of these to hold an explosion of pests in check, especially when natural predators fall prey to the toxins and the genes of insects become immune. In all such cases the market fails to work and for the same underlying reason. The personal short-term gain experienced by the microcosm combines to create a catastrophic longer-term deficit for the macrocosm. Each farmer needs to keep his pests at bay more effectively than competitors, yet this every contest could poison the whole environment they share. Each "fix" for the drug addict brings pleasure, but the accumulation brings death. The fact that customers may be desperate for drugs or pesticides and cannot face life without these does not mean that a wise society should allow them to be supplied.

Again, this is not an argument against profit as an ingredient within a developing economy, but only an argument against regarding profit as an unqualified good, not to be interfered with or qualified by meddlesome persons. The fact is that any country that targets pollution-control technologies today, before the demand is heavy, will probably enjoy a handsome stream of profits into the next century when, very predictably, we all start to choke and the horrendous warnings will multiply. We will make these profits in the future by taking a broader view of creating wealth and value in the present, by seeing that the ultimate customer is the environment itself, that in evolutionary survival "the unit" which survives is people plus their environment. The limitation of profit as currently conceived is that it strips the profiting person away from his or her environment and allows the first to "gain" notionally at the expense of the second.

The place of profitability in the race to learn

Profitability is one crucial ingredient in a strategic synthesis of values designed to create wealth as broadly defined. It is similar to yeast in its capacity to make a combination of ingredients rise. We should be neither ashamed of profit nor exultant at its making. It is a far better description of a successful economy than it is a prescription for what we should form strategies about.

If the real race is to learn, and if the competition will be won by those who create the most valuable configurations of knowledge in the shortest time, then profits are needed to pay "the school fees" to sponsor the next generation of learners and the next. They are clearly a mundane necessity – but an inspiration? Business is on the verge of a virtual renaissance which will make the methods of early philistine industrialists and the doctrines of Grantham grocers' daughters into vestiges of the past. To reduce these extensive skeins of knowledge to measures of more or less money paid to persons not even present in the organization and not, for the most part, known as individuals with recognizable faces is to reduce a culture to an abstraction and a community to a set of accounts. This will produce not only a diminution in the energy and creativity with which we work but a loss in the potential of all of us to find meaning in our lives. The hunt for the unicorn is a doomed quest, for no pure unambiguous essence of business virtue exists. We are like jugglers with more and more balls in the air, who will drop them all if we get fixated on one.

Conclusion

There are two kinds of profitability. There is profit as private gain and profit as a somewhat rough guide to mutual satisfaction between the corporation and its stakeholders. It is the latter which has kept the west far ahead of statist economies. An imperfect feedback loop is better by leagues than no feedback loop at all. Yet multiple feedbacks are more effective still. Profit as one element of multiple measures of what is valuable is the way forward strategically. It is the only way toward sustainable development.

References

European Management Forum 1985: *Annual Report on International Competitiveness*. Geneva: European Management Forum.

Hampden-Turner, C. M. 1983: The trap of ideology. In *Gentlemen and Tradesmen: the Values of Economic Catastrophe*. London: Routledge and Kegan Paul, ch. 10, 182.

Porter, M. F. 1980: *Competitive Strategy: Techniques for Analyzing Industries and Competitors*. New York: Free Press, ch. 2.

Thurow, L. C. 1985: *The Zero Sum Solution*. New York: Simon & Schuster, 172.

PART V

As a Society – From Complexity to Sustainability

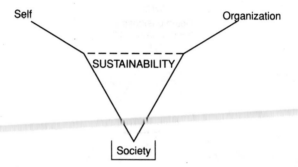

From complexity to sustainability

16

Achieving Sustainable Development
John Davis

Introduction: Environmental Concerns Emerge

The early 1970s saw the publication of *Limits to Growth* (a Report of the Club of Rome), the Report of the 1972 Stockholm Conference of the United Nations on "The Human Environment," and the late Dr E. F. Schumacher's book *Small is Beautiful* (1974). These can now be seen as seminal events that triggered a debate leading, in the late 1980s, to a global agreement – ranging from the supermarket shopper in the High Street to the General Assembly of the United Nations. It is now believed that if there is a continuation of the kind of development so far known and enjoyed by a quarter of the world's population, it is very likely to lead to such widespread environmental and ecological damage as to amount to the destruction of a large part of the earth's life support system. Thus it is said that the traditional form of economic development, based on a particular set of assumptions and beliefs having the six characteristics listed below (pages 326–7), is unsustainable:

Not since the dawn of civilisation some 8,000 years ago has the earth been about 1°C warmer than today. To find conditions like those projected for the middle of the next century, we must go back millions of years. If current trends in "greenhouse gas" build up continue, we will have committed earth to a warming of 1.5° to 4.5°C by around 2030, the upper end of this range being the more probable. In short, if the "greenhouse-effect" turns out to be as great as predicted by today's climate models, and if current emission trends continue, our world will soon differ radically from anything in human experience. (The President, in World Resources Institute, 1989.)

Panel 17.1
A Bleak Prospect for the Year AD 2000

1 Per capita consumption of food in South East Asia, the Middle East and much of Africa will not improve, and in some places it will decline from its present inadequate level, despite an increase of 90 percent in global food production.

2 A 25 percent shortfall in the supply of firewood will have devastating effect on the quarter of the human race that depends entirely on the use of wood for fuel.

3 Around 40 percent of the remaining forests will have been destroyed, with the result that many countries will have increasingly erratic supplies of water.

4 An area the size of the state of Maine is becoming barren wasteland each year, and a fifth of all plant and animal species could be lost.

Source: The Global 2000 Report, prepared in 1980 for the President of the United States by the Department of State and the Council for Environmental Policy.

Many more study reports, conferences and books have followed the Global 2000 Report, culminating in the 1988 Brundtland Report (World Commission on Environment and Development, 1988). Its most important recommendation is that "the principle of sustainable development must be built into all activities."

Sustainable development: changing assumptions and beliefs

An understanding of the complex idea of sustainable development can best be approached by contrasting some of the underlying assumptions and beliefs of conventional economic development that affect sustainability. As Schumacher repeatedly pointed out, and as practical consequences demonstrate, each of the six below is flawed.

1 **Increasing indiscriminate growth of financial transactions will produce benefits and prosperity for all.** (In fact, we can see that it widens the gap between rich and poor, and a progressively smaller proportion of the world's population are enjoying the fruits because the "trickle-down" theory does not work.)

2 **Natural resources are believed to be unlimited, and they can be exploited unconditionally; the environment is also unlimited in its capacity to withstand human activity in all its forms.** (The consequence is that important nonrenewable resources are being rapidly exhausted, and the environment is being destabilized by the activities of only a quarter of the world population.)

3 **Capital-intensive manufacturing is universally more efficient and productive than labour-intensive repair and reconditioning services.** (In fact, the capital-intensive manufacturing system that has been produced is immensely wasteful and environmentally damaging. It has been sustained by some fundamental fallacies in the ways the productivity and efficiency have been measured.)

4 **Earning a living is inevitably a demanding activity. All that is needed to satisfy workers is an adequate financial reward; the nature of the work required is of no great importance.** (The consequence has been a total failure to optimize the human contribution to wealth creation in the mix of men, money, and machines. Human creative effort has far more to offer, if properly organized and employed, both to the economy and to personal satisfaction.)

5 **People have an unlimited hunger for possessions. So long as they conform to fashion they are an acceptable mark of social status and the principal means of personal satisfaction.** (In fact, as the late Fred Hirsch pointed out (see Hirsch, 1977), the value placed by individuals on particular desires declines the more widely they are shared by other people. When desires become frustrated they lose their attraction, and life becomes a series of frustrations. Once material needs have been satisfied, self-fulfilment has to be gained in nonmaterial ways.)

6 **So long as growth and/or a good return can be obtained on savings, people are in general not concerned who invests them nor what purpose they are intended to serve.** (The consequence has been that personal financial power has been given away to impersonal financial institutions; they use it for their own purposes, which often do not correspond with the real interests of the individual or the general community good. Ethical investment schemes indicate that a growing number of people are not happy to leave investment choice entirely in the hands of others.)

If these are the underlying assumptions and beliefs that underpin an unsustainable kind of development, what are the concepts which can be used to replace them in order to promote a sustainable economic development? Panel 17.2 suggests some assumptions and beliefs.

Panel 17.2   Some Assumptions and Beliefs for Sustainable Development

(a) Of economies

- Economic activity should not only be efficient in its use of all resources but should also be socially just, and environmentally and ecologically sustainable.
- The purpose should be to satisfy all human needs – physical, mental, emotional, and spiritual – through personal responsibility, mutual aid, and governmental enabling, with minimum consumption of scarce resources.
- Communities need to develop economic self-reliance as a basis for dignity and self determination.
- Inter-trading should primarily be for an exchange of materials and skills that are naturally maldistributed.
- Activities that do not involve financial transactions are no less important than those that do. Consequently, there is no justification for the maximization of financial transactions.
- The interests of future generations, and of other communities, must not be jeopardized.

(b) Of businesses

- The essential purpose of a business is to provide goods and services to meet some of the needs of a defined sector of the market.
- The essential purpose of a business is to provide goods and services to meet some of the needs of defined sector of the market.
- The continuity of a business that is performing satisfactorily in fulfilling its purpose should be protected.
- The well-being of all other stakeholders is as important as that of equity shareholders.
- Through the technologies that are used, operations should enhance the environment rather than damage it, and contribute to ecological balance.

- All forms of waste should be minimized, and renewable energy and materials should be used as much as possible.
- A company does not own all its resources: it holds them in trust to make the best possible use of them on behalf of the community, where it has "citizenship" responsibilities.
- Managers and employees together are the players in the business game. They should be enabled to participate to the limits of their abilities and have a sense of "ownership with dignity."
- Operating units should be kept as small as the maintenance of efficiency allows.
- Companies should be dynamically innovative, striving to achieve higher levels of excellence and quality in all aspects of their business, and making the best use of human skills and technologies to that end.
- Investment must place equal weight on the long term as well as the short.
- Company Boards of Directors should be guided by a general purpose clause that reflects these assumptions and beliefs.

Note that these two lists are not intended to be a dogmatic credo. They are intended only as examples of the assumptions and beliefs that are needed to underpin sustainable development.

Discriminating development

All who are able and fit to take part in the generation of real wealth – both financial and nonfinancial – must be enabled to play their part for the benefit of themselves, their families, and their local communities. Their activities cannot be indiscriminate. They must be discriminating in the use of resources in order to minimize waste and prevent environmental and ecological damage. Using "appropriate technologies," wealth-generation can be much more evenly spread, fully satisfying all material needs and opening up a prospect of unlimited development in areas that are not energy- or material-intensive.

Conserving resources

A clear distinction has to be made between renewable and nonrenewable materials and energy sources, with preference being given to renewables wherever possible. There should also be a bias toward locally available resources. Care must be taken to ensure that when renewable materials are taken from the natural stock a balance is maintained by restocking:

> The ways in which resources are extracted, processed, used and finally disposed of, must be planned with a view to an avoidance of damage to nature and to the maintenance of ecological balance.
> By increasing energy efficiency measures, consumption of energy per unit of GDP could be reduced in the UK by 60% at least by 2025. (Leach, 1979)

Maximizing repair, reconditioning, re-use, and recycling (4Rs)

Consumption of virgin materials and manufacturing energy will be minimized if things are designed for maximum durability and repairability. Full advantage of those qualities can be realized if the 4R services are used to the full.

Creative work

Work should be organized in a variety of ways to make the fullest possible use of human talents and energy in the satisfaction of all kinds of human needs. Technology used by people in their work should be skill-enhancing and "user friendly." People in employment should be able to identify with it and with its purposes.

Nonmaterial growth

Although material growth has to be limited within the bounds of sustainability, no such limitations need apply to those forms of human activity and personal or community development that need not be material- or energy-intensive (e.g., health care, the arts, social services, sport, hobbies, and education).

Table 17.1   Unsustainable and sustainable development

Unsustainable development	Sustainable development
Indiscriminate development	Discriminating development
Unconstrained use of resources and the environment	Resource conservation and care for the environment
Maximization of manufacture	Maximization of the 4Rs
Unskilled work	Creative work
Maximization of material growth	Maximization of non-material growth
Impersonal investment	Self-directed investment

Self-directed personal investment

To enable discriminating development to take place, opportunities must be available for people to direct their savings into investments that will facilitate such a development. In effect, this will mean placing money primarily to serve the needs of individuals and communities, rather than making these needs serve a financial purpose which may or may not accord with the wishes of individual investors or the needs of their community.

Sustainable Development Accentuates the Positive

Table 17.1 summarizes the difference between these two forms of development. One way to contrast their overall meaning is to say that it is a moral choice between "eat, drink, and be merry for tomorrow we die" and "let us live responsibly now so that others may also live in the future." This formulation immediately seems like a straitjacket. It actually means being liberated, because the positive aspects greatly outweigh the negative.

For yourselves in businesses, as the main agents of economic development, the negative aspects may sound like bad news. It may seem like the denial of freedom to invent and innovate in any way that can be commercialized. It is, of course, inevitable that old things must give way to new in any fundamental change. We shall have to stop doing certain things. However, much as we might personally regret such constraints, they become entirely acceptable once we remember that they are not arbitrary. It is an imperative placed upon us if life on the planet is to continue with any kind of dignity. In the words used by Margaret Thatcher to the UN General Assembly in November 1989, "it must be growth which does not plunder the planet today and leave our children with the consequences tomorrow." Happily, as we shall see later, the positive aspect, which is dominant, opens up marvellous new opportunities.

Sustainable development challenges the entire industrial and commercial system to restructure itself, based on a completely new set of assumptions and beliefs about the ways we must conduct our economic affairs. We should be making a profound mistake if we perceived the change in terms less fundamentally radical than that. Some may be tempted to think that sustainable development means little more than insulating our houses, fitting catalytic mufflers to our cars, and buying so-called "green" produce from the supermarket. That would be for change to continue along conventional lines, leaving all the erroneous beliefs and assumptions untouched. The effect would be so marginal as to have little influence on the future of life on the planet, other than to delay the consequences for a generation or so. The magnitude of the per capita reduction in the consumption of fossil energy and nonrenewable materials that is needed long-term in the industrialized nations cannot be achieved by tinkering with the problem. A reduction to about one-third of present levels of consumption is required in Europe for sustainability; in the USA it is considerably greater.

The challenge that sustainable development poses to the world's business community must be taken up in its entirety, and at a level of basic assumptions and beliefs. Only in this way can the business sector hope to prove that it is feasible. As the President of the International Chamber of Commerce said (see Wallenburg, 1989), the onus of proof rests with the business sector because it alone controls most of the technological and productive capacity that is needed to bring it about.

The future of sustainable development is one of intense innovation – inventing a new and different age. Innovation will be in the lead, with administration playing its supporting role of serving the needs of people and the planet. It is a prospect full of opportunity for dynamic management:

> We have reached a stage in human development where our future technological progress must be based to an increasing degree on the

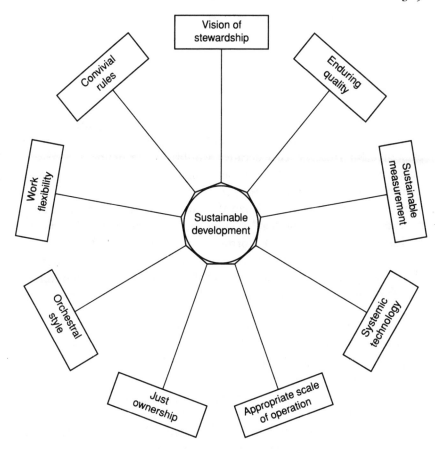

Figure 17.1 Transformation strategies for sustainable development

rational needs of our civilisation rather than let our civilisation be driven about aimlessly by haphazard invention[1].

Radical Business-transformation Strategies

An effective approach to this new age of opportunity requires not only dynamic management of innovation, but also a radical transformation in a number of critical areas of business life. Figure 17.1 lists nine such areas for which sustainable development has vitally important implications. We need here to see in what ways there are connections with sustainability arising out of the new set of assumptions and beliefs.

Vision of stewardship

For some time it has been widely recognized that companies benefit from published "mission statements." Those that have been in existence for the past two decades would, in the majority of cases, place emphasis on developing the business to obtain growth and a high return on the investment of equity shareholders within a defined product or service sector. When development was constrained only by the limits set by the legal system, no more needed to be said to indicate recognition of other forms of restraint, such as those arising from the need to conserve certain types of material or plant species. When the quality of goods or services to be marketed was mentioned, reference might be made to the aim of being leaders in performance, style, or fashion, and perhaps to reliability and value for money. Seldom would there have been an explicit expression of ambition to be leaders in durability, repairability, or energy efficiency. There might have been an intention to be a dynamic and innovative company, but it is unlikely that any reference would have been made to the motivation for dynamism and innovation, or to the "stewardship" obligations of the company for the general well-being and to the communities within which it operated. For many years there have been such expressions of corporate social responsibility in a small number of organizations, but they have been the exceptions.

Generally speaking, conventional mission statements have been narrowly written. The visions they have embodied have failed to suggest a vital and responsible engagement in a creative endeavor necessary for the general benefit. A company lives not only by its mission statement; it also operates with a set of common values. They vary somewhat from company to company, but in general they reflect the conventional underlying common beliefs and assumptions of trade and industry. The radical change arising out of the moral choice to pursue a course of sustainable development must result in a change both in the shared values and in the vision of most commercial enterprises.

Two examples may serve to illustrate, in part, the relevance of "vision and values" to sustainable development. The vision of the public electricity supply industry has been a narrow one: that of delivering power reliably at minimum unit cost to customers every hour of the day and every day of the year. If its vision had been different, to remain a reliable source of supply, but to make maximum use of renewable sources of energy and only where necessary to use a fossil-fuel input, it would have been an entirely different business. Had the vision gone further and anticipated that generation from fossil fuels would be carried out in combination with generation of heat wherever that was taking place, it would have been even more different.

The domestic heating business is the second example. The conventional approach is for each competing fuel supplier to seek to maximize the volume of sales of fuel to customers. Although advice on efficiency of use may be available on request, the decision whether or not to improve it is left with the householder. If, however, the supply company had a vision of providing customers with a comfortable indoor environment temperature at minimum cost, instead of simply supplying a product, the business would not be the same at all.

Each of the alternative visions of these two illustrations would accord with the kind of approach needed for sustainable development. The value systems underpinning these visions would also be different.

Appropriate scale of operation

Sustainable development raises questions about the nature of business operations, not least about size. The many influences that have been at work over the past century have tended toward increasing the scale of operation in almost every sector. The finance and investment system has been a very big influence, but the main justification for the increase has been that so-called economies of scale make it inevitable. Nevertheless, managers in these large organizations are well aware of the difficulties that size and complexity create. One of the most serious problems for any company that has to be intensely innovative is the inertia a large organization experiences in making rapid responses to the need for frequent change.

Since a change of direction toward sustainable development necessarily means that innovation in all kinds of business will become more intense, it is important to consider carefully the optimum size of operation once the top management has made a commitment to change direction.

The food-processing and food-distribution industries provide a good example of the ways in which a re-examination of the size factor could produce movement toward sustainable development. Over many decades a very fragmented system has been replaced by a concentrated and capital-intensive industrial system based on large processing plants and a massive international distribution system. It appears that when he was Chairman of the Cadbury Schweppes Group, Britain's Sir Adrian Cadbury made a careful study of what was required for the future. He came to the conclusion that the historic process needed to be reserved. Siccolt Mansholt, one of the architects of the European Common Agricultural Policy, has studied the primary food-production end of the business. His conclusion has much in common with Sir Adrian Cadbury's. He has been quoted as saying that large-scale, energy- and chemical-intensive agriculture has been a mistake, and that quite different and more environmentally harmonious forms of farming need to replace it – another reversal of a historic trend!

Sustainable measurement

Every company's management is equipped with a set of measuring instruments for planning, monitoring, and controlling the business and its future development. Some of these measurements are common to all businesses. For example, every company needs to know the annual return on the average capital employed. Other measurements are specific to particular kinds of business. The important criterion of sales revenue per square metre of shelf space in a supermarket is obviously of no interest to the manager of a coal mine. Neither is the latter's interest in the hourly output per metre of coal-face of any interest to a supermarket manager.

All the various measurements that play a vital part in the daily lives of managers have been devised to provide the kind of information you require to run your businesses in accordance with the assumptions and beliefs about what is important and unimportant in economic life in general and business life in particular. With a new set of assumptions and beliefs, and a new vision and set of common values for the company that are a basis for sustainability, you will need to modify some of the measurements they use daily and eliminate others. Some new measurements will need to be introduced. Without such changes a company is likely to continue on a "business as usual" course, no matter what the expressed intentions to change may be, or how sincerely they are held.

Three examples can illustrate the radical effect that a change in measuring instrument may have. Discounted cash flow (DCF) has been a widely used method of evaluating investment projects. In its very nature it puts less weight on the future than on the present. A sustainable form of development cannot accept that view; an alternative to DCF will have to be found. Unit cost of production is another common number used of most products. To reflect the importance of product durability for sustainable development, consider, for example, the cost per hour of useful life of electric light bulbs; if this replaced unit costs of bulbs, products of higher first cost would perhaps be produced. If the vision of the manufacturer also aimed to produce bulbs that minimized electricity consumption, a still different kind of bulb would be produced. The third example concerns the building industry and could have even more dramatic effects. One of the traditional, principal objectives in building construction is to minimize first cost. In so doing, buildings have been produced which are vastly more inefficient thermally than they need be. Had "total cost of construction, maintenance, and operation over a 50-year period" been used as an alternative criterion for minimization a very different stock of buildings would be in existence.

Thus the measurements that are used in businesses will be crucially important for sustainable development.

Work flexibility

Kinds of work rearrangements that are likely to be beneficial for intensely innovative activity are already taking place in some companies. The monolithic, entirely self-reliant, hierarchical form is being replaced by multidimensional arrangements. These are capable of great flexibility and adaptability. They leave as many options open as possible for coping with uncertainty. The potential of information technology will enable the new arrangements, with their looser non-bureaucratic systems, to cope effectively.

New work arrangements will have to do more than merely provide greater flexibility and freedom for managements. They will have to take full account of the changing expectations and attitudes of a work force that is increasingly composed of a variety of specialist skills. The marriage of business needs with the needs of the work force will frequently produce companies with small core operations that employ, on contract terms, the services of a cluster of specialist suppliers of skill, knowledge, technology, and effort.

A comparison of the old MG car company and the Morgan car company provides an illustration of different work arrangements in the same business of sports-car manufacture; one was a traditional monolithic firm, doing itself as much of the job of designing and manufacturing as it could, whereas the other concentrated on design and final assembly on a low-capital, high-labor basis, with much of the manufacture being contracted out. Lord Nuffield chose to use much the same kind of high-capital production system of his sports cars as he used for the mass-market, popular Morris models. Morgan chose to use a much less capital-intensive system, with a small, highly skilled, and enthusiastic team of production workers for the small volume production job, relying on their design skills to fill a particular market niche. Morgan still has a healthy business with its well-adapted organization of work; MG was unfortunately forced to cease trading some years ago.

Not only is more and more work being subcontracted, but some companies will increasingly benefit if some of their in-house "core" activity is carried out by employees working from home rather than from a company plant or office.

Orchestral style

In the best companies, autocratic and paternalistic management styles have been gradually changing to more consultative forms. With the emergence of "total quality management" a further advance is being made toward greater participation at all levels.

The challenge of sustainable development requires that movement toward a participative style of new-paradigm management should accelerate in all kinds of company. The principal reason is that "man management" becomes an even more critical factor than it has always been. Comparatively small teams of highly skilled professionals in a wide variety of specialisms can only be led successfully with the kind of leadership – such as is displayed by the conductor of an orchestra – that inspires full participation. Management of multidisciplinary R&D teams provides a useful business model in which a similar kind of leadership is practised.

It is not uncommon to find such styles of management in some computer-software companies. It is a mistake to think that similar leadership is inappropriate in more traditional forms of business, with their different history of organizational development. Changing styles in such companies, from autocracy to participation, is not an easy job. Happily, there are examples where it has been achieved very successfully. One outstanding example is Britain's Baxi Heating. Before it was converted into a Partnership Company, the Baxi Heating Company was a traditional family firm, founded in the 19th century to make a patent coal-fire system. When the business was taken over by Phillip Baxendale, the grandson of the founder, he began to encourage participation. As a result the firm became increasingly successful and prosperous as an innovator in the domestic gas-heater business. Phillip Baxendale believes that participation made a big contribution to the success.

Just ownership

An "absentee landlord" system of ownership that came into existence with the invention of the joint-stock limited-liability company has become the dominant form of ownership in free market economies during an era of indiscriminate economic growth. Unconstrained investment and growth were well matched. Discriminating growth for sustainable development requires responsible, long-term investment from sources that have both a vested interest in the corporate agent and a legal obligation to serve the common good as well as the stakeholders. The "absentee landlord" system, as it presently operates, is not best suited to that role; alternative forms of ownership need to be promoted.

There are other practical reasons, but there is also an important moral consideration. The choice being made for sustainability is based on principles of natural justice and equity. For this choice to be effectively pursued similar principles must be employed within the agencies that are engaged in the task. Thus businesses must be seen to be operating on just and equitable principles. This requires some fundamental changes in the dominant company law covering joint-stock limited liability. To use George Goyder's term (Goyder, 1987), we need just enterprises.

Examples of different ownership structures already in existence may be useful conversion models. The Baxi Partnership is an attractive model for any family company contemplating a change of ownership. The Body Shop and other franchising examples point the way to alternatives that, to a greater or lesser extent, decentralize control and obligation, thereby creating a closer relationship between investment and a particular small group of workpeople. Although employee and management buy-outs have become more common in recent years, and will probably continue to increase, the main part of the private-company sector is likely to remain substantially intact. A major change in company law will be needed to bring about a more just relationship between employer and employee, and restore an element of public benefit accountability and linkage between ownership obligations and rights. Cashbuild in South Africa, as we saw in chapter 11, is a very good case in point.

Enduring quality

Some of the things that are happening in the food production, processing, and distribution industries illustrate how environmental issues and product quality are inseparable. Farming is beginning to undergo a major reformation. Processing is rapidly having to move away from additives, and marketers are suddenly faced with customer demands for biodegradable and recyclable packages. Processes themselves are under public scrutiny; for example, the radiation treatment of foods and the chlorine whitening of paper products are being questioned.

The value changes that are both explicit and implicit in a move toward sustainability will have profound effects on the meaning of quality and its expression. Across the entire business spectrum the concepts of quality are likely to undergo very many changes, from the rather narrow contemporary concept to questions of resources and environment, new codes of good practice, and new standards for managers and professionals.

The implications of sustainability for business professional Codes and Standards are considerable. For example, the main constraints that professional engineers have traditionally insisted on have been concerned with health and safety, together with compliance with minimum standards required by official regulations. Construction engineers and architects have for a very long time had the know-how to erect buildings requiring only a fraction of the space-heating energy used in existing buildings. Automotive engineers have had the know-how to design cars that would use about half the amount of fuel consumed at present, and which would also last two or three times as long. The imperative of sustainability will surely add maximization of durability, repairability, and energy efficiency to health and safety, as things that professional codes require.

Convivial rules

The rules that govern the operation of businesses have been designed to foster the indiscriminate growth that is leading toward environmental and ecological damage of global proportions and the rapid exhaustion of some nonrenewable resources. They have also led to concepts of quality, types of technology, instruments of business management, and systems of corporate ownership that appear to be inappropriate in a period of discriminating economic growth.

The business game rules obviously reflected the old assumptions and beliefs that were listed earlier in this chapter. For example, on the grounds of so-called economies of scale, it was believed that there would be natural advantage in linking large-scale marketing with large-scale manufacturing operations. According to that belief it would obviously be disadvantageous to interfere, through official regulations, by restraining the discount that a retailing chain might obtain from a manufacturer for a nation-wide, big-volume contract for a particular product. Similarly, the same generalized belief in economies of scale rules out interference in all but a very few examples of company takeover.

Under a new set of assumptions and beliefs about what principles must apply if sustainable development is to be achieved, existing rules of business must be carefully reviewed and tested against the new principles. If "horses for courses" is to replace "the bigger the better" in the optimization of size of operation, there may be cases in which limitation of discounts and restraint on takeovers would be beneficial.

Systemic technology

From what has already been said in previous sections, it is clear that technological development will be transformed by a decision in favour of sustainability. Technology is by no means neutral. It serves whatever purpose we expect of it. It can be an immense contributor to good; or it can be frighteningly destructive. The peaceful purposes for which we have so far used it have done much good, but unwittingly it has also been the direct cause of the serious environment and ecological threat. It is clear that, in future, much more careful attention will have to be paid to any new technological developments. In particular, all possible side-effects will need to be studied in great detail before widespread use is allowed. However, if development objectives are embodying principles of sustainability, side-effects should be a major problem. The new developments will not only be about things that have never been done before. By far the majority will be ways of doing most of the common things that fulfil human needs and wants, but in ways that serve the new purpose of sustainable development. This makes the challenge to scientists, technologists, and engineers very widespread and very profound.

In two particular ways, the change is revolutionary. Since the beginning of the Industrial Revolution the process of development has become increasingly fragmented as knowledge and experience have accumulated and individuals have become more specialized. As a result the focus of attention has tended to be on the achievement of progressive improvements in elements of the total system. For example, much effort has been put into the development of better and more efficient domestic heating appliances. Unfortunately, too little attention has been paid to the thermal design of the complete building, with the result that most of the space-heat continues to be wasted. The result would have been quite different with a "systems approach" to development rather than the traditional "blinkered approach." Instead of maximizing the performance of one element of the system, we would have optimized the whole system. For the future the process of fragmentation in development needs to be reversed. A "systems approach" has become increasingly necessary.

A second revolutionary change concerns the type of material and the sources of energy that we use. The first industrial revolution was based on a switch from renewable wind, water, and wood to nonrenewable fossil fuels as sources of energy. It also depended on the use of an expanding range of highly processed, nonrenewable materials in place of natural materials. For example, synthetic fibers have to a considerable extent replaced natural fibers. Synthetic alcohol based on petroleum feedstocks has taken over much of the market previously supplied by fermentation alcohol. Plastic materials have displaced paper products in some types of packaging. In the second industrial revolution, as we seek to contain environmental and ecological damage while making space of an improvement in the living conditions of three-quarters of the world's population, the recent historic process will need to be reversed by using more renewables.

Summary

Recognition of the necessity of a form of development that is sustainable demands a fundamental break from some of the important assumptions and beliefs that have underpinned traditional development since the beginning of the Industrial Revolution. A new set of assumptions and beliefs will be needed to guide development toward sustainability. Success or failure depends primarily on businesses which have control over the human skills and the material, financial, and technological resources that are capable of effecting the change.

Sustainable development is a complex idea which, from a business point of view, can be described as something that:

- uses renewable resources in preference to nonrenewables
- uses technologies that are environmentally harmonious, ecologically stable and skill enhancing
- designs complete systems in order to minimize waste
- reduces as much as possible the consumption of scarce resources by designing long-life products that are easily repairable and can be recycled; and
- maximizes the use of all the services that are not energy- or material-intensive, but which contribute to the quality of life.

All of this profoundly challenges companies everywhere and at all levels. Nine reorientations in business life are required. They are toward:

- a corporate vision of stewardship
- an appropriate scale of operation
- the measuring of sustainability
- flexible work arrangements
- an orchestral style of management
- enduring quality
- just forms of ownership
- convivial rules of the business game
- systemic technology

Each involves a separate task for a company, out of which a transformation program should be produced. Although, inevitably, there are new constraints, these are more than offset by the vast range of new opportunities to be seized by imaginative firms as we move toward the information society.

Note

1 HRH the Duke of Edinburgh, The Melchett Lecture of the Institute of Fuel, London, 1979.

References

Goyder, G. 1987: *The Just Enterprise*. London: André Deutsch.

Hirsch, F. 1977: *Social Limits to Growth*. London: Routledge and Kegan Paul.

Leach, G. 1979: *A Low Energy Strategy for the UK*. Science Review Limited.

Meadows *et al.* 1972: *The Limits to Growth*. A report of the Club of Rome.

Schumacher, E. F. 1974: *Small is Beautiful*.

Wallenburg, P. 1989: *Sustainable Development – the Business Approach*. Stockholm: ICC.

World Commission on Environment and Development 1988: *Our Common Future* (the Bruntland Report).

World Resources Institute 1989: A matter of degrees. Research report.

17

Toward a Synergistic Society
Yoneji Masuda

The Information Society

The information society will be one that develops around the production of information values, according to Japanese futurist Yoneji Masuda, and will therefore differ fundamentally from the agricultural and industrial societies of the past, which developed around the production of material values. More precisely, the term "information society" refers to an economy in which:

1 Information is the core of society's economic needs.
2 The economy, and society itself, grow and develop around this core – the production and use of information values.
3 The importance of information as an economic product exceeds goods, energy, and services.

This economic structure could be called an "information-axis economy."

Change to an Information-led Industrial Structure

Firstly, there will be a change from an industrial structure centering around goods, energy, and services to an information-led type of industrial structure, a change that will pass through three stages of development (see figure 18.1).

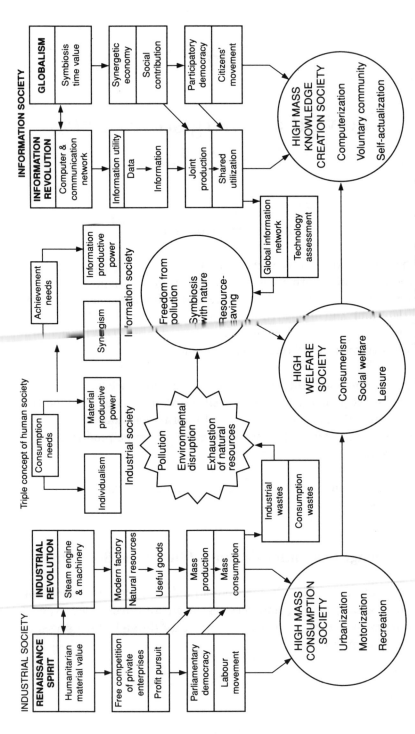

Figure 18.1 Transformation process from industrial society to information society

The appearance of information-related industries

The first stage will be the formation of information-related industries. In an information society the information-related industries will become the leading industries, which will develop to the point of the formation of quaternary industries as a new classification.

The concept of "quaternary industries" is necessary as a category, in that a clear line of demarcation must be drawn between service industries and information-related industries. There is a general tendency to characterize the major change in the structure of post-industrial society as an expansion of tertiary industries (i.e., service industries) with their importance exceeding that of the secondary manufacturing industries. In this context, information-related industries could be classified as tertiary industries only because they are industries which do not produce goods. But it is highly probable that information-related industries would develop beyond the service industries in an information society. It is reasonable, therefore, to distinguish information-related industries from service industries, and classify them as quaternary industries, to provide a clear concept of the industrial structure of an information society.

What would be the composition of the quaternary industries, as leading industries of the future? Quaternary industries can be divided broadly into four main industrial groups: (a) information industries; (b) knowledge industries; (c) arts industries; and (d) ethics industries. Of these four, the information and the knowledge industries will become the key industries of the future. Figure 18.2 gives a breakdown of all information-related industries.

The first "information industries" will primarily be industries that produce, process, and service cognitive information, or produce and sell related equipment. Here, the information industries are restricted to cognitive information because a separate industrial group, the arts industries, will be established for affective information. The core of the information industries will comprise the information-machinery industries, including the computer and peripheral equipment industries, and LSIs (large-scale integrated circuits) and micro-processors. Such information-machinery industries will probably displace the automobile industry to take first place as the largest manufacturing industry.

In parallel with this, the industries concerned with information-

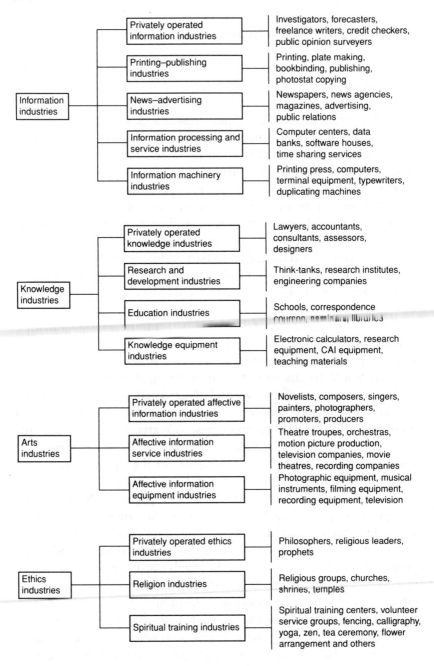

Figure 18.2 The quaternary industries (information-related industries)

processing services and systems development, software, telecommunication services, and computer centers, will also undergo unprecedented development. The present mass-communications industry of newspapers and publishing, which dominate the information services today, will probably enter an era of stagnation.

The second group, the "knowledge industries," can be expected to develop after the information industries have come into being. The core of these will be of two types, that is, education industries and research-and-development industries. The education industries and the information industries together will be the pillars of the information society. The reason for this is that in the information society human values will change; material values will be superseded by time values, and greater importance will be attached to the development of new abilities and the improvement of human life. Research and development industries will greatly expand in response to the need to solve problems of resources and energy, an example of which would be resources-recycling technology, or the need to improve human welfare through integrated social systems.

The third information-related industrial group is the "arts industries," such as the mass-communications industries (newspapers and publishing). These seem to have reached a peak now, and it is likely they will be declining industries. The reason is that in an information society the expansion of individual creative knowledge will flourish, and society will be able to escape from the present fad-oriented, sensory, television-dominated society of today. The future of television is probably that it will be linked with the computer and function more as a medium for cognitive information. One main use, for example, would be for citizen participation in decision-making on social problems.

The fourth group, the "ethics industries," by contrast, will become growth industries, among which religion will form a particularly important part. In this case, while moving away from belief in the existence of a supernatural god, religion will be epochally significant, in that human life will be elevated through renewed belief in the existence and strength of humanity. In the information society, on one hand, each person will attach more importance to scientific thought, and on the other, will be humble before an absolute existence that transcends human abilities. The very basis of this humility will be the global concept, the harmony and symbiosis – as reflected in the previous chapter – of man and nature on this finite planet, earth. Whether one calls this globalism a religion or calls it the awareness of a supra-human existence, we believe the future will call for religious thought and an ethical content that are new and clothed in new attire.

In the information society of the future, the industries in these four groups, together with the computer industries, the information-processing and service industries, the education industries and the religion industries, will form a core group the major function of which will be in the growth and development of the quaternary industries as a whole.

The formation of industries with installed information equipment

The second stage will be marked by the formation of industries with installed information equipment. This means the informationaliza-tion of industries through utilization of the machinery, with infor-mation equipment forming part of it. The development of machinery and equipment capable of exercising information functions has been made possible through the invention of LSIs and microprocessors. We have already reached the stage at which a wide range of machinery with installed information equipment, such as electronic calculators, electronic watches (digital or other), automatic cameras, cash dispensers, games machines, and facilities containing infor-mation equipment are coming into extensive use in medicine, education, pollution control, traffic control, and all industrial areas. As this process continues, various kinds of robot-operated and control machinery and equipment will certainly be created.

The development of systems industries

The third stage will be the development of systems industries. Analyses of the industrial structure have, in the past, generally been based on a quantitative assessment setting out the ratio of constituent industries, and the shift from low- to high-technology industries.

But the structure of the systems industries will consist of a complex of industries formed by linking up existing industries with information industries. This means a qualitative change in the industrial structure, one example of which is seen in automatic warehousing, which has combined warehousing with the information industries. The systems industries may range from the relatively simple, such as automatic warehousing and automatic diagonsis systems, to the highly complex, such as the health industry and the opportunity industry.

The "health industry" will comprise a system that includes food, pharmaceuticals, medical services, sports, and information, combined organically. The medical-care industry of the future will not mean simply the treatment of disease. The emphasis will be on early diagnosis and the maintenance of health. Medical care, through the integration of new systems and technology, such as frozen-food technology, preventive medicine, hospital automation, health-diagnosis centers, and athletic clubs, can be expected to develop into a health industry that operates as a systems industry.

What we have called the "opportunity industry" will be an integrated industry the functions of which will be to open up personal possibilities for the future, and, like the health industry, will be one of the systems industries that offers the possibility of personal growth.

The four major opportunity industries will be (a) education, (b) information, (c) ethics, and (d) finance–insurance, each with its own function. The education industries will promote the development of individual abilities. The information industries will supply information that will enable new opportunities to be discovered and created. The ethics industries will provide behavioral standards and guide in the molding of character, and the finance–insurance industries will provide the necessary capital and risk cover. The education industries will not operate on the current uniform system of school education, but will become a more diverse and dynamic system of education. Home self-learning, labor re-education and computer plazas (where people can use the computer freely) will make their appearance. A mechanical data bank of enormous range will be established as an information industry, and the accumulation of information will proceed on everything necessary for opportunity development, from analysis of individual potential and work references to the location of educational facilities.

Training facilities for the ethics industries will be provided, along with community centers where values and behavioral standards, thought, religion, and ethics are the focus of interest. The finance–insurance industries will be equipped to provide opportunity loans, the capital needed for the application of ability and opportunity development, and opportunity insurance as a guarantee against the risk of the loans.

The labelling of such systems industries should not be according to industrial categories used for traditional types of goods; the systems should be related to traditional categories of industries by means of a matrix. If the traditional categories of industry from primary to quaternary are placed on a horizontal axis, and systems industries on a vertical axis, the relationship can be established. Table 18.1 sets out this new industrial matrix.

The primary industries, divided into agriculture and forestry, stock-farming, fishery, mining, and manufacturing industries, are placed on the top portion of this industrial matrix. The more specific industries in each of these, such as mechanized agriculture and the broiler industry, are included. The industries shown in the matrix are those that bear some relation to the systems industries, which are on the horizontal axis. This matrix enables a multifaceted quantitative and qualitative analysis of the industrial structure to be made in a way that has not been possible before.

Expansion of the Public Economy

The second change in the economic structure will be an expansion of the public economy. Expansion of the public economy refers to an increase in the public side of economic activities, with the emphasis on economic activity for the public benefit rather than on profits to be made. This expansion of the public economy will occur in four ways.

Strengthening of the infrastructure

The first form of expansion will be the strengthening of the infrastructure. In the current industrial society, gas, water, communications, roads, parks, and schools are typical examples of the infrastructure. But in the information society many other kinds of facilities and services will become important parts of the infrastructure. The most significant, needless to say, will be the information utilities.

In the information society, information utilities will be the driving force of social development. The information utilities themselves will basically assume the nature of an infrastructure, which alone will become a decisive factor in the transformation of the economic structure from the present private economy into a public economy in the information society.

In addition, lands may also become part of the infrastructure because these are limited basic resources that will take on the character of public assets, as a result of the separation of land ownership from use.

Of special note as infrastructure will be do-it-yourself facilities. These will be public facilities where many things can be done: carpentry, woodworking, ceramics, fabric dying, weaving, and even machine construction. These facilities will satisfy people's need to make things for themselves. Such places will be equipped not only with tools for handicrafts, but with highly sophisticated machinery and the necessary technology for people to make things for themselves that may take several months to complete. Hobbies for leisure-time activities are becoming more and more popular even now, but the information society will greatly increase free time, and so it is expected that these do-it-yourself facilities will develop to an astonishing degree, in sharp contrast with the anti-human automation-based production in present-day industrial society.

Basic-materials industries join the public economy

The second form of expansion will be that basic-materials industries join the public enterprises. In the future information society, steel, oil refining, petrochemicals, fertilizers, synthetic fibers, aluminium, and other basic-materials industries will probably all come into the public sector, for which there are two impelling reasons:

1 The growing threat of shortages in basic material supplies, due partly to the depletion of natural resources, changes in climate, increases in population, and other factors. No matter how sophisticated technology becomes, it will not be possible for technology to produce adequate supplies of resources artificially, or resources will

Table 18.1 Matrix industrial structure

		Systems industries →	Opportunity development industry	Health industry	Fashion industry	Leisure industry	Space industry	Marine industry	Environment industry	Regional development industry	Housing industry	Integrated transport industry	Distribution industry
By products		**By systems**											
Primary industries	Agricultural industries	Mechanized agriculture		●									
		Broiler industry		●									
	Fisheries industries	Fish hatcheries		●				●					
	Mining industries	Offshore oil wells						●					
		Underwater mining						●					
Secondary industries	Light industries	Manufactured foods (margarine, etc.)	●	●			●						
		Frozen foods											
		Clothing			●	●	●						
		Cosmetics			●								
		Medical supplies		●			●						
	Heavy, chemical industries	Artificial organs		●			●						
		Medical engineering equipment		●									
		Anti air-pollution devices		●					●				
		Construction equipment							●	●	●		
		Ambulances		●						●			
		Disaster prevention devices		●						●			
		Rack-style warehouses							●	●		●	
		Deep-sea submarines						●					
		Space devices					●						
		Communications satellites					●	●	●				
		Traffic signal equipment							●	●			
		Automated commuter transport				●				●		●	●

	Construction industries	Prefabricated houses
		Mobile homes
		Hospitals
		Highways
		Land development
Tertiary industries	Utility (light, heat and power)	Atomic power
		Solar energy
		Natural gas
	Traditional public utilities	Regional heating and air-conditioning facilities
	Freight industries	Monorail
		Container transport
	Communications	Data communications
	Commerce	Supermarkets
		Distribution centers
	Warehousing	Warehouses
	Finance and insurance	Opportunity loans
		Housing loans
	Personal services	Medical care
		Human docks
		Athletic clubs
Quaternary industries	Information industries	Data banks
		Computer centers
		Software
		Computers
		Terminal equipment
	Knowledge industries	Think tank
		Consultants
		Audiovisual teaching equipment
		CAI equipment
		Color television
	Arts industries	Movies
		Plays
		Records
	Ethics industries	Spiritual training centers
		Religious groups
		Volunteer service groups

Source: Y. Masuda, Information Economics (Tokyo, Sangyo Noritsu University Press 1976) inevitably become a major socio-economic factor, restricting the free economic activity of the private enterprise system.

2 Another reason why basic industries will become public is that in these basic-materials industries automation by the use of computer technology will make very rapid progress. Already automation in industrial production has reached a fairly advanced stage, and before the beginning of the 21st century there will probably be massive – even complete – automation in basic industries, where the merits of scale are great, such as in the steel, petroleum, petrochemicals, cement, and electric-power industries.

The increasing shortages in the supply of resources, combined with the further expansion of productive power by applied automation will result in increased contradictions between the profit principle of monopolistic private capital and the public interest.

Expansion of social consumption

The third change in the public economy will be the expansion of social consumption. The dominant form of consumption in industrial society at present is individual, as evidenced by food, housing, and automobiles, all of which are commodities of personal consumption. Examples of social consumption are parks, roads, schools, and hospitals, but individual consumption carries far greater weight than social consumption.

In the information society, however, social consumption will constitute a far larger portion of total consumption than individual consumption, influenced by two factors. The first will be that individual consumption will reach saturation point, with increased social disutility. In developed countries, the share of individual consumption is rapidly decreasing. And social disutility, which includes air pollution, urban congestion, and the destruction of nature, is increasing in inverse proportion to the increase in material consumption. As these conditions increase, people will attach more importance to social utility, thus imposing restraints on individual consumption and enhancing the tendency for an increase in social consumption.

The second factor to encourage social consumption is that the basic characteristic of computer information is as a service offered by a public utility. In the information society this computer information will be used extensively by people in general through the information utility. There will also be a large number of social-information network systems, such as the medical-care information system and the education information system, that will be essential to the maintenance of health and the development of capabilities.

The shift to a synergetic economic system

We now consider the shift from a free economic system to a synergetic economic system in the information society, i.e., the total transformation of the economic system itself. This will be the final form, comprehensively encompassing the transformation of the economic structure so far outlined.

For the most part, the current economic system in industrial society has tended to be a liberalistic economic system characterized by:

- free competition of private enterprise
- pursuit of profits
- commodity production
- supply and demand as the determinant of prices

In the future information society, however, this liberalistic economy will be transformed into a new economic system, a synergetic economy, which is an economic system based on synergism. The three aspects of this are as follows.

Synergetic production and shared utilization

The transformation from a commodity economy to a synergetic production and shared utilization economy means that the production of goods is at the core of economic activity, with production and consumption wholly separated. But future society will mean synergetic production and shared utilization, as constituting the primary economic system. The realization of this will be encouraged in two ways, one of which will be the development of information utilities. In the information society, information utilities will form the core of economic development. The unique production system of the information utilities will be structurally quite unlike factory production. As has been said, the production of information by the information utilities will differ structurally from the production of material goods by factories, in that it will be man- and-machine-based production of information, characterized by self-multiplication. Information utilities will not merely provide extensive information processing and service to the general public. The information utilities will be used by the people themselves to produce the information they require. In addition, the programs produced by the people and the data they have collected will be available for shared utilization by all other persons. When this occurs, information utilities will advance to the synergetic production and shared utilization of information accumulated by the citizens. This unique production structure of the information utilities will not determine merely the production structure for information goods; it will broadly determine the structure of the consumption and distribution of information goods. Producers will also be users, and in this way the economic goods produced will be shared and utilized. Because the information utilities will be the axial institutions in the economy of the information society, the joint production and shared utilization of information goods will greatly influence the economic structure as a whole.

One more thing to be emphasized is that people will voluntarily participate in the synergetic construction of public facilities. In the information society, it will become quite normal for the synergetic labor of citizens to construct public facilities such as homes for the elderly, parks, roads, and schools. Of course, national and local governments will provide part of the materials and funds, but the main characteristic of this kind of construction will be that the share of funds and physical and mental labor voluntarily contributed by the citizens themselves will be greater.

Voluntary synergy to achieve a shared economic goal

The second aspect is that, corresponding to free competition, there will be voluntary synergy. This refers to individual economic subjects carrying on economic activities synergetically in order to achieve a shared economic goal.

In industrial society, private enterprises carry on business activities freely. The result has been that this free competition has meant the development of the national economy as a whole, and provided national economic welfare. This free competition in the micro-enterprise economy has functioned effectively, without conflicting, on the whole, with the orderless macro-national economy, because the law of price, Adam Smith's "Invisible Hand," has guided and adjusted business activity. Behind Adam Smith's law of price, however, was the tacit economic assumption that resources are limitless, and if demand expands, the production of goods will go on expanding indefinitely.

This economic assumption is now proving to be invalid; Smith's Invisible Hand is not functioning as effectively as in the past, because we have begun to recognize that resources are finite. The gigantic productive economic subjects have to give priority to carrying on economic activity to reach shared economic goals, which, in one sense, means voluntary synergy corresponding with free competition.

Autonomous restraint of consumption

The third aspect is the autonomous restraint of consumption by the people. One economic principle of industrial society is the raising of consumption levels by mass production and mass consumption. But in the information society, autonomous restraints on the consumption of goods will apply, to ensure stabilized development of the economy. The economic ethics of ordinary citizens will require that the limited natural resources must be used efficiently, and inflation prevented. The idea that the problems of shortages of natural resources and inflation will be resolved not by law imposed from above, but through voluntary restraints, presents a new economic concept, worthy of the information society, and it is the concept and idea of the synergetic economy that lies at the base of this system.

Increased management and capital participation

The fourth aspect will involve an increase in management and capital participation. The tendency for labor and the general public to participate in enterprises has already become a historical fact, and in the information society this tendency will certainly increase. The private side of private enterprise will decline, and the social side will increase as the public nature of economic activity expands from management participation to capital participation by labor and the general public. As this tendency progresses, there will be a change from authoritarian synergy to functional synergy in economic units.

The synergetic relationships in economic groups in the existing economy are relationships of authoritarian synergy between the owner of capital, who has the right of management, and the employed workers. The lower stratum has followed directions from above. But economic groups of the future will move toward an economic community of people who participate voluntarily and share the same goal. The synergetic relations that come into being will not be authoritarian but purely functional, which will probably come about in stages by various methods and means; there will be management and capital participation by the general public, as well as autonomous management. What can be said clearly is that the managerial class in the information society will not be a privileged class backed by monopoly ownership of capital and therefore the right of management, it will be a functional class that has the job of management.

Conclusion

This chapter has provided a general outline of the fundamental characteristics of the synergetic economic system. However, the synergetic economy will not suddenly replace the existing economy in the developing information society; rather, elements of the liberalistic economy will continue for a long time. For example, the pursuit of profits and the free prices and free markets of commodity production will not just suddenly disappear. We are referring here to a gradual shift from the present economy to a synergetic economy in the sense that the hub of the economy in the information society will be a synergetic economic system, with the trinity of contribution motive, voluntary synergy, and synergetic production with shared utilization. The new-paradigm manager, who embodies this synergistic approach, will have a particular orientation.

18

Doing Business in the New Paradigm

Jagdish Parikh

A Synthesis of Western Science and Eastern Wisdom

Managing congruence: values and "isms"

The essence of doing business in the new paradigm (or in the emerging view of the business world) is functioning from a level of consciousness or awareness which intrinsically implies the integration of the basic values implicit in the pursuit of economic objectives, ethical behaviour, and ecological sustainability. Doing business in the new paradigm starts with managing your self. A conceptual overview as a summary of the major elements of managing your self is provided in figure 19.1. At the top, you can see the world systems or "isms" within which you create and manage your life. Several such societal "isms" or ideologies have been advocated and practised in different parts of the world during this century, with varying degrees of success or failure. In fact, they represent different combinations of two basic parameters, values and ideologies, as shown in figure 19.2.

The vertical "value-laden" axis covers the whole spectrum of values, ranging from the spiritual (emphasized in eastern cultures), to the materialistic (dominant in western thinking), from a self-denying to a self-centered approach. The horizontal "ideological" axis covers a different range of ideological stances. These extend from freedom of the individual on the one hand, to integration with society on the other, ranging from competition to collectivism, or from capitalism to communism. In fact, none of the value sets or "isms" have been able to achieve their stated objectives, namely societal growth and/or individual welfare, on an equitable or durable basis.

In this context of the existing paradigm of values and "isms",

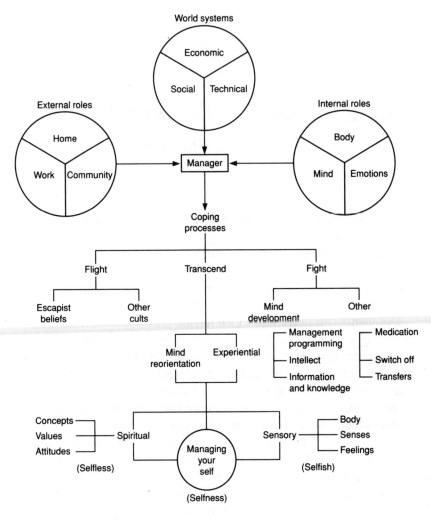

Figure 19.1 Self in the world

then, what is the average manager's approach to life? In order to cope with the rigor of accelerating change and uncertainty, complexity, and conflict, managers generally adopt "coping" approaches consisting of either fight or flight. In other words, you either try to orchestrate external events (inevitably frustrating) or to escape from them (self-limiting). And for internal satisfaction, you either try to "acquire more knowledge" (with a hope of behaving differently) and/or take to medication, drink, or smoking, and so on. In other

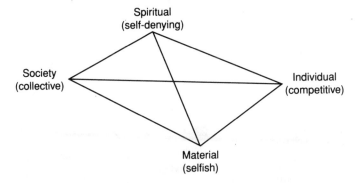

Figure 19.2   The values–ideology axis

words, you basically try to gain some comfort and peace from external sources – the result is continuing stress and frustration.

What is really required is a strengthening of your self, whereby you generate the capability within you to cope with accelerating change, and to overcome conflicts. The only "ism" that can work for everyone is a form of "pragmatism." This implies no ideological or value bias, either western or eastern, northern or southern, and no compromises in between, but a cooperative synthesis of them all, at the top, as shown in figure 19.3.

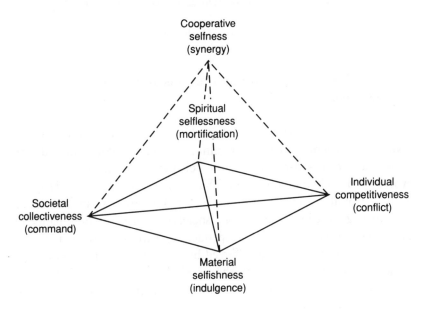

Figure 19.3   Self-managed pragmatism

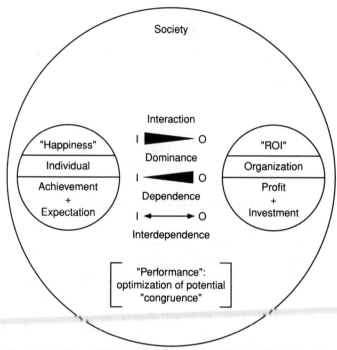

The individual needs the organization to achieve his full potential
The organization needs the individual to achieve its goals
Society needs organized individuals to attain a rising quality of life

Figure 19.4   Quality of life

Essence of the new paradigm; the consequence of "cooperative selfness"

Behind or beneath managerial life styles are your mind styles. These involve a reorientation of your mind, or your thinking, in order to transcend both self-centered and self-denying extremes, thereby evolving "detached involvement." Such a managerial style is designed to bring about an optimization of your potentials – as an individual, in your organization, and in your society. In place of dominance or dependence is congruent interdependence, seen in figure 19.4.

This congruence can be achieved by a synthesis of the technology of how to make a living with the psychology of how to live; of the science with the art of management; reaching beyond business manager to business yogi!

The Paradigm Shift

"Raplexity"

This is the direction in which the world seems to be moving, almost imperceptibly but quite unmistakably. This is the paradigm shift which is being increasingly talked about now in mainstream business forums. The list below will facilitate translating these basic trends into meaningful implications at the micro-level, for managers:

I • quantitative	transience "raplexity"
• qualitative	revolutions:
	agricultural → industrial → technological
	information − − → consciousness
II • world view	mechanistic → holistic − − → holographic
• concept of man	economic → social → humanistic →
	holistic − − → transpersonal
• values	competitive − − → cooperative
• thinking	analytic → creative − − → intuitive
• living	survival − − → resonance
III • concept of wealth	land → cattle → money →
	information − − → consciousness
• role of business	power-driven → purpose-driven − − →
	planetary
• organizational culture	power → role → achievement − − → support
	purse/person − − → vision
• management style	control and aggression (threat/stress)
	caring and connection (trust/energy)
• role of manager	problem-solving − − → leadership
	fear of losing − − → joy of doing

The constant change that is going on around you is both *quantitative* and *qualitative*. The magnitude and pace of quantitative change is so great that it has been described as "raplexity," meaning a combination of rapidity and complexity. The nature of the qualitative change consists of layers of simultaneous revolutions, ranging from the agricultural to the informational.

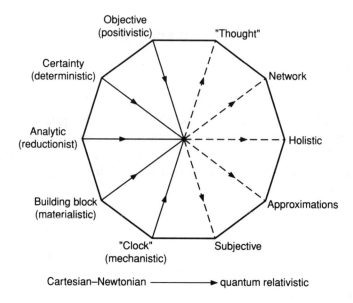

Figure 19.5   The paradigm shift: changing world views

The most commonly acknowledged contemporary change is the "information" revolution. However, there are already significant signs of a thrust toward a "consciousness" revolution. In fact, Willis Harmon describes today's paradigm shift as a movement from the first to a second "Copernican revolution." The first Copernican revolution created more accurate awareness and understanding of "outer space" and the positioning of the earth as a satellite in the Solar System. The second "Copernican" revolution is expected to generate greater insight and consciousness into your "inner space," thereby positioning your "self" and your life space in the context of an appropriate "reality."

The *world views* or the paradigms of "reality" are also changing from the "mechanistic" ones that have prevailed over the past few centuries, based on the Cartesian–Newtonian model, to a holistic and holographic world view based on the quantum relativistic model (see figure 19.5). This was also referred to in chapter 14.

The mechanistic view has been based on the notion that "to understand the whole, you must understand the part." The holistic view maintains that "to understand the part, you must understand the whole." Finally, the holographic view suggests that "the part *is* the whole." The old paradigm's focus is on management of observed systems: the new paradigm could be viewed as management of observing systems.

It is interesting to note the convergence of this view, based on quantum physics, with the ancient Indian vedantic wisdom. One of the Sanskrit verses in ancient Indian literature states: "This is the whole; that [part] is a whole. The whole [part] emerges from the whole. Even if the whole [part] is taken away from the whole, the whole still remains."

What is the relevance of all this to business? Business policies and management thinking are based on particular assumptions about human nature. These assumptions have been changing during recent decades from a narrow *concept of man* as an economic entity to a broadened view – ranging from "social" to "humanistic" to "holistic." With the resultant growing interest in the whole person, a human being is now viewed not as independent of and separate from nature, but as an autonomous subsystem through which consciousness is manifested. Furthermore, consciousness is no longer a product of chance mutation amongst particles, but is considered as the ultimate reality. This is the transpersonal view of "man" who has both a self-(ego-) centered existence and an ego-transcending, or transpersonal, self.

It is in the context of such a concept of man that the *values* in business seem to be moving from adversarial competition toward more cooperative competition. This is manifested at the inter-organizational level, by the growth in mergers and strategic alliances and, within organizations, by the shift toward interfunctional teams and networking. As a corollary, the focus in managerial *thinking* is moving from the earlier emphasis on analytic problem-solving to a recent orientation toward creative abilities, and now toward intuitive insights. In fact, the whole attitude toward *life* is also changing from one of just surviving to one of meaningfully thriving and thereby "resonating" with all the other interrelated elements in life. This implies that "richness" or "*wealth*" is no longer evaluated in terms of traditional measures such as land, cattle, money, or even the contemporary notion of "information." Increasingly, "riches" are being assessed in terms of your capacity to experience higher levels of vision and consciousness.

This is being evidenced by a perceptible shift, as Charles Hampden-Turner has suggested, in attitudes toward the purpose and *role of business*. From earlier orientations toward profit and power, to a more recent focus on people, we are now seeing business leaders seeking greater alignment with global and ecological concerns. The internal corollary of such external "turning" is the growing interest in creating an *organizational culture* based on support systems, networks, and shared values, rather than on power, money, or personal ambition – changing outlooks through deeper insights.

There is therefore a rapidly growing shift in *management style* away from one based on control and aggression (which inevitably generates threats of "losing," leading to negative stress) toward one based on "caring and connection." Through the resulting team spirit and a "connective consciousness," you come to view your colleagues not as adversaries, in the management game of succession, but as co-creators of success. This in turn generates trust and therefore positive energy. Such are the qualities and competencies that are now being sought in *managers*. As more and more problem-solving skills are being taken over by computers and expert systems, it is leadership skills which are being increasingly required.

This is the essence of the new paradigm: the role of management is to create within the organization a climate, a culture, and a context in which corporate enrichment and individual fulfillment collaborate and resonate progressively in the development of a creative and integrative global community.

Managing Paradoxically: Transcending Conflicts

Doing business in the emerging paradigm, then, implies a basic shift in perceptions, purpose, and profiles of the organization and the managers from those in the old paradigm. Some of the contrasting characteristics of a business organization and individual managers, under the old and the new paradigms, are shown in figure 19.6 and table 19.1.

To initiate and achieve such a shift, individual managers need to cultivate almost contradictory or apparently paradoxical qualities, such as:

- converging divergence
- constructive discontent
- flexible persistence

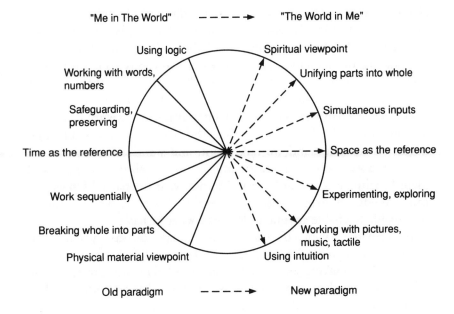

Figure 19.6   Doing business in the new paradigm

- confident humility
- relaxed attention
- "mindless" perception

How can you bring about such a radical qualitative shift into a corporate culture? How can you cultivate such apparently paradoxical qualities in a manager? This is where the relevance and

Table 19.1   Contrasting management and paradigms

Characteristic	Old paradigm	New paradigm
Strategy	Planned	Entrepreneurial
Structure	Hierarchy	Network
Systems	Rigid	Flexible
Staff	Title and rank	Being helpful
Style	Problem solving	Transformational
Skills	To complete	To build
Shared value	Better sameness	Meaningful difference
Focus	Institution	Individual
Source of strength	Stability	Change
Leadership	Dogmatic	Inspirational

significance of the concepts of the self – our real identity – becomes clearer. As already discussed, you have the potential to experience different levels of consciousness, and therefore self-identities. With the practice of meditation and centering, you can remain "in touch" with your "deeper or observing self" – the self that is your "constant" secure pivot – and function through your ego, or operating or changing self. Isn't it interesting that we are described as "indivi-duals!" This also resolves the paradox of our conflicting urges: on the one hand we talk about, and want to, change; at the same time we want the security and comfort of all that we have and identify with, and at that level we do not want to change! Unless we can provide an experience of something better it will be almost impossible to enable anyone to let go of what he has!

By providing yourself with an inner image of, say, a lemon (or whatever happens to be your favorite fruit), saliva happens to you, without your making any effort to create it! Similarly, by operating with such a dual or expanded consciousness, that is, with detached involvement, you are able to cultivate even apparently contradictory qualities and become a master manager or a "business yogi." As such you gain, on the one hand, a synthesized experience of the nonchang-ing, undying, perennial, transpersonal self, a constant river of joyous energy, while interacting on the other hand through the ego-self with constantly changing phenomena. This not only enables you to cope with change, complexity, and conflict, but also to master it. This transforms not only the quality of your mind but also your emotional profile and your physical chemistry. In effect you lead, or bring about change, through a synthesis (not a compromise) of several opposing or conflicting parameters, not only externally but also within yourself.

The common or traditional approach to conflict resolution has been one of compromise "in between" the opposing interests or viewpoints, which usually results in a win-lose or even a lose-lose settlement. Therefore, such "settlements," whether intrapersonal, interpersonal, or intergroup, are most often neither satisfying nor durable. The synthesizing, synergistic, or "win-win" approach involves enlarging the "context" of any problem or conflict in any situation and enabling an understanding "above" or beyond the opposing or conflicting interests. This is illustrated below:

| sympathy | _____ | antipathy |
| excitement | _____ | depression |

blind optimism	_____	fearful pessimism
rebellion	_____	submission
self-depreciation	_____	arrogance
intellectual doubt	_____	dogmatism
license	_____	depression
weakness	_____	violence

Based on the above, you will find that the usual approach is to find a compromise, somewhere midway between opposing or conflicting elements of sympathy and antipathy, in the form of indifference. The genuine resolution, however, would be one of benevolent understanding of the broader context which causes sympathy or antipathy and thereby, through sincere *em*pathy, find a lasting solution which satisfies both the extremes. This is possible if you are able to detach or distance yourself sufficiently and involve yourself adequately rather than experience indifference. Similarly, you can, with such inner experience, bring about serenity, clearer vision of reality, and transcendence. These "triangular relationships" are shown in figure 19.7. The natural consequences of this are the paradoxical qualities we expect in a master manager – they happen to you!

Synthesizing the globe

Such an "understanding" can also help us in taking a "clear stand" on some of the basic issues facing us today:

- Are you, as a manager, living for business or are you in the business of living?
- Are you interested in adding years to your life, or life to your years?
- Is your main interest in making yourself a living, or in making a life for yourself?

To be able to achieve a synthesis, beyond such either/or propositions, so as to secure a larger and inclusive "both," you have to combine the technology of "how to make a living" (western/northern management expertise) with the technology of "how to live" (eastern/ southern philosophical traditions). You require a synthesis of the earning potential of corporations with the living potential of individ-

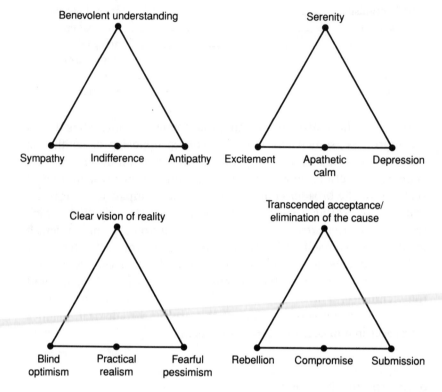

Figure 19.7 Triangular relationships

uals. This also resolves the paradox of the old and new paradigms by enabling not only a symbiosis but a synergy between the two.

In other words, you should not only be "efficient" but also "effective," not only, as we saw in chapter 4 do things right (a good manager), but also do the right things (a good leader). How do you ensure this? You may pursue money, power, and prestige – the symbols of success. As discussed earlier, these are pursued in order to feel happy. But, despite getting more of these we do not feel proportionately happier! We are, in a sense, going up the "ladder" but are we sure that the "ladder" is against the right wall?

The real issue is to remember that "success" of getting money, power, and prestige can get us:

- Food but not appetite
- Clothes but not beauty

- A beautiful house but not necessarily a happy home
- Books but not wisdom
- Medicines but not health
- Beds but not sleep
- Even partners but not love; and
- Maybe all the luxuries of life, but not happiness!

Human beings, not human havings!

Happiness can never come from "outside." This may be obvious – perhaps even a blinding glimpse of the obvious – but it is the obvious that is often overlooked! After all, you and I are described as "human beings," and not as "human havings," or even "human doings!" This is the essence of detached involvement. It is the missing link between success (getting what you want) and happiness (wanting what you get). Management by detached involvement (see chapter 3) enhances the drive to get what you want and, at the same time, enables you to thrive on what you get. Being to become!

Clearly, living and managing by detached involvement requires courage. You have to change before you need to, and make your own space in time. Courage is the key, but fear seems to be the common reaction. Courage implies not absence of fear, but mastery over it. We therefore want to conclude by expressing an earnest wish that you enhance your courage to change what you can; enhance your serenity to accept what you cannot change, and, above all, always have the wisdom to know the difference. Perfection is sometimes described as the ability to live in harmony with the unchangeable imperfections in life!

Today is the first day of the rest of your life. Yesterday is a dream, and tomorrow is a vision. Today, well lived, as if it is the only one you have, makes every yesterday a dream of happiness and every tomorrow a vision of hope. What you do now determines what you will be in the next moment!

Index